MOON MADNESS

MOON MADNESS

by PAUL KATZEFF

ROBERT HALE · LONDON

First published in Great Britain 1990

Robert Hale Limited
Clerkenwell House
Clerkenwell Green
London EC1R 0HT

Printed in Great Britain by
St Edmundsbury Press Limited, Bury St Edmunds, Suffolk
Bound by WBC Bookbinders Limited

Table of Contents

Introduction: The Silver Watch

PART ONE—LORE AND MYTHOLOGY 1

Chapter 1: Green Cheese 3
Chapter 2: Lunacy 7
Chapter 3: Lunar Sympathy 11
Chapter 4: "The Moon Is God" 23
Chapter 5: Fertility 39
Chapter 6: Moisture 47
Chapter 7: Lycanthropy 51
Chapter 8: Hungry Dragons 73
Chapter 9: Epilepsy 81

PART TWO—THE MOON AND ITS EFFECTS 85

Chapter 10: Selenology 87
Chapter 11: Ocean Tides 93
Chapter 12: Atmospheric Tides 97
Chapter 13: The Eiffel Effect 99
Chapter 14: Earthquakes 103
Chapter 15: Moon Weather 107
Chapter 16: The Aquatic World 115

Contents

Chapter 17:	Aboard Noah's Ark	135
Chapter 18:	Diana's Green Thumb	145
Chapter 19:	Reproduction	151
Chapter 20:	Male Periods	165
Chapter 21:	Murder and Mayhem	175
Chapter 22:	Madness	187
Chapter 23:	Suicide	199
Chapter 24:	Biological Rhythms	203
Chapter 25:	Bleeding	217
	PART THREE—A SEARCH FOR THE MECHANISM	223
Chapter 26:	Moonlight	225
Chapter 27:	Biological Tides	237
Chapter 28:	"P.I." in the Sky	241
Chapter 29:	Weather Effects	247
Chapter 30:	Magnetism and Electricity	251
Reference notes		267
Bibliography		311

Acknowledgments

I want to thank the many people who provided me with assistance, especially my friends, for their patience. My special thanks go to John Langone and to Anne Katzeff for her professional assistance in preparation of the manuscript.

Portions of the following works are reprinted with the kind permission of their publishers.

Burrows, William, "Periodic Spawning of 'Palolo' Worms in Pacific Waters," *Nature,* 1945, *155,* 47–48, reprinted by permission of *Nature,* London.

Fox, H. Munro, "Lunar Periodicity in Reproduction," *Proceedings of the Royal Society of London, Series B,* 1923, *95,* 523–550, reprinted by permission of The Royal Society, London.

Hartley, William, and Hartley, Ellen, "Moon Madness," *Science Digest,* September 1972, pp. 28–33. Reprinted by permission from *Science Digest,* Copyright © 1972 The Hearst Corporation. All Rights Reserved.

Kelley, Douglas, "Mania and the Moon," *Psychoanalytic Review,* 1942, *29,* 406–425, reprinted by permission of Human Sciences Press, New York.

McDaniel, Walton Brooks, "The Moon, Werewolves, and Medicine," *Transactions & Studies of the College of Physicians of Philadelphia,* 1950, *18* (Fourth Series), 113–

122, reprinted by permission of the College of Physicians, Philadelphia.

Sadger, Isidor, *Sleep Walking and Moon Walking,* trans. Louise Brink (Nervous and Mental Disease Monograph Series No. 31. Washington, D.C.: Nervous and Mental Disease Publishing Co., 1920), reprinted by permission of the Smith Ely Jelliffe Trust, New York.

Sarton, George, "Lunar Influence on Living Things," *Isis,* 1939, *30,* 495–507, reprinted by permission of the History of Science Society, Philadelphia.

Small, Collie, "A Full Moon Can Beam Disaster," *Boston Herald American,* December 13, 1978, p. 15. Distributed by Special Features. Reprinted by permission of The New York Times Syndication Sales, Inc., New York.

Stahl, William Harris, "Moon Madness," *Annals of Medical History,* 1937, *9,* 248–263, reprinted by permission of the Medical Department of Harper & Row, Publishers, Inc., Hagerstown, Maryland.

Summers, Montague, *The Werewolf* (Secaucus, N.J.: University Books, 1960). Selection reprinted by arrangement with University Books Inc.

"I do not know whether I understand your meaning when you say 'Astrology.' I do not know all the influences which go from body to body. I do know that if man is not affected in some way by the planets, Sun and Moon, he is the only thing on Earth that isn't."

—ROBERT A. MILLIKAN, 1924
Nobel Prize winner and President
of the California Institute of Technology

Introduction

The Silver Watch

The day a Cornwall, England, ditch-digger named Charles Hyde was hauled into court on a housebreaking charge in 1953, his lawyer argued that Hyde couldn't help himself because the full moon had made him do it.

Hyde's barrister went so far as to portray his client as "a Dr. Jekyll and a real live Mr. Hyde."[1] He insisted Hyde was a faithful father, husband, and worker. "But he suffers from a kind of moon madness. He seems to go off the rails when the moon is full."[2]

Remarkably, the court bought this defense and let the laborer from St. Columb Minor in Cornwall off on probation. Regrettably, Hyde was back in court one year later, accused of breaking probation. Just before a full moon, he had skipped England and joined the French Foreign Legion, ending up at Sidi-bel-Abbes in Algeria. Back in Cornwall, he was placed on probation a second time, but on May 3, 1954—the night after a new moon—he burglarized his brother-in-law's home, making off with a checkbook and wallet. This time he was sentenced to eighteen months in prison.[3]

* * *

When more than a hundred young Iranians attempted suicide during a single day not long ago, there was a full moon over the Middle East.

A surgeon in Tallahasee, Florida, examined the hospital records of some 1,000 tonsillectomy patients to see what he could learn about patients who suffer unusually heavy bleeding after surgery. What the good doctor saw was that more than eight out of ten problem bleeders had gone under the knife during a full moon.

* * *

Skeptical? You may dismiss the full moon's legendary power. You may file the British burglar, the anguished Iranians, and the surgeon's survey in the nonsense bin along with black cats, four-leaf clovers, and warts from masturbation. You may.

But you'd be wrong.

The myths and old wives' tales may not always accurately describe the mechanisms by which the moon influences terrestrial life, but contemporary science is proving that the effects themselves often do exist. And there are more effects than many people would imagine. The full moon is more than an accomplice to barroom brawls and general craziness. As predictably as the full moon climbs above the earth every 29 days, 12 hours, 44 minutes, and 3 seconds, human violence, despair, disease, lust, births, and madness also rise. It is the full moon that decides which stalk of corn shall grow tallest. It is the full moon that tells monkeys, worms, cows, mayflies, rats, grouse—and humans—when to mate.

To be sure, its sinister influence is present where we do expect it. A Miami psychiatrist-psychologist team, for instance, found that the murder rate in surrounding Dade County, Florida, was highest over a fifteen-year period at the full moon. They found a similar pattern over thirteen years in Greater Cleveland, Ohio. A New York study found that robbery, assault, and car theft all peaked at the full moon. Hockey players start slugfests most often at the full moon. Julius Caesar was assassinated during the full moon phase. And the people of My Lai, Vietnam, were massacred beneath a full moon.

But the full moon also commands us to make love, not just war. A medical survey of women in a prestigious Connecticut college community revealed that a huge majority preferred to have sex at the full moon, which is also when most women ovulate. That discovery was borne out by the results of three separate studies of nearly one million births in New York City. More by far were around full moons than any other time of the lunar month, which makes perfect sense because human gestation lasts a period equal to nine lunar months.

The moon itself is often a fanatically jealous lover. Researchers in Buffalo, New York, have found that people in surrounding Erie County who commit suicide usually take their lives during a full moon. Most suicides in a major Ohio urban area were at the full or new moon.

Nor does mankind have a unique relationship with the full moon. In the forth century B.C. Aristotle said that sea urchins (aquatic cousins of starfish and sand dollars) in the Mediterranean reach sexual maturity—and taste best—at the full moon. No one bothered to check Aristotle's claim, however, until the twentieth century, when a British biologist proved him right. Nova Scotia fishermen have long known that the biggest catches of North Atlantic herring are usually at the full moon. And the luminescent Atlantic fireworm illuminates the waters around Bermuda when it swarms near the ocean's surface at each full moon in the spring. The sun may have set on the British Empire, but the full moon certainly hasn't.

There is more to the moon, though. Its power is not confined merely to one day or phase, the full moon. Just as the moon raises tides every day, people, animals and plants are always under the moon's influence. Birds use its ceaseless tug to navigate. A snail-like dweller of the deep Pacific needs the moon to know when to grow another chamber on its spiral shell each month. The moon tells potatoes how much oxygen to breathe each day of the lunar month. A Japanese bus and taxi company discovered that once every lunar month its drivers, all male, had *periods* that affected their ability to drive. When the company rearranged drivers' schedules around their respective lunar cycles, traffic accidents disappeared like moonlight on a cloudy night. And in California, the biological functions of a blind man voluntarily confined to a hospital room without any clues to tell him what time of solar day it was drifted into a daily timetable equal in length to the 24-hour, 50-minute lunar day. Sometimes it is blatant, sometimes it is covertly hidden behind more obvious solar rhythms, but one way or another so much life on earth operates on a lunar schedule, it is as if the moon were a silver-plated watch suspended for all to see in the sky.

Of course, the ancient world claimed to be perfectly aware of the entire range of the moon's influence, paying as much attention to its beneficial effects as to its deleterious ones. People believed the moon—the full moon, in particular—could drive men mad, cause epilepsy, and metamorphose men into werewolves, but also increase the fecundity of everything from timber to stud bulls. The moon was consulted before starting war or visiting a barber. Any fool could tell you that if you wanted something to grow, flourish, or survive, you should prune, plant, or paint it at the full moon; if you didn't give a damn—or it it was something grown underground like a carrot or onion—the new moon would do just fine. The Druids worshiped the moon and, like so many other peoples, revered the full moon as the patron of prosperity, a symbol of good luck.[4] German Jews in the Middle Ages would marry only during a full moon.[5] An in Gaelic, the word for "full moon" is the root for the word meaning "good fortune."[6]

In the fourth and fifth centuries B.C., Hippocrates, the father of modern medicine, advised that no physician be allowed to practice before he had studied the moon and stars and planets.[7] The Greek physician Galen, second only to Hippocrates among the early pillars of medicine, went so far as to develop a diagnostic procedure which presumed that certain days of each lunar phase had their own unique effects on illness or medical treatments.[8] Sailors since the time of Pliny have been afraid to sleep on deck exposed to moonlight for fear of any number of dire consequences, from insanity to blindness. And a physician in that most maritime of nations, Britain, studied seamen aboard ship some years ago to see if there were any basis for their fears.[9]

The Hottentots of South Africa are one of several peoples who blame the moon for death as well as disease, and they'll tell you it's all because of a rabbit. Their legend goes that the moon told the rabbit to go to earth and tell the people that they would be reborn after death, just as the moon comes back to life after every new phase. Unfortunately, this was one dumb bunny and he delivered the moon's message incorrectly. He told men and women they would only go 'round once in life, and when he returned from his mission the moon was furious and threw a stick at him, splitting his lip, which is why to this day the rabbit has a split upper lip. The Hottentots say that's also why the moon has spots: before the rabbit split, split lip and all, he swiped the moon's face with his clawed paw, and the marks remain for all to see.[10]

In an Indochinese tale that bears a remarkable resemblance to the story of the Tower of Babel, the moon is blamed for the diversity of languages and dialects.[11] The story recalls the time when all people lived in one big village and spoke the same language. During a council session, however, the people agreed that the moon's phases were an inconvenience. At the new moon, for example, cattle theft and warfare were more common, so the people decided to capture the moon and make it shine permanently. They began to build a tower that became so tall after several years that workers remained on their respective levels all the time instead of commuting up and down. Food was relayed up the tower to them and naturally it didn't take long for people on different levels to develop their own customs and languages.

Then disaster struck. The moon realized what the people were up to and grew mighty offended. It raised a terrific storm that shattered the tower and scattered the people everywhere. The survivors, of course, simply built new villages wherever they landed and perpetuated their new customs and tongues. The tower's rubble? Well, that became the foundation for the mountains that separate Burma from the Bay of Bengal.

Not surprisingly, there are still people everywhere who try to solicit the moon's aid—or at least avoid its disfavor—as if it were some rotund, all-powerful Eastern potentate. The women of rural northwest New Guinea use the moon to help assure the safety of their menfolk when the men have departed on some journey. The wives and sisters of the traveling men sing to the moon and accompany themselves with melodic gongs. They start two or three days before the new moon and continue until the second or third day after it, when the first sliver of the waxing crescent appears.[12] They feel that their music has helped bring the new moon back to life. If it weren't for that, their men would disappear—like the new moon.

The men of some tribes in New Guinea fish on lagoons at the full moon. What they do is poison the water with the pounded root of a certain plant which has a potent narcotic effect that stuns the fish and makes them easy prey. But while the men are at work on the moonlit water, the people on shore must keep as still and silent as death, with their eyes fixed on the fishermen, and no pregnant woman may be there because a single glance by her at the water will nullify the poison's effect.[13] Even the full moon can't correct that.

At the new moon, some Alaskan Eskimo boys are responsible for leaving the family igloo and heaping a handful of snow into the kettle. This is supposed to help hunters capture seal and bring it home.[14] At least as recently as the 1940s, some Armenians feared the fickle moon enough to try to ward off its influence on children by performing magical ceremonies outdoors beneath the moon.[15] The Oglala Sioux say that merely dreaming of the moon is an invitation to calamity.[16] An in the Tarot, the sign of the moon is usually evil.[17]

A more benign use of the moon is in timekeeping. Whereas our notion of "day" depends on the coming and going of the sun's light, the moon gave us the concept of "month," something illustrated by prehistoric cave-wall drawings of the moon used as calendars, as well as the later Egyptian hieroglyphic, a lunar crescent, which designated one month, and similar symbolism used by some American Indians.[18,19] The moon's quarters may also be the basis for the idea of "weeks," though many scholars point out that each quarter is longer than seven days.

At any rate, some people still use the moon to influence as well as to mark time. Natives in parts of New Guinea throw stones and spears at the moon to hasten its movement, which they are convinced will also hasten the return of friends who are away from home.[20] Many societies continue to measure time by lunar months, instead of the solar year. The Muslim calendar does this, relying on twelve lunar months to constitute a year even though that results in a year with only 354 or 355 days.[21] The ancient Chinese calendar (also used in Vietnam) is nearly identical, and it is certainly no mere coincidence that China's Senior Vice Premier, Teng Hsiao-ping (Deng Xiaoping), made his historic visit to the United States on January 28, 1979, the day of the Chinese New Year, a day his countrymen associate with good luck.[22,23] The Hebrew calendar uses both the sun and moon to keep track of time. It is based on a year of thirteen lunar months; New Year's Day is the day the new moon appears nearest to the autumnal equinox.[24,25] Modern Christian holidays also rely on the moon; the full moon helps determine the date of Easter.[26]

The trouble with lunar calendars is that their years don't equal solar years in length. In a lunar calendar of twelve lunar months, for example, seasons and holidays will keep arriving earlier every solar year. That is what has prompted every reform in the evolution from primitive lunar calendars through the Roman calendar to our Gregorian one. Nevertheless, the changes have not always enjoyed public support. When England got around to adopting the Gregorian calendar in 1752, eleven days had to be dropped from the new calendar. That incited the people of Bristol to riot because they believed they were being cheated out of eleven days of life, not to mention wages.[27]

The world's literary luminaries have consistently paid tribute to this illuminated orb's power over humankind. Shakespeare was no exception. When Romeo swears by the moon that his love for Juliet will never end, pragmatic Juliet suggests he find something a little more consistent than the ever waxing and waning moon to pledge by. Othello curses the moon for making men mad. And it is to the moon that Enobarbus confesses guilt and regret for his treachery against his friend Mark Antony.

Lord George Byron trusted the moon much less. He accused it of harboring the devil, while John Milton and Percy Bysshe Shelley both considered it the cause of "moon-struck madness." Francis Bacon, on the other hand, was sure his own intellect grew as the moon waxed full. Dickens's Mr. Peggotty is simply fatalistic about the moon. He assures David Copperfield that Mr. Barkis will die promptly at the lunar-pulled ebb tide.

Of course, we could dismiss all that as merely so much poetic license, which we expect authors to exploit. But what makes all of this more than an empty exercise in the occult is the increasing receptivity of contemporary scientists to this idea that lunar influence is more than hollow superstition. We are not talking about the sort of "science" that thinks the pyramids were beacons for prehistoric spacecraft or that the Axis lost World War II because Hitler was born under the wrong star. We are talking about meticulous clinical and statistical research, fastidiously performed and dutifully reported in books and the professional journals of the scientific community. Many of the most important advances in this research have taken place during the past two decades. A number of these have been accidental spin-offs of the space program or of such otherwise routine biological studies as, for example, the methods birds use to navigate on cloudy days.

But if legitimate research has validated ideas about the moon's power, why has that research remained unheralded and largely unknown to the public? Precisely because old prejudices die hard. Since the idea that the moon could affect anything other than ocean tides has been condemned as superstition for so many years, any professional scientist undertaking research along that line has risked having his or her reputation marred by that taint. Professional credibility has always been precious, but especially in a day when university tenure and government research funds are as difficult to obtain as a free trip to the moon, many scientists have been reluctant to engage in or publish research about lunar cycles.

Take the Australian radiophysicists E.E. Adderley and E.G. Bowen. In 1962 they published their discovery that heavy rainfall occurs at set intervals every lunar month. Their work had actually been completed years earlier but, as they explained in the journal *Science,* fear of professional ridicule made them decide not to publish it earlier.[28] As late as 1970, zoologist John D. Palmer wrote, "As it turns out there have been few scientific studies designed to examine the possibility of the effect of the moon on human life. Even the hint of interest in such an investigation would generate condemnation from fellow scientists. . . ."[29] Biologist Frank A. Brown, Jr., faced the same threat. While working toward his 1934 doctorate at Harvard University, Brown was warned by an older colleague of the professional dangers in pursuing his interest in the lunar rhythms of living organisms. "So, dutifully, I turned to more conventional areas of biology and worked until I had achieved a full Professorship, a good salary, permanent tenure—could not be fired—and then, in 1948 I returned to the rhythm problem."[30,31] Brown says he has no regrets. Had he gone ahead with his rhythm research before being armed by tenure, he might well have made it impossible or at least more difficult to pursue a career that has brought him distinction, especially for his research in crustacean endocrinology and, as we'll see in succeeding chapters, in lunar cycles.

That reluctance seems to be passing. The accumulation of hard-nosed evidence in recent years has simply encouraged more investigators to step into the field. The result: more scientists have swung away from positions of hostility toward the idea of lunar influence to a posture of open-mindedness and, in a growing number of cases, outright conviction that the moon does indeed play a brilliant role on mankind's stage. Debate surely continues to swirl around this subject; not every question has been answered by any means. But most of the scientific discussion has moved from "Is there a correlation between lunar phases and the behavior of life on earth?" to "Why *is* there a correlation, and what causes it?" If the moon does what if really seems to be doing, how does it do it?

By moonlight? Researchers in metropolitan Boston have shown how women with unpredictably long menstrual cycles can stabilize them at 29-day intervals by leaving a bedroom light on during the fourteenth through seventeenth nights after ovulation. The lamp's light apparently is comparable to the full moon's.

Perhaps the moon's influence is due to tides in our bodies like those in the oceans. Not only are several types of emotional disturbance more common at full moons, but physicians have found that some disorders, like manic depression, can be treated with drugs that normalize levels of body water. Or perhaps the moon alters our mental climate by influencing the weather. The lunar rainfall pattern discovered by Adderley and Bowen is not the only meteorological rhythm seemingly synchronized with the moon, and we'll see that men and women have a hard time weathering several of these weather events. We'll also take a close look at what happens to humans when the moon fiddles with such geophysical phenomena as the earth's magnetic field.

In fact, the more exotic the theories become, the more popular they are with scientists. New knowledge in the vanguard of astronomy and biology is now suggesting mechanisms for the moon's influence that scientists heretofore never dreamed of. Their importance can no longer be ignored.

Wrote the medical researchers Walter and Abraham Menaker: "The day of geophysical biology and medicine is at hand. What may appear of merely theoretical interest in this field today may have considerable practical value tomorrow"[32]

PART ONE

Lore and Mythology

This book is organized into three parts. In Part One we'll deal with the lore and mythology that have surrounded the moon like an ageless halo. These stories are not merely a random assortment of legends and mythical explanations for the nature and workings of the moon. Instead, most fall into one of several specific areas, which we'll examine individually as chapters in this section.

Part Two considers facts about the moon: selenology (lunar "geology" and astronomy), tidal effects, and the scientific studies that have found correlations between lunar phases and everything on earth from man's sexual habits to the weather.

The final section will present theories about how the moon exerts its influence on the earth and its inhabitants.

1

Green Cheese

Galileo could not work in peace. People were so intrigued by the moon that when Galileo brought his first telescope to St. Mark's Church in Venice, a savvy crowd spotted him in the tower and guessed exactly what he was up to. When he came down, the crowd took away his telescope and would not let either the man or his instrument go until every person there had had a chance to gaze through the new spyglass, and that took several hours. When Galileo finally took his first telescopic look at the moon in May 1609, the news of that event caused more excitement than the discovery of America had.[1] Italian authorities expressed their pleasure by immediately granting Galileo life tenure at the university in nearby Padua and doubling his salary.[2]

Fascination with the moon is as old as mankind, and people have speculated about what the moon is and why it behaves as it does since first setting earthbound eyes on it. Its most dramatic and most mysterious habits are its waxing and waning, and there has never been a shortage of explanations for that. Aborigines of what is now Encounter Bay, near Adelaide, Australia, once said that the waning moon is actually a woman whose endless partying causes her to lose weight. The moon is new when she wisely decides to go away and rest awhile.[3]

The Klamath Indians of Oregon say the moon wanes as it breaks to pieces. The Dacotahs believe that once the moon is full, mice begin to nibble away at it until they've eaten it all. Then a new moon is born and grows to maturity, only to share its predecessor's fate.[4] Some people in the Balkans of Europe tell the same story, substituting wolves for the mice.[5] Similar myths were as common as wampum among many Indians of North and South America; only the hungry animals change.[6]

Greenlanders tell the tale of Malina and her brother, Anninga. One day Anninga seized his sister by her shoulders, a gesture of courtship in Greenland, and Malina, horrified at the prospect of incest, fled to the sky, becoming the sun. Anninga chased her, and became the moon. He is still pursuing her, and the incessant hunt makes him hungry and thin until he's forced to rest. That's the new moon. He hunts seals and relaxes until he's fit, fat, and strong again, and that's the full moon.[7,8]

The Slavic tale is just the reverse. The male moon cheats on his wife, the sun, who in anger turns and cuts him with a sword.[9] Eskimos have a story about a powerful magician who left earth with his beautiful sister and precious Fire, which became the sun, his new home in heaven. At first he and his sister lived happily together, but he gradually turned cruel. Then, one day, they fought and he burned one side of her face. She ran away, of course, and became the moon, who shows us her burnt side at the new moon, her healthy half when the moon is full.[10]

The Wongibon people of New South Wales believe the waning moon is the bent back of an old man who injured himself falling off a rock.[11] The ancient Egyptians believed that the waning moon is all that men can see of the god Osiris's destruction by his enemies.[12] Early Semites thought seven demons ganging up on the moon gradually broke it down.[13]

Even the familiar nursery rhyme of Jack and Jill is interpreted by scholars as an allegory for the moon's waxing and waning. On the one hand, if you stare at the face of the crescent moon, the dark seas and lighter surface features may begin to resemble the silhouette of Jack and his pail. Jill appears as the moon becomes full. Linguists, however, say the modern nursery tale evolved from an old Scandinavian legend, which describes how the moon kidnapped two earth children, Bil and Hjuki, as they were carrying water home in a bucket. The Norse name Hjuki, it seems, was pronounced as "Juki," which has been corrupted into "Jack." "Bil" became "Jill," because "Jack and Jill" sounds better than "Jack and Bil." The fall of Jack and Jill in the rhyme simply represents the disappearance of one moon spot after another as the moon wanes.[14,15]

But there's more. One European archeologist and folklorist says that Jack and Jill gave birth, allegorically, to the Old Man in the Moon. After Jack and Jill evolved from the Scandinavian myth, they themselves gradually lost their identification with the moon. Then, sexism being nothing new, Jill faded passively into the background and Jack aged into a wizened old man whose bucket became stolen sticks or vegetables.[16]

A nineteenth-century English clergyman wrote that in Hebrew tradition the Old Man in the Moon is Jacob, Abraham's venerable grandson and prophet.[17] The Creek Indians believed that a man and dog lived together on the moon, and the Selish Indians of mountainous eastern Washington State believed that a toad inhabited the moon. He got there in one mighty leap he was forced to make to escape the pursuit of an amorous wolf.[18] The ever-polite Selish have never said what they thought about the wolf's romantic preferences.

People who never had access to anything like Galileo's telescope have relied more on vivid imagination than scientific observation to explain the moon's spots. South Pacific islanders thought they were "splendid groves."[19] The ancient Greeks viewed them each as Elysium, pockets of paradise, where all people retire in friendship after life.[20] In Malayan mythology, the spots are a hunchbacked man sitting under a banyan tree.[21] The Khasias of the Himalayas say the spots are punishment for the moon, which is a man who falls in love with his mother-in-law once a month. That righteous lady rewards his sin with ashes, thrown reprovingly in the moon's face.[22] The Greenlanders perpetuate a similar story, involving again that brother-sister couple, Anninga and Malina. In this version Malina smears her brother's face with soot from a lamp because he has been teasing her.[23] With a sense of humor like that, one wonders what it is that Anninga sees in her.

For the Greeks, the moon's passage across the night sky was

easy to explain. It was the moon goddess Selene hurrying to her slumbering lover, Endymion. In other Mediterranean cultures, the moon was lovely Europa fleeing from (or being carried by) her suitor, the solar bull. Once a month, her sturdy suitor caught up and the two celestial bodies were in conjunction, in more ways than one. Moreover, this consummation of marriage between the king and queen of the sky was celebrated with special fervor every eight years. The moon and sun may be in conjunction (that is, a new moon) every month, but each new moon is in a different spot in the sky until about eight years pass, when it is once again in exactly the same place. Some scholars say this is why the Athenians had to sacrifice seven girls and seven boys to Minos every eight years as tribute.[24]

The Tahitians, whose sense of tragedy was less dramatic than the Greeks', used to imagine that the sun and moon were happily engaged in lovemaking during any eclipse.[25]

In general, the moon is often thought of as an animal, and most often as a rabbit. Sometimes the moon's spots are explained as rabbit's tracks. The toad, mouse, cat, lion, bear, and fox are other animals "seen" in the moon.[26] The Egyptians signified the moon as a white cow in some hieroglyphics because that's what the horns of the crescent moon reminded them of. Pictures of the moon goddess often showed her being drawn by a team of cattle.[27]

Ironically, one outrageous image of the moon is not at all based on some outlandish concept of what the moon is like. "The moon is made of green cheese" is actually a proverb nearly as old as Modern English. It cropped up first in English in the works of the eminent statesman and author Sir Thomas More (1478–1535). The French humorist Francois Rabelais (1495–1553) also used it. Both men, though, were probably repeating something they had heard used in speech by ordinary people.[28]

In any case, "green" does not refer to the color of the moon. It means a cheese that is new, one that has not had time to age. In the early days of cheesemaking, such a new cheese might resemble the moon in shape and mottled color.[29]

And a new cheese is almost certainly uncut, still whole and round. Like the full moon.

2

Lunacy

This happened to a Chicago physician at a suburban cocktail party. It was summer, and he was standing on the terrace with friends admiring the bright yellow disc of the full moon in the star-spangled night sky. Suddenly, the hostess excused herself, explaining that she had to pull the shades in her son's bedroom or the boy would end up sleeping with the moon shining "right on his face."

When one of the guests asked her whether that wasn't just superstitious malarky, not only did she stand firm but several other people backed her up. They all agreed that moonlight shining on the face during sleep can cause bad dreams, nightmares even insanity.[1]

The good doctor was amazed. Bedouins of the desert would not be. They believe staring at the moon will drive a strong man mad. So, too, rural German housewives say the moon makes maids careless enough to drop fragile dishes.[2]

A Scandinavian fairy tale, "The Magic Mirror," describes the plight of King Alting, who behaved like a wild beast once a month. The culprit was the full moon.[3]

And in Iceland the saying goes that if a pregnant woman sits facing the moon, her child will be wacky.[4]

The equation of lunacy with the moon, especially the full moon, is one of the oldest and most deeply rooted beliefs of man. We only have to look as far as the linguistic roots of the word itself for proof. *Luna* is both the name of the Roman goddess of the moon[5] and the Latin word for moon.[6] It is found in the French *avoir des lunes,* the German *mondsuchtig,* the Italian *lunatico,* and the Latin *lunaticus.*[7] It is also obvious in such current English colloquialisms as "moonstruck," meaning crazed; "moony," for dreamy or absent-minded; "mooning," as in wandering aimlessly or a lover's distraction; "mooncalf," being someone born deformed or retarded; not to mention "loony."

The belief is ancient. In the Mediterranean world insanity was often blamed on gods and demons from the moon who visited or possessed a person's mind.[8] Dreams and nightmares were often considered the result of sleeping in the full moon's light.[9] The Babylonian-Assyrian god Sin was the deity both of wisdom or light and of the moon. The Egyptian god Thoth governed intelligence and understanding as well as the moon.[10] It was also the Egyptians who said the cure for insanity was to make meatballs out of the flesh of a particular common snake and eat them beneath the light of the full moon.[11,12]

Hippocrates, the father of modern medicine, wrote that nightmares are caused by visitations from the Greek goddess of the moon.[13] Plutarch later wrote that anyone who sleeps in moonlight is liable to pay for such obvious folly by becoming and out-and-out numbskull.[14] Even the Bible concurs with all of this. The Hebrew Talmud warns people not to sleep in moonlight.[15] Psalm 121 sings of the moon's danger at night.[16] And the New Testament preaches about connections between the moon and insanity.[17]

Nor is it only ignorant, ill-educated people who have perpetuated this idea that the moon is a main cause of insanity. The educated elite of every age have also embraced it. The respected Welsh historian Giraldus (1147–1230) wrote that lunatics are people whose madness can be observed once a month, whenever there's a full moon.[18] The sixteenth-century physician Paracelsus blamed insanity on the moon's attraction, which extracts a person's lucidity the way the north pole pulls on a compass needle. This is the cause of every mental ailment from excessive sexual passion to hallucination, he wrote, and the problem is worst at the new moon.[19] The eminent eighteenth-century French psychiatrist Joseph Daquin took the lunar connection for granted. So did Italy's Cesare Lombroso.[20] Benjamin Rush, who had signed the Declaration of Independence and was one of the brightest lights of medicine and politics of eighteenth-century Philadelphia, initiated a study of the moon's effect on mental patients.[21] In 1882 the German psychiatrist Koster published a monumental study of the correlation between hundreds of cases of insanity and the moon's phases.[22]

The British, however, gave the most prominent recognition to the moon's role in insanity. In the 1600s, Sir Matthew Hale (who would later become Chief Justice of England) argued before a court that lunacy was most assuredly caused by the moon, particularly the full moon "and in the change of the moon" at the equinoxes and summer solstice.[23,24] And in the eighteenth century, Sir William Blackstone's definition of lunar lunacy was written into law after the legal eagle had dazzled his colleagues with an explanation that distinguished between a "lunatic," whose madness is monthly—usually at the full moon—and someone who was "insane," which meant perpetually and hopelessly psychotic.[25,26]

3

Lunar Sympathy

The women of Naples, Italy, pray to the moon's ripening orb for a sexual, sensual favor. According to the late, Harvard-trained classics scholar Walton Brooks McDaniel, a young Neapolitan woman who wishes to increase the size of her bosom is likely to step onto her apartment's balcony or rooftop without a stitch of clothes on and recite a certain incantation.

"If she would perform this operation of magic with any hope of success, she has to be alone and quite naked," McDaniel wrote. "Furthermore, the well-known inability of heavenly powers to recognize that they are being addressed requires her to hold up her hands in obvious petitioning to the moon. Simple nudity itself can be so easily misinterpreted. The further inability of the powers to take in readily and precisely the purpose of a prayer makes her press her breast as she says *questa,* and makes her reinforce this deictic gesture by repeating the whole business . . . nine . . . times."[1]

This phrase she must repeat is, *"Santa Luna, Santa Stella, fammi crescere questa mammella,"* which means "Holy moon, holy star, make this breast grow for me."[2] Imagine the young lady standing beneath a starlit sky, praying that the waxing moon make her breast grow as it increases its own bulk. The light of the moon and a million suns barely illuminates her pale flesh, and she speaks hesitantly because her throat is tight with anxiety, anxiety over being discovered and, as McDaniel wrote, from concentrating so hard on not making a single mistake, which would wipe out the chant's effect. From a distance you can see her shoulders and head move while she implores the moon for help, and each time she touches her breast the soft skin ripples. As for the effectiveness of this ritual, that's—well—hard to say. McDaniel would only admit, tongue clearly in cheek, that he had "not been privileged to know either by . . . sight or through the personal assurance of any flat-breasted damigella . . ."[3]

Still, it's the thought that counts, and the thought behind this bit of lore from modern Naples reflects a mythological theme that is older than the city itself: the moon dispenses good luck and makes living things flourish while it waxes, and just the opposite while it wanes; the fuller it has grown, the more luck and sustenance it has to give away.[4] The full moon brings out the fullest potential of things on earth. The new moon is itself drained and thus has nothing to offer anyone or anything on earth. This is the concept of lunar sympathy.

The clearest illustrations of lunar sympathy have always been in agriculture. Farmers and gardeners have believed that it is during a waxing moon that you should plant something you want to grow. Anything you want to dry or cure should be cut while the moon is on the wane.[5] McDaniel explained how this rule was applied in the old Latin world:

> Roman farmers paid close attention to the changes of the moon. The time to fell timber and to cut, gather, and store all vegetable products was while its orb was on the wane. Manure was not be touched except at that season. On the other hand, the crops were thought to grow more vigorously as the moon increased. That is the period during which a graft should be inserted. . . .
>
> The changes of the moon were to be scrupulously observed in the raising of animals. Gelding should be done at the time it was on the wane. Both the planet [that is, the moon] and the beast were losing something. On the other hand, one should put eggs under a hen at the new moon if they were to mature into a good brood of chicks. We are advised that, if meat be salted while the orb is waning, no worms will ever invade it.

Shellfish were said to increase and diminish in plumpness under the influence of the moon.[6]

An understanding of this principle of lunar sympathy was considered so essential to one's success in daily affairs—certainly in farming and fishing—that everyone seems to have considered it important enough to publicize. The Greek poet Hesiod, in a work of verse dating back almost to the time of Homer, provided one such list of lunar *dos* and *don'ts* in which he discussed the right time of lunar month for everything from cutting wood to shearing sheep, gelding rams, and reaping grain.[7] Horace, just before the time of Christ, advised that "honey apples picked during a waning Moon preserve a finer blush."[8] Horace, the naturalist Pliny, and the satirist Lucilius thought that shellfish and certain starfish grow fatter during a waxing moon.[9,10] Aristotle argued that animals are colder during the waning moon.[11] And it was Pliny who said that ants never work at the full or new moon, and a new streak grows on the liver of rats every lunar day.[12]

The physician Galen reminded farmers that animals born when the moon was sickle-shaped would be weak and short-lived, whereas those born at a full moon will be healthy, vigorous, and long-lived.[13] Virgil recommended that vines (such as grapes) be planted during a waning moon; on the seventeenth day after a new moon, to be exact.[14] Cato, too, suggested that vines—as well as fig, apple, olive, and pear trees—be planted after a full moon and during an afternoon when there is no south wind blowing, but that timber be cut around a new moon.[15] Marcus Terentius Varro, whose interest in politics and literary endeavors made him a sort of Roman William F. Buckley, Jr., felt that the best time to shear sheep and strain sediment from olive oil is when the moon is waning.[16]

There was hardly anything untouched by this doctrine. The waxing moon was supposed to enlarge the eyes of cats and cause onions to wither. A waning moon would prompt onions to throw out their buds.[17] Pliny and Aristotle said that earthquakes usually occur at the new moon.[18] And *everyone* seems to have understood that medicinal plants and herbs would be most effective if plucked at the full moon.[19]

Common as such Greek and Roman examples are, the concept of lunar sympathy was not at all confined to the Mediterranean world. The Druids, for instance, also put immense faith in it. This was demonstrated by the way they timed their worship of mistletoe in oak trees, which they believed was a holy remnant of lightning sent by their gods. Nothing was more sacred, so the precious shrub would be harvested six days after the new moon, when the waxing phase had built up a powerful head of steam and could be relied upon.[20] Two white bulls would be sacrificed afterwards, and a potion prepared with mistletoe was believed more than adequate as a fertility drug for animals and women, an antidote for poison, a cure for ulcers and epilepsy—and a fire extinguisher.

Both the Druids and the Romans figured that since mistletoe was sent by the gods, its resting place must have been chosen by the gods. Indeed, anything this divine substance lived on had to be godly in itself. Thus, the Druids identified mistletoe-bearing oak trees with the god Balder; the Romans, with Jupiter, "who had kindly come down from heaven in the lightning flash to dwell among men. . . ."[21] It just so happened that the sacred tree beside Italy's Lake Nemi, where the principal temple to the moon goddess Diana stood, was oak. This allowed Diana, in her form as the silvery moon, the convenience of being able to gaze upon both her temple and the nearby embodiment of her divine liege, Jupiter.

That's probably also how we got one of our own most popular religious traditions. Mistletoe became increasingly identified with Diana and love; then, as the rites of new religions absorbed some fragments of old rituals and discarded others, mistletoe became identified solely with love. As a result, today we kiss beneath mistletoe at Christmastime.[22]

Diana is also one reason why the harvest moon is so well known today; the notion of lunar sympathy and orgies conducted in ancient farm fields are the other two reasons. Astronomically, the harvest moon is the full moon nearest the fall equinox, when farmers are harvesting. This moon is rising soon after sunset, which gives farmers (especially in temperate latitudes) extra hours of light to work by. Two thousand years ago, farmers gave that full moon credit for actually ripening produce. William Stahl, a medical historian, explains: "Our expression 'harvest moon' testifies to our once popular belief that the moon is responsible for the ripening of fruits. Among the Romans the harvest moon was especially venerated, for Diana's day fell at the time of the harvest full moon and offerings were made to her for bountiful aid. In the spring time a successful planting was assured by a festival to Anna Perenna at the March full moon. Drunkenness and sexual promiscuity in the fields were thought to bring fertility to man, beast and crops. Ovid tells how bystanders, meeting the merrymakers as they staggered homeward along the road, called them 'blessed' because they had worshipped well."[23] And to think that today people settle for a platonic ride in a haywagon.

Naturally, the idea of lunar sympathy has always applied to man, as well as beast and field. In some ways, the moon's influence is simply physical, as it is with so many animals and plants. The Emperor Tiberius, for example, called in his barber only during a waxing moon.[24] It may have been *easier* to fell timber during a waning moon, but when it came to one's own handsome locks the Romans did not want hair to get into the habit of falling out. For that very reason, Varro advised all men to get a haircut only at the full moon; otherwise, they risked going bald.[25]

The general idea was that not only do things grow better as the moon grows, but that living things are actually stronger, more resilient and resistant to damage during a waxing moon, and weaker, more vulnerable as the moon wanes. The fifth-century politician and philosopher Ambrosius Macrobius put it this way: "[T]here is no doubt that the Moon is the author and framer of mortal bodies, so much so that some things expand or shrink as it waxes and wanes."[26,27] Ptolemy tried to put this into medical terms by saying that the moon's waxing and waning was responsible for the expansion and contraction of "the bodily humors,"[28] which determine a person's ability to resist disease and his overall state of health. No one less than the great seventeenth-century scientist Robert Boyle agreed, saying that the human brain itself grows bigger and smaller as the moon waxes and wanes.[29]

The practical applications of this were numerous. Warts were supposed to be easiest to remove during a waning moon. Likewise, most diseases were easiest to cure.[30] For that reason, Marcellus Empiricus (court physician to Emperor Theodosius whom William Stahl describes as a "prince of quacks") believed that the most effective time to administer medical treatment was during a waning moon.[31] Here's his prescription for arthritis and sciatica, which was supposed to be prepared and taken by the patient only during a waning moon: take the dung of the chamois, a small, goatlike antelope, and crush a handful of it in a mortar. Add 25 grains of finely crushed pepper, some honey, and wine. Mix well, and use for seven consecutive days. If that didn't cure you, it would probably kill you—immediately and quite painlessly.

In contrast, a French physician published a study showing that epidemics spread quickest during a waning moon, as if diseases picked up strength like the growing moon.[32] Arguments for both sides litter the medical literature landscape, although the idea that a man's strength ebbs as the moon wanes was most widely accepted. The waning moon was considered an especially tough time for women.[33] Aristotle said that was because all body functions become sluggish during a waning moon.[34] Similarly, Aristotle was only the first in a long line of medical pundits to argue that men and women were most likely to die during ebbtide of the nearest body of water.[35]

The waxing moon is more than a celestial fertilizer, though. Its influence is not just physical. It brings good luck as well as good health. The Greeks considered the day of the full moon the best day for marriage.[36] When Agamemnon, who commanded the Greeks in the Trojan War, was asked in Euripides's play *Iphigenia,* what day he would choose for marriage, he answered, "When the bless'd season of full moon is come."[37,38]

The full moon was also considered the best time to have babies by the Greeks and Egyptians, among others. One writer has said, "Among the [ancient] Jews the full moon was believed to be lucky. . . . 'The full moon,' says the Rabbi Abravanel, 'is propitious to new-born children, but if the child be born in the increase or wane, the horns of that planet cause death; or, if it survive, it is generally guilty of some enormous crime.' "[39] How's that for a concept of Original Sin?

Armies of German barbarians would consult the moon before making any military moves. In a personal journal, Caesar recalled the time one of his armies was being bloodied by one such German horde until the Germans unexpectedly withdrew from the battle. They had acted on the sudden advice of their seers, who had "learned" that the Germans could not win any fighting begun before the moon was waxing, which would not happen for several days more.[40] It was a disastrously self-fulfilling prophecy.

The principle of lunar sympathy was sometimes carried to what seems today like nit-picking extremes. Pliny the Younger (the elder Pliny's nephew), for example, said that hyenas should be captured only during one particular combination of zodiac signs and waxing or waning phases, and ivy cut only during an entirely different set of cosmic combinations. Of course, he explained, that applied only to ivy that would be used to cure varicose veins.[41]

* * *

Not everyone considered the full and waxing moons beneficial. Some ancient American Indians placed the full moon in the same category with black cats and the number 13. Pictures on early Peruvian urns that portrayed the full moon often showed the moon in conjunction with the hieroglyphic representing the puma, which personified evil[42] and conjured an image of bad luck. This sounds like the way we think of the full moon today, associated with misfortune and evil. Just ask any cop, bartender, or hospital emergency-ward worker, who will tell you that the full moon brings out anything *but* the best in people. Still, the doctrine of lunar sympathy probably has more adherents today than, say, the doctrine of America's Manifest Destiny.

Since the new moon ushers in the fortuitous waxing moon, many Scottish women curtsy to it.[43] In 1937, one medical historian made the cavalier observation that "the negro [*sic*] is cheered by" the new moon.[44] Without explaining this crude generalization, the writer did go on to say, "He possesses a lore about the new moon, showing money to it and associating the first glimpse of the new moon over the right shoulder and through the trees with good luck." At any rate, all sorts of city folks still turn coins in their pockets at the new moon, and, in England, "one can still find old country folk who . . . insist that cauliflower must be planted only when the moon is new, and root crops when it is full or waning."[45]

Some Germans think that the time to pull or fill an aching tooth is during the waning moon because that's when the "pain" is weakest and most vulnerable to manipulation.[46] In contrast, it is a custom among Hindus of northern India to place food on their rooftops at the full moon of the month of Kuar (September-October). After this food has had a chance to absorb the rays of the full moon, they distribute it among their relatives, who are supposed to be able to live longer after eating food saturated with the energy of this most propitious of all moons.[47]

Then there are the Swedish housewives who still slaughter their family's poultry. They will not, however, perform this chore while the moon is waning for fear that the animal's meat will shrivel and melt away in the cooking pot.[48] That brings to mind an old Malaysian legend, that in the beginning of time no man died; a person merely grew thin like the waning moon and fat as it waxed.[49] The Malaysian equivalent of man's expulsion from Eden was the end of that eternal idyll. The English poet John Milton believed something similar. He was sure his intellect was sharper during the full moon.[50] Frederick II, the thirteenth-century Holy Roman Emperor, thought his advisors' wits would be sharper during a waning moon, and that was the only time he would consult them on crucial issues.[51]

As for the ancient Greek belief that the full moon is the best day for marriage, that's still the conventional wisdom among rural Germans.[52] Antique Roman, Egyptian, and Hebrew notions about which phases of the moon are best for birth would sound familiar today in Bolivia, New Guinea, and parts of Africa. Mothers of the Guarayos Indians of eastern Bolivia's gloomy rain forests and the Baganda people of the Central African Republic hold their newborn children to the new moon so the babies will grow like the waxing moon.[53] Some New Guinean mothers hold their children up to the full moon so that their bodies will be inspired by the robust orb.[54]

Aristotle's idea that human life ebbs and flows with the lunar-born tides is also still alive and well today. People in Spain say no one can die unless the tide is going out, and the rural Dutch believe that thin people are most likely to pass away during an ebb tide and fat people during the flood.[55] An English physician touring Peru around the turn of the century learned that mule drivers would not unsaddle their beasts during a waxing moon until the animals had cooled down; otherwise, the mule was believed almost sure to develop sores.[56]

The idea of lunar sympathy still is probably most widely accepted by farmers and gardeners. Just consider the continued success of *The Old Farmer's Almanac,* whose leaves of wisdom include planting tables that indicate the best times of the lunar month to plant, cultivate, or harvest particular plants.[57] There are also a cornucopia's worth of books like Dr. Clark Timmins's *Planting by the Moon,* which has detailed planting charts and reviews of similar charts made as far back as the 1600s. For example, Timmins relays the advice from *The Wonders of the Heavens,* by Camille Flammarion, the turn-of-the-century astronomer and lecturer, that such plants as cucumbers, radishes, turnips, leeks, lilies, horseradish, and saffron grow best during a full moon, and herbs plucked during a waxing moon will be strongest; in contrast, onions do most of their growing during a waning moon.[58] Such contrary behavior was the reason ancient Egyptians were so wary of eating onions, Flammarion said.

One writer says many otherwise modern farmers still watch the moon closely for the birth of their livestock.[59] They believe that a calf born around the new moon will be similarly debilitated and soon die. They'll often try to sell it before that happens.

Ironically, two very well-known things which don't seem to have anything to do with the concept of lunar sympathy actually commemorate an historic moment in Western history that took place precisely because of that concept. It was the Battle of Marathon in 490 B.C., memorialized by a race in the Olympic Games and one of the world's greatest amateur athletic events, the Boston Marathon.

The march into battle was ordered about a generation before the Golden Age of Athens, when Athenians would erect the Parthenon and Sophocles would write his tragedies, by a warrior-king who ruled much of the civilized world. Darius of Persia was lord of all Asia Minor. His empire stretched from northwestern India and parts of central Asia to southeastern Europe.[60] Greece stood just beyond his rule across the Aegean Sea from Turkey.

In 499 B.C., however, his authority was challenged by a revolt among the Greek colonies in Asia.[61] When the rebels went so far as to attack Sardis (located about where the Turkish city of Izmir is), the Athenians and Eretrians supported them.[62] Darius smothered the rebellion, but his anger against the Greeks now burned. He organized a huge army to invade Greece, only to have it shattered at sea by a storm off Mount Athos in 492 B.C.[63] Two years later, Darius was ready to try again. He assembled a large army of 30,000 men[64] and sent them to Greece under two generals, Datis and Artaphernes, with strict orders recorded by the historian Herodotus: " 'enslave Athens and Eretria and bring the slaves into [my] presence.' "[65] Dead Greeks they could feed to the vultures.

Datis and Artaphernes followed their orders well. Eretria, which is on the island of Evvoia and about 30 miles north of Athens, was placed under a punishing siege and soon taken, then taken apart. The Persians leveled the city and enslaved all of the survivors.[66] Finished there, the Persians returned to their boats and in September of 490 B.C. landed cavalry, archers, and infantry[67] along the coast about 24 miles northeast of Athens.[68] Athenian scouts on the surrounding hilltops could only watch as 20,000 of Darius's soldiers assembled on the beach below.[69] After a few days, part of the Persian fleet and the remainder of the army set sail for the Bay of Phalrum to form the southwest side of a pincer attack on Athens.[70] But here, north of Athens, all that separated the Greeks and Persians was a long, narrow plain called Marathon.

Back in Athens, the citizens did not need to consult the Oracle of Delphi to know the Persians' battle plan. They also knew they were badly outnumbered and, unless they could recruit the support of allies, Eretria's fate awaited them too. The Athenians decided to send some 9,000 heavily-armed infantry to Marathon while a garrison was kept behind to defend the city itself.[71] They also sent a runner, the Olympic champion Pheidippides, on to Sparta to enlist aid. He traveled for two days and two nights, jogging and walking roads, swimming rivers, and climbing mountains along his route.[72] But when he arrived, grim news greeted him. The Spartans said they could do nothing for six days,[73] when the moon would be full. The Spartans, who believed it was folly to make war before a full moon, would wait until then before sending troops.[74] In fact, the Spartans would never even appoint military commanders or commence a march to battle before a full moon.[75,76]

The Athenians were on their own, reinforced only by 1,000 Plataeans.[77] Worse, their command could not agree on a strategy. Five generals wanted to wait for the Spartans before taking any action, and five wanted to attack as soon as possible. It was Callimachus, the civilian commander-in-chief, who broke the stalemate by voting to act at the first opportunity,[78] and right away the Greeks moved to nullify the advantage Persian cavalry would have on the open plain. Under cover of night, the Greeks cut trees and moved them onto the plain, creating obstacles and narrowing the distance to the enemy. Incredibly, the Persians failed to retaliate.[79]

Historians believe the day of battle was probably September 21.[80] That morning, before the break of dawn, the Greeks charged one mile across the plain.[81] As they ran over the open land, Persian bowmen showered them with arrows. Their shields and bronze armor, though, were adequate, and when they reached the Persian lines, the Greeks found the invaders clad only in turbans, tunics, and trousers, carrying shorter spears and swords and wielding wicker shields. In minutes, the Persians' numerical superiority became meaningless. Six thousand four hundred of Darius's soldiers were slain while the rest were driven back through the surf to their fleet. The Greeks lost only 192 men.[82]

When the Spartans did finally reach Athens, the full moon was past and so was the battle.[83] If Callimachus or the Athenian generals had shared their Spartan neighbors' notions about the full moon, today Tehran might be the capital of the Western world and the Ayatollah our President.

4

"The Moon Is God"

It was an odd location for a wedding, this campground with bald spots showing through its grassy cover. No matter. This was no ordinary marriage. Two hundred and fifty worshipers had gathered in this place outside Demotte, Indiana, at the full moon of July 9, 1979, to witness and participate in a wedding conducted in the name of the moon and sun and performed by a pagan priest and priestess.

As the wedding throng formed a circle around the bride and groom and chanted the Hindu mantra, "Om," the gods and goddesses of the four elements—air, water, earth, and fire—were invited by the priest, priestess, and their co-celebrants to bless the ceremony by their presence. During the ceremony, the wedding couple (two chiropractors from Marietta, Georgia, in their twenties) were sprinkled with holy water and given "communion" with bread and wine. Then they fastened blue ribbons around each other's heads. A silver crescent representing the moon was affixed to the woman's; a gold medallion symbolizing the sun to her groom's. Finally, they jumped over a broomstick and were pronounced man and wife.[1,2]

This sort of pagan wedding is called a "handfasting," and it was one of the high points of the Third Annual Pan Pagan Festival, a veritable witches' brew of 325 paganists, occultists, and witches from twenty-six states and Canada.[3] The handfasting's timing was no mere coincidence.

"The moon is seen by us as representative of a certain type of energy flow, which peaks every twenty-eight [*sic*] days," says priestess Selena Fox, of the Church of Circle Wicca in Madison, Wisconsin. "We try to plug into that energy at the full, and sometimes new, moon. . . . Christians come together on Sundays; that's when their energy peaks. Our peak is at full and new moons, when we feel energy peaks."

"We don't have any specific requirements on this," priest Jim Alan adds. "We just follow the wishes of the couple, but most do want their marriage at the full moon."[4]

Lunar worship is alive and well in the twentieth-century industrial world. Fox and Alan are members of a neo-paganist church, whose members revere the forces of the natural world. Fox says nine to thirteen people join them for most full moon celebrations. As many as fifty participate in celebrations of the full moon that coincide with other major pagan holidays. Fox and Alan are both quick to emphasize that their church has nothing to do with the sort of bloodthirsty occultists who pop up on TV shows like "Starsky and Hutch," drooling for a chance to kidnap Starsky's latest girlfriend and use her for a human sacrifice. Their own worship, Fox and Alan say, has nothing to do with Satanism or any of the other malevolent practices people often associate with occultism and paganism.

Exactly how much company Fox and Alan have is hard to pinpoint. They themselves receive correspondence (letters, newsletters, pamphlets, and so on) from several like-minded groups. A more panoramic head-count comes from the Institute for the Study of American Religion, which estimates there may be as many as 40,000 practicing pagans in the United States.[5] Many of those people may worship the sun—or Pan, or Apollo, or Osiris—above or instead of the moon, though. Those whose primary reverence is for the moon may practice what they preach with varying degrees of commitment. They may make their living at such conventional jobs as bank-telling or bartending, for example, whereas Fox and Alan live on a farm, plant by lunar tables, and support themselves by hosting a local radio and a local TV show on metaphysics and holistic health and with proceeds from gardening, lectures at their farm and elsewhere, "and donations, like any church."

Some lunar worshipers may go uncounted altogether, says Fox, because they conduct their ceremonies in secret out of fear of harassment or ridicule.

Indirect evidence provides more clues to the number of lunar worshipers. Nancy Passmore of Boston has published a lunar calendar for each year since 1977. The first thousand printed for 1977 sold out, and so did the second printing of 1,500. All 3,000 printed for each of the following two years also sold out, and at least that many were planned for 1980. The months are lunar months of 29.5 days, showing the date and times of specific lunar phases. The calendars also have brief essays on such topics as planting by the moon, mythology, sexual cycles, and astronomy.

Passmore believes many of the people who buy her calendar are women simply interested in charting their menstrual cycles, but she says she has had correspondence from some 100 groups and individuals of lunar worshipers.[6]

The moon is also a source of quasi-religious inspiration to certain political and cultural movements. Take the women's movement. Some feminists take a strong interest in moon lore and cycles because they associate lunar worship with respect for women. As we'll see later in this chapter, the moon has traditionally been identified with women, especially in religious matters. Since, as some feminists believe,[7] many societies which have engaged in moon worship were outright matriarchies or societies which at least gave women an equal shake, feminists say the lunar roots of those societies should be examined with an eye toward imitating their desirable features. Some of Passmore's correspondence is from feminist individuals and groups having just that perspective.[8] And that's the view of at least one female author who suggests that women ought to pay attention to the moon and its lore in order to gain political power over their own lives, for in order to make themselves politically stronger women must bolster their pride in themselves; they need to see themselves as the historical central figures in societies, religions, and nature.[9]

Many American Indians are also seeking more independence through political power and pride in self, and at least one Indian group, Voices From the Earth, of the Mohawk Nation near Rooseveltown, New York, publishes its own lunar calendar.

* * *

Of course, the moon's role in religion is as old as religion itself. Cavemen at the end of the Old Stone Age made incisions on reindeer bone, mammoth ivory, and ornamental stone as well as on the walls of caves and rock shelters that were used as lunar calendars; the markings also refer to the moon as god.[10] Archeologists have found thousands of these, dating roughly from 8,000 to 40,000 B.C. The engraved bone, stone, and ivory resemble notched wooden rulers, but instead of small lines marking every eighth of an inch and large lines the inches, these prehistoric implements have short marks for individual solar days and long ones for the full and new moons. The paintings on cave and rock-shelter walls are more elaborate. At Abri de las Vinas, Spain, for example, the whole picture looks something like a human ear. There's an elongated oval vaguely resembling a human silhouette in the center of the picture. Assorted dots, crescents, and check-marks surround it. Each one represents a day in the lunar month and every shape has significance. "Each crescent faces in the precise direction it would face to a man looking south [at the moon], the first crescent curving right in the western dusk sky, the last curving left in the eastern dawn," explains a report in *Science.*[11] A thin slash designates the new moon day; a cluster of three dots indicates the days of and after the full moon. This was no lame-brain Fred Flintstone at work here. This Paleolithic Spaniard was perfectly capable of achieving the precision he desired. And that applied to the silhouette in the center, too. *Science* identifies it as "the humanoid 'god' or anthropomorph common in Magdalenian and Azilian [i.e., two stages of this Upper Paleolithic period] art. This is the first clue towards an understanding of this 'god' "[12] The same symbolism is present in the earlier paintings and notchings, as well.

Much later, around 2,000 B.C., Stonehenge in southern

England was used as a sort of lunar and solar temple. Various alignments of certain stones were used to predict the occurrence of solstices, equinoxes, eclipses, and other long-term lunar events, many of which were essential to the religious, agricultural, medical, calendric, magical, and artistic ceremonies conducted by people like the Druids, one of several groups to use Stonehenge.[13]

This capacity for predicting crucial events would help any priest class stay in power and make Stonehenge and the moon whose movements it times all the more important to those religious leaders. Some scholars think Stonehenge might even have been used to predict nothing less than the moon-god's visits to earth every nineteen years, the span of time mentioned by Diodorus in his *History of the Ancient World*.[14] That span of time has the right ring to it since it is almost exactly the amount of time to the Saros cycle, the time between eclipses in precisely the same spot in the sky.

The Anasazi Indians of New Mexico built a similar structure that played a crucial role in their agricultural and ceremonial lives from A.D. 950 to 1300.[15] The structure, atop an isolated butte in arid Chaco Canyon near several pueblo villages, consists of three crude stone slabs six to nine feet tall leaning against the face of the butte. They're aligned, though, with *astonishing* precision. Only during specific solstices, equinoxes, and eclipses, light from the sun and moon shines between the precisely positioned slabs onto a ceremonial spiral pattern carved into the butte wall behind.

Even aspects of the great Western faiths seem to have emerged from worship of the moon. Stephen Langdon, an astute student of mythology, has said that the earliest seeds of Judaism, for example, are in the worship of the moon, sun, and Venus. "[T]he three principal and perhaps the only deities originally worshipped by the Semites are the Sun, Venus, and the Moon, all astral deities. . . . It is, therefore, certain that Semitic religion in its most primitive form begins with three astral deities, Sun, Moon, and Venus. . . ."[16]

Later, while that primitive Semitic theology was evolving into the Hebrew faith, roots of words used by then to denote God came from words which had earlier referred to the moon as god. "[T]he South Arabian deity Ilâh, or Il, which is also the common Semitic word for 'god,' and corresponds to the Hebrew and Aramaic deity El, Elōhim, is one of the names of the Moon-god," Langdon wrote in *Mythology of All Races.* "The North Arabic alilah=Allah, who became the supreme and only god of Mohammedan religion, and El, Elōhim of the Northern Hebrew tribes who with Yāw, a deity of the Southern Hebrew tribes, became the supreme deity of Hebrew monotheism, would thus originally denote the ancient and prehistoric Moon-god."[17]

Scholars have noticed the same linguistic identification between words for "God" and words for "moon" on clay tablets from the time of Hammurabi, the great codifier of laws who ruled Canaan in the days of Abraham,[18] and Hammurabi's father. Some scholars translate a certain passage to read, "Yahveh is God," while others read it as 'The moon is God."[19]

The early lunar influences reflected by that language were gradually absorbed into the emerging Judaic religion (and later, the Islamic). The Hebrew calendar, for example, is still lunar oriented, as are many of its holidays. Howard D. King made this observation in the *Medical Record:*

> The Hebrews held the moon in great religious and superstitious veneration, considering lunar influence superior even to that of the sun; in fact, the moon was worshipped as a Deity. The new moons, or the first days of the month, were kept with great pomp and ceremony as national festivals. The people were obliged to abandon work on those days. The feast of the new moons was a miniature of the feasts of the prophets. The Jews, who were not acquainted with the phenomenon of eclipses, whether of the sun or the moon, looked upon them as evidences of divine displeasure.[20]

Evidence of this heritage of moon worship in the early Hebrew religion is even right there in the Bible, J.W. Slaughter wrote in the *American Journal of Psychology.* "There is frequent reference in the Scriptures to the 'host of heaven,' to the 'queen of heaven,' to Astarte or Ashtaroth, the moon-goddess of the Phoenicians. Ancient writers, as Lucian and Herodian, identified the latter deity with the moon. There is reference in

Genesis to Ashtaroth-Karnaim, meaning Ashtaroth of two horns. The symbol of Astarte was the heifer with the crescent horns, the worship of which continued almost throughout Hebrew history. The crescent was one of the most common of Ornaments."[21]

Even the day and name for the Hebrew Sabbath comes from the religious importance of the moon, the full moon in particular, to the Babylonians.[22] They called the day of the full moon, which was the fifteenth day of their month (the day of the new moon was day number one), "sapattu." The Hebrew "sabbath" also originated in moon worship, and, Langdon wrote, as a day of rest was probably an adaptation of the Babylonian "sabattu." This would have happened when the Israelis were enslaved by Babylonia. The Israelites gradually applied this Sabbath not only to the day of the full moon but also to the days of the new moon, first quarter, and third quarter.

Christianity also shows vestiges of lunar worship. Slaughter and another scholar pointed out that a fourth-century sect of Christians "worshipped it [i.e., the moon] in the person of the Virgin."[23,24] Slaughter went on to say, "The lower classes in the middle ages openly worshipped the moon, identifying her with the Virgin. In the Missal [i.e., the Church's official prayer book] Mary is spoken of as 'Sancta Maria, coeli Regina, et mundi Domina,'[25] which means, "Holy Mary, Queen of Heaven, and Mother of the World." And apparently that identification survives today. In a 1974 masters thesis, Doris Ann Stahl wrote, "The Blessed Virgin Mary is called 'The Moon of the Church,' 'The Spiritual Moon,' 'The Perfect and Eternal Moon.' "[26]

We even find the moon gaining the attention of some of Christianity's great theologians. Several medieval thinkers, for example, went to considerable lengths to explain why the devil tries to frame the moon for his own sins while at the same time letting it be known that the moon is acting at his behest. This was actually just an early, erudite version of that old plea, "The devil made me do it," only in this case it was supposed to be the moon and not a person who was asking for understanding.

Theologians thought Satan had an excellent motive for this devilishness, namely, to make God, Who controls all the planets and stars, look bad. According to Douglas Kelley in *The Psychoanalytic Review,* that was the prevailing view by church scholars, expressed by the *Malleus maleficarum,* a compendium of the devil's tricks, which appeared in twenty-eight editions between 1486 and 1600.[27] Kelley, in turn, quoted medical historian Gregory Zilboorg:

> One of the greatest difficulties of the time which the Malleus had to cope with was the increasing influence of astrological views and fantasies. Somehow it was necessary to bring the Malleus into a certain state of harmony with the various trends: a proper place had to be preserved for the lunatic, a proper significance retained for the stars, and yet while not depriving the devil of his influence, he was not to be endowed with any authority over the astral bodies which were under the direct control of the Lord. To quote the Malleus, ". . . there are two reasons why devils molest men at certain phases of the moon. First, that they may bring disrepute on a creature of God, namely the moon, as S. Jerome and S. John Chrysostom say. . . ."[28]

Similarly, Kelley observed, "The superstition that the moon at certain phases caused diseases, especially epilepsy, was combated by the explanation that the disease was actually caused by demons whose activity is connected with the phases of the moon. St. Jerome was the chief exponent of this idea, and he claimed that 'lunatics were not really smitten by the moon but were believed to be so, through the subtlety of the demons, who by observing the seasons of the moon sought to bring an evil report against the creature that it might rebound to the blasphemy of the Creator.' "[29]

These intellectual gymnastics were impressive. Yet, ironically, Old Man Moon had the last laugh over the devil. As Kelley pointed out, by the seventeenth century learned men were discounting the notion of a devil with widespread power over health, but medical literature continued to pay close attention to lunar influence.[30]

Semitic religions and their descendants, however, are hardly the only theologies which paid heed to the moon. The Druids in Britain and Ireland worshipped the moon; so did the Chinese and other Asians.[31] In Burma, the greatest festival of the year is still at the full moon of October, following the Buddhist Lent season, when sexual intercourse is prohibited.[32] Indians throughout the Americas also worshipped the moon.[33] There were those Anasazi, with their butte-top "Stonehenge," and the Blackfoot Indians, who revered the sun as their prinicipal god. But four days before the new moon of August the Blackfoot halted their annual migration and suspended all hunting. The people fasted and took spiritually and physically purifying steam baths. Finally, the nation chose a vestal virgin—or the next best thing, a woman who had had only one husband—who represented the moon and was married to the sun. And you better believe the Indians took this as seriously as the nuns Archie Bunker remembers from parochial school. Any maiden found to have lied about her purity was put to death.[34] The Romans had a similar ceremony, in which the moon priestesses and sacred harlots escorted a girl to the temple of the Moon Mother, where her virginity would be sacrificed to the goddess Diana.[35]

Many primitive peoples today also consider the moon a great deity, whereas the sun is viewed with little or no veneration.[36] For instance, the people of Bali, an island east of Java, hold public mass expulsions of local devils about every nine months at a new moon.[37] On the designated day, the citizenry gather at a local temple while food is set out at the nearest crossroad. The priests pray, and celebrants blow horns to summon the devils. Then men light torches at the high priest's holy lamp and spread out through the countryside like so many Paul Reveres, alerting their neighbors, who respond with a rising crescendo of noise by beating on doors, beams of wood, blocks of rice, and anything else they can pound. The fiends flee this racket and pause at the food laid out for them, but, wouldn't you know it, it's an ambush. The high priest leaps out from the temple and curses the devils so loudly that he frightens them away. The people of Fiji have a somewhat similar practice.[38] And, except for its synchronization to new moons, the whole thing sounds a lot like the way American politicians respond to any local crisis.

Moon worship also thrived in Egypt long before the pyramids became mere tourist attractions. "Among the ancient Egyptians the sun and moon worship seems to have been the earliest form of religion," Slaughter wrote. "There were two moon-gods, Khonsu and Thoth. All representations of these deities show them with the crescent, and Thoth was the keeper of time. The cat, well known as one of the sacred animals among the Egyptians, was dedicated to the moon."[39] In hieroglyphic literature or in art, moon deities took the moon's form, a crescent, or were depicted near a crescent. Often the importance of a deity or some other special entity was indicated by how close to the moon or a moon-god it was located. Other times a moon-god might be depicted as something resembling or suggestive of a crescent. In that case, the moon and sun, which were thought of as the eyes of heaven, might be represented as a cow or bull straddling the earth;[40] from front to rear hoofs the animal would have a crescent form. At one early stage, the Egyptians even considered the moon and sun the same object. The moon was simply the less brightly illuminated appearance of the sun at night.[41]

Today, we can still thank the Egyptian moon-gods for one of our most beguiling, if least logical, popular expressions. It turns out that ancient Egyptians desiring greater intelligence would pray to the moon-god Thoth because he was considered not only the keeper of time but also the god of wisdom. And since a man's heart, not brain, was supposed to be the seat of intellect, ancient Egyptians would beg Thoth to give them more "heart." Thus, our own expression, "to learn by heart."[42]

In ancient Babylonia the moon was worshipped above the sun, and there, too, the moon was closely associated with intellect and understanding. The moon god's name was Sin, and he was regarded as the God of Wisdom. His best known nickname was "the Illuminator," and the Babylonians believed that his light revealed the dark traps laid for men by evil spirits.[43]

That makes the moon out as a kind of celestial Sherlock Holmes. Other times the Babylonians depicted the moon as a goddess whose physique would be the envy of any modern stripteaser and whose worship resembles a college frat party. That's the view which sees the moon as goddess of fertility, both in the farm field and in the bedroom. Moon goddesses like the Babylonian Ishtar, the Phoenician Astarte, the Phrygian Cybele, the Greek Artemis, and the Roman Diana were patronesses of childbirth, whose temple "images frequently represented them with a crescent moon on the head or beneath the feet, and with bodies covered with breasts. Their ritual was marked by orgies of notorious profligacy, really festivals of primitive magic to induce fertility."[44]

The Chaldeans, who were early Semites of southern Babylonia later absorbed into the Babylonian state, were also moon worshippers, who named their lunar deities Sin and Hur. "The latter was also the name of the Chaldean capital," wrote Slaughter. "The name for the moon in Syriac at the present time is Sin. Many think it appears in Sinai, and that this mountain was consecrated by the moon. The fact is very important in view of the part Sinai played in the Hebrew religion."[45]

For most Westerners, the most familiar lunar deity is Greek. This is the Artemis of classical mythology, goddess of love, fertility, and child birth. She was, as William White wrote in "Moon Myth in Medicine," "the moon goddess pausing in her nightly course across the heavens to stoop and kiss the sleeping Endymion, the setting sun."[46] We like to think that even Socrates was charmed by her. When dim-witted Meletus accused him of irreligion at his infamous trial for the corruption of the youth of Athens, Socrates replied, "You strange man, Meletus, are you seriously affirming that I do not think Helios and Selene [one of Artemis's incarnations] to be gods, as the rest of mankind think?"[47] Many writers have cited this as evidence of Socrates's adoration of the goddess. But the truth is that Socrates was no mark for mythology, and he probably was mocking Meletus with facetiousness. Still, Socrates's bluff *is* evidence that "the rest of mankind" did indeed believe in Selene.

Like any beloved character, Artemis had several nicknames. It was as if the ancients wanted to have more of her, so they created her over and over in different guises under a number of names. To the Greeks she was sometimes Artemis, sometimes Selene. To the Romans, Diana, sister of the sun-god Apollo, or Luna. But Walton Brooks McDaniel explains that her name at any moment would depend on what she was doing and where she was doing it—and so many of these identities suggest the more ominous things, like insanity and witchcraft, that the moon is still associated with:

> [C]haste Dian *[sic]* is not always such a simple and exemplary maiden. She does not always figure in ancient literature as a friendly deity of light, a sort of female Apollo, whose companions were the lovely nymphs and her favorite occupation hunting. You are also told that while she was Greek Selene, Roman Luna, in the sky, and Artemis or Diana on the earth, she was that dreadful goddess Hecate in the world below. As mistress of Hell, she was the patroness of sorcery. She it was who made the black art work. Witch and wizard worshipped her at the crossroads, so that in addition to bearing the epithet Triformis because of her triple aspect and character, she is often addressed as Trivia, goddess of the place where three ways come together. It is there that her devotees would summon spirits from the infernal regions and perform magic operations of a bloodcurdling sort. Diana of the Crossways was Hecate, Queen of the Ghosts. Her appearance among men was heralded by the yelping of her hell-hounds. These were proper companions for her, since, as everybody must know, dogs even now see the spirits of the departed when they may be quite invisible to the human eye, and a dog is truly dumb if it is not sufficiently excited by the rays of a full moon to bay at it loud enough to awaken the very dead. In wild parts of Greece where animals have not been so fully christianized as with us I have heard the dogs calling to Hecate and her pack at all hours of a moonlit night and have cursed them into Hecate's abode in vain.[48]

Nevertheless, the most enduring image of Artemis is as Selene, the lovely goddess of the moon in heaven. Slaughter quoted this description of her beauty by another writer:

> She is the beautiful eye of night, the daughter of Hyperion, of Pallas or of Hellos, the sister of Phoibos Apollon. Like the sun, she moves across the heaven in a chariot drawn by white horses from which her soft light streams down to earth, or she is the huntress, roving like Alpheios, over hill and dale. She is the bride of Zeus, and the mother of Pandia, the full orb which gleams in the nightly sky; or as loving, like him, the crags, the streams and the hills, she is beloved by Pan, who entices her into the dark woods under the guise of a snow-white ram. In other words, the soft whispering wind, driving before it the shining fleecy clouds, draws the moon onwards into the sombre groves.[49]

The moon has often been thought of as the divine eye of god through which the heavenly host can see and know all, making the moon a kind of divine judge and jury rolled into one. The Chinese emperor Ming Li of the House of Wei, for example, once scolded himself early in the third century A.D. for ignoring the admonitions of this celestial magistrate. In a letter to civil administrators serving him, Li reminded his countrymen that heaven sends warnings to an emperor who is not fulfilling his obligations. A partial eclipse of the moon, such as the one that had recently occurred, is most certainly such a warning, Li wrote. He then conceded, "Ever since We ascended the throne, Our inability to continue the glorious traditions of our departed ancestors and carry on the great work of civilization, has now culminated in a warning message from on high. It therefore behooves Us to issue commands for personal reformation, in order to avert the impending calamity."[50] That was followed by imperial orders intended to set Li's ship of state back on the right course.

The same notion of an omniscient moon pops up in Iceland. The people have a story about a sheep thief who was eating a leg of ill-gotten mutton in his hiding place. Feeling very content with himself, the thief held a piece of meat impaled on his fork up to the moon as if to boast, "I've got it and you don't." But such impertinence just angered the moon, which threw a red-hot key at the thief and hit him on the cheek. It burned a vicious mark on his tender flesh, one which still hasn't gone away, and that's supposed to have been the start of the practice of branding thieves.[51]

Civilizations past and present have believed that the moon not only judges man, but does so with a vengeance—and the classical appeasement to a vengeful god is a human sacrifice. This was the case among the Toltec or Aztec Indians of Mexico.[52] In Cholula, the people were especially zealous in their worship of the god Quetzalcoatl. The god's image was enthroned atop a lavishly decorated pedestal inside the city's main temple. He had the body of a man, but the head of a bird, with a red beak, yellow face, black band from its eyes to below its beak, and lolling tongue. Gold jewelry shaped like butterflies hung around its neck. The god's feet were protected from contact with the earth's common dirt by sandals made of gold.

Quetzalcoatl's festival was in February. Forty days before the auspicious day the city's merchants chipped in and bought a slave, a well-built, muscular, healthy slave without any moles, sores, or other blemishes, whom they bathed twice in a lake, then dressed up in lavish duds similar to Quetzalcoatl's own. For forty days, this sucker lived the life of Riley. He was given companions for conversation, allowed to dance and sing his way through the streets, and pelted with flowers and praise. On the fortieth day, Quetzalcoatl's priests slipped him a Mickey Finn containing the dried blood of previous sacrifices, danced him until he was dizzy, then, at midnight, held him on an altar and cut out his heart. That's right, still alive. The priests held it aloft as an offering to the moon, then threw it against the idol of Quetzalcoatl, where it must have gone *splat* like a rotten melon. The slave's body was dropped off the altar, down the temple stairs. Afterwards, his body was embalmed.

That out of the way, the merchants and other townspeople sat to a joyous banquet at daybreak.

Tibetan Buddhists and Albanians have had similar sacrificial ceremonies, although in Albania this has probably all but died out.[53,54] In ancient Egypt, the otherwise reviled pig was sacrificed to the moon once a year.[55] Until at least earlier this century, farmers near Oldenburg, Germany, would purge themselves of any abnormal bony growth by stroking it crosswise three times in the name of the Christian Holy Trinity, then pretending to throw it at the moon, which the farmer hoped would keep the excrescence.[56]

As alien as such practices may sound to us, they all (except for that last example) have one thing in common that should be familiar: the victim is a Christlike martyr whose divine mission is to relieve the people of their guilt and sins. The Christian religions have a built-in martyr; other faiths feel obliged periodically to provide one.

The Greeks also believed the moon could be a vengeful deity, though not a bloodthirsty one. Hippocrates warned that "one who is seized with terror, fright, and madness during the night is being visited by the goddess of the moon."[57,58] Some medieval Europeans envisioned the moon as the seat of hell.[59] In fact, that's where one of the stories about the Man in the Moon comes from. It goes like this: a man was gathering wood in the forest one Sunday when he should have been in church instead. Before long, another man in his Sunday best came along and asked him why he wasn't in church. When the woodgatherer replied that he didn't care whether it was Sunday or Monday, the stranger (who was apparently an angel) banished him to the moon as a warning to all Sabbath-breakers.[60]

Far more often, though, the moon has been considered heaven.[61] In the Egyptian *Book of Respirations,* the goddess of fertility and motherhood, Isis, prays that the soul of her brother Osiris might rise to heaven, which is on the moon. Lucian the Greek described the moon as a great big round and shining island, hanging in the air, whose inhabitants were called Hippogipians and whose king was Endymion. Plutarch said that the moon absorbs the souls of dead men and women just as the earth absorbs their bodies. And Johanna Ambrosius, the German peasant-poet, prayed in one of her poems that when she died she could spend eternity in the moon.

Likewise, the Polynesians of Tokelau claim the moon is the abode of their kings and chiefs who have departed earth in death. Captain Cook found that many South Pacific islanders regarded the moon's spots as splendid groves of now-extinct trees which used to grow on Otaheite, an island paradise-on-earth. Other islanders thought the moon a beautiful country where the "aoa," the most stately object in a Tahitian landscape, grows. And like those Tokelauans, the Guaycurus Indians of South America revered the moon as the home of their deceased medicine men and chiefs.

But the vision of a lunar heaven which we may be able to appreciate best is the one still beloved by another nation of South American Indians, the Saliva. They, too, believe the moon is paradise. And how do they know? Simple. That's where, they say, you'll find no mosquitoes.

5

Fertility

Our modern myth about the stork, the most famous of all obstetricians, seems to have hatched from primitive myths about the moon. The people of Niger in West Africa, for example, believe babies are delivered to their mothers by the "Moon Bird," which is sent on its way to earth by the "Great Moon Mother," who keeps watch over people from her lunar roost.[1]

° ° °

In ancient Italy, the most famous shrine to the goddess Diana was at Lake Nemi. The lake is surrounded on all sides but one by a steep, densely wooded slope, and the entire setting is splendid. Julius Caesar briefly enjoyed a costly villa there.[2] Caligula passed many pleasant hours aboard two floating palaces he had moored on the lake.[3] Tourists from Egypt even established shrines there to Isis and Bubastis, two of their own moon-goddesses.[4] But it is for Diana that the site is best remembered.

Her sanctuary was built in a grove on the only accessible shore.[5] Women were its most frequent visitors. At the full moon of August they approached the shrine in a torchlight procession. The trove of clay and stone phalli, female genitalia, figures of women with infants on their laps, and pregnant women that archeologists have unearthed is mute testimony to the prayers for help in becoming pregnant and bearing children that were whispered or sung there.[6]

* * *

Once a year the ancient Zimbabwe of what is now Zimbabwe, Africa, murdered their king. That was his lot in life. Days of luxury climaxed by a ritual regicide. He was their Christ, dying for them.

But before his death, the king was expected to marry and enjoy a productive sex life. To make sure of that, the time for marriage and moments of princely passion were strictly scheduled according to lunar phases.[7] These lunar rituals were important enough to be worth commemorating with paintings and incisions on the walls of caves.[8]

* * *

The point, of course, is the moon's association with human fertility, which is another of the most extensively developed mythological themes about the moon. It has been believed capable of making women fecund, of making childbirth easier, and of making maidens pregnant. Its aid has been sought by those seeking motherhood, and its power believed so strong that women not wanting to become pregnant have behaved as warily toward it as if it were a celestial Casanova run amok.

The basis for this faith has been primarily visual. As the moon increases from a slender crescent to a full, rounded orb, its changing shape suggests the progression of a woman's pregnancy. Also, mothers in ancient Greece and Rome kept track of their pregnancies by counting off "ten moons," or ten lunar months.[9] Human gestation does coincide with nine lunar months, and the ancients were certain that such an exact correlation between gestation and lunar phases could not be mere coincidence. Another reason has been the widespread belief that the moon causes menstruation,[10] bringing on the flow of blood just as it controls the ocean tides. Moreover, the moon has often been considered a nocturnal counterpart of the sun, similarly responsible for life and growth as its brighter diurnal companion.[11] Anyway, who besides the moon, lord over the mysterious night, could be responsible for something as mysterious as birth?

How does the moon make women pregnant? As any man would. Speaking of peoples past and present, Douglas Kelley wrote in *The Psychoanalytic Review,* "It is almost universally accepted among primitives that the moon has carnal knowledge of woman, and the full moon is generally considered the commonest offender. . . . [T]he fertilizing power of the satelite [*sic*] is demonstrated in the ceremonies involving virgins and the common lunar charms to promote childbearing."[12]

Many people of Greenland, for example, have certainly believed in this lunar "carnal knowledge." They believe that the moon visits their wives at specific intervals and makes them pregnant.[13,14,15] They also believe that a maid who stares at the full moon will become pregnant.[16,17,18] In *The Golden Bough,* James George Frazer gives one of the most explicit accounts of this idea. "According to the Greenlanders the moon is a young man," Frazer wrote in his multi-volume work on mythology, "and he 'now and then comes down to give their wives a visit and caress them; for which reason no woman dare sleep lying on her back, without she first spits upon her fingers and rubs her belly with it. For the same reason the young maids are afraid to stare long at the moon, imagining they may get a child by the bargain.' Similarly, Breton peasants are reported to believe that women or girls who expose their persons to the moonlight may be impregnated by it and give birth to monsters."[19]

Certain Asians, Polynesians, and Eskimos also believe the Man in the Moon is quite a playboy. One medical journal put it this way:

> The belief of the Mongolian Buriats is the most extreme, for they assume that the moon can fully replace the human male on the conjugal. Women of other tribes evidently rebel at such a physically Platonic relationship; they believe impregnation is a result of teamwork between their earthly husbands and the

> heavenly spouse, the former first rupturing the hymen or dilating the vaginal passage in a thoroughly satisfying manner in order that the moonbeam, the real fertilizing agent, may enter. This convenient modification of the legend is accepted by such widely separated peoples as the Maoris of tropical Polynesia, the Eskimo Ahts, and their arctic brethren of Greenland. Incorrect theory of etiology has led these latter tribes to adopt somewhat inefficient prophylactic measures; when food becomes scarce or there are too many tousled heads about, the women believe that contraception of further progeny may be accomplished by not looking at the moon or by rubbing spittle on their abdomens. On the other hand, women who want babies expose themselves to the light of the moon or make offerings to the celestial neighbor and invoke its aid.[20]

Germans in the Middle Ages were convinced the moon not only could help a man trying to become a father, but that only a fool would ignore its advice. That faith was best expressed by the twelfth-century visionary mystic Saint Hildegard, who was abbess of Bingen and a sort of medieval Ann Landers. Her essay, "Causae et Curae," warned men to consider the moon's phases when trying to have a child. The essay, whose title translates to "Causes and Cures," also specified what would happen to children conceived on each day of the lunar month. Males conceived on the first day of the month, for example, would grow up "proud and strong, healthy and honored, [and] will not have outstanding weaknesses, but will not live long. Females will be strong in body, but when they do take sick, will suffer severe pain and usually die. They will dislike those about them in the household and will highly esteem strangers." Males born two or three days after a full moon, the Saint cautioned, would be idiots "cherished about the house as a plaything. [They] will be easily weakened in the marrow and will not live to a very old age. A female will be stupid and quarrelsome, sometimes (rarely) kind, and will not live to be very old." As for a boy conceived four days after a full moon, he "will always be a thief and desire not his own, but what belongs to others. He will be healthy and will live to a good old age. A female will have the traits of a fox, will not speak her innermost thoughts, but will deceive, and will even lead good men to death. She will be strong, sometimes suffering spells of insanity, and will live to a good old age."[21]

Women have often treated the moon like a midwife, seeking its aid in childbearing. European peasants at one time nicknamed the moon, "the Moistener" and the "Dew Bringer," in the belief that it could lubricate an expectant mother, making her child-delivery easier.[22] Sometimes the best help a human midwife could offer was her knowledge of prayers and offerings to the moon, the patroness of childbirth.[23]

Women in southern Italy still wear crescent-shaped charms or amulets to obtain the Moon Mother's assistance in labor,[24] a practice also common in our own antebellum South and, apparently, for some time after the Civil War. There, plantation slaves wore necklaces of "birth beads" to help ease childbirth. "This talisman had been brought from Africa by slaves and [had] been handed down from generation to generation; it consists of roughly carved beads that are symbolic of power, and includes the lunar crescent."[25]

Naturally, since people believed the moon played such a large part in the successful outcome of sex, it had to be important to marriage as well, which sanctified that oldest of all sports. Sure enough, the ancient Greeks, Romans, and Jews thought the best time for marriage was the full moon; Polynesians are among those who still feel that way.[26,27,28]

The moon was also believed capable of helping a woman become pregnant by making her fertile in the first place. It was the job of moon priests and priestesses to persuade the moon to do its best so their congregations would be blessed with many children.[29] Likewise, the moon was responsible for the fertility of farm land and animals, fishing waters, and wild growing things everywhere. Roman farmers, fishermen, and hunters prayed to Diana with special fervor. ". . . Diana was . . . a patroness of wild beasts, a mistress of woods and hills, of lonely glades and sounding rivers," wrote Frazer. "[C]onceived as the moon, and especially it would seem, as the yellow harvest moon [which is a full moon], she filled the farmer's grange with goodly fruits, and heard the prayers of women in travail. In her sacred grove at Nemi, as we have seen, she was especially worshipped as a goddess of childbirth, who bestowed offspring on men and women. Thus, Diana, like the Greek Artemis, with whom she was constantly identified, may be described as a goddess of nature in general and fertility in particular."[30]

A paradox emerging from all of this is that the moon is depicted as neither exclusively male nor female. John Oliven, in the *American Journal of Psychiatry,* makes the observation that the moon has been worshipped as "The Great Mother" in the form of such female deities as Diana, Artemis, Ishtar of Babylonia, Asthoreth of the Phoenicians, and Cybele of Phrygia, while some cultures have venerated the moon as a male deity who can make their women pregnant.[31] William White points out that in French and Italian the word for moon is feminine, whereas in German it is masculine. Similarly, many Eskimos believe that the moon is male (the brother of the sun, which is a maiden), whereas many Malaysians believe that the moon is a woman and the stars her children. South American lore describes the moon as the sun's husband.[32] White also says the Khasias people of the Himalayas believe the moon is a man, Greenlanders see the moon as the female sun's brother, and that to the ancient Egyptians and in Peruvian lore the moon was both brother and husband of the sun.[33] In contrast, the Chinese understand the moon to be "feminine and passive," an idea embodied in the concept of yin-yang. White quotes the "Yih King":

> The yih is capable of representing all combinations of existence. The elements of the yih, yang the positive principle and yin the negative principle, stand for the elements of being. Yang means "bright" and yin, "dark." Yang is the principle of heaven; yin is the moon. Yang is masculine and active; yin is feminine and passive. The former is motion; the latter is rest. Yang is strong, rigid, lordlike; yin is mild, pliable, submissive, wifelike. The struggle between, and the different mixture of, these two elementary contrasts, condition all the differences that prevail, the state of the elements, the nature of things, and also the character of the various personalities as well as the destinies of human beings.[34]

In short, it seems that where the moon god is believed to act on its own—like the lunar god of Greenland, who seduces women without being invited to—then its gender is male. But where people have to approach the moon for help as a deity, then that deity is female.

What makes all of this so poignant today is that these are not myths and legends which have become impotent with time's passage. Instead, they are timeless beliefs, which spring up even in the modern world. Consider the examples spotted by psychiatrist J. Sadger. Sadger found several patients of his who thought the same things about the moon as did Diana's ancient worshippers and as Eskimo Ahts still do. They were sleepwalkers, whose trances were frequently triggered by the sight of a full moon. In that near-hypnotic condition, their impressions of the moon were like repressed primal instincts, temporarily freed.

One patient, for instance, thought of the moon as a mother-fertility figure, whose ample endowment is reminiscent of the anatomically exaggerated statuettes dedicated to the goddess Diana at Lake Nemi. Sadger wrote that this patient was a twenty-two-year-old heterosexual woman who, beginning at age nine or ten, had fallen into a walking trance whenever she saw a full moon. In that condition, she would stare at the full moon. And what did she see? "[A] woman's smooth body, the abdomen and most of all the buttocks. It excited me very greatly if I saw a woman from behind. Whenever I am fondling anyone erotically and have my hand on the buttocks—I always think then of a woman—the moon always occurs to me but in the thought of a woman's body."[35]

John Oliven, in the *American Journal of Psychiatry*, was quick to compare that and other patients' imagery to the "conception of the moon as The Great Mother," which is personified by such lunar deities as Diana, Ishtar, Ashthoreth, Artemis, and Cybele.[36]

Sadger also discussed another female patient who experienced similar trance states. She was boating on a lake with her brother one day when she found herself staring at the moon's reflection in the water. It reminded her of having lain in bed recently, more asleep than awake, but still managing to sing to the moon. She told Sadger the lyrics, which were plainly lusty and romantic. The song ended, "Thou Moon, most beautiful and best, save me, take my maidenhood, I am not evil to thee. Draw me mightily to thyself, do not leave off, thy kisses have been so good to me."[37] The song, Sadger observed, was an offer of her virginity.[38] He didn't need to point out that the Mongolian Buriats and South Pacific Maoris also imagine the moon to be some sort of heavenly Don Juan.

In fact, they rather relish the thought.

6

Moisture

The people and animals that populate the fortune-teller's Tarot cards are like tiny time-travelers, returned from the future to tell the reader his or her destiny. They seem suited to the task. Their elongated bodies and mysterious faces appear contorted from the effort of defying space and time.

Besides, their exotic appearance helps the kerchiefed gypsy sell her scam to rubes, tourists, and college students out for a laugh.

Still, look what tradition has perpetuated. Card Number 18 designates the moon.[1] It shows the full moon suspended in a blue sky. Below it are drops of falling dew or blood and two vicious dogs howling on the ground. A road winds its way to the horizon between two tall towers. This is the treacherous road of life, surrounded by bloodthirsty horrors. Dogs baying at the moon are a common superstitious prediction of death. And the number "18" stands for the Hebrew letter, *tsade,* which means the "end" or boundary of the mind. A curious concoction of symbols, but one with a long history. And a central feature is that association of the moon with dew or blood falling like rain.

That association is no accident. It is one of the oldest ideas about the moon: the moon is a wet world which brings moisture in many forms to earth's inhabitants and affects the earth's own moisture, its oceans and rain and morning dew. It is such a broad notion that it overlaps with several mythological themes we've already looked at. In pre-Columbian Peru, for example, one word could be used to say "woman," "sea," and "moon."[2] Where do we file that? Here or in the "Fertility" chapter? And can you blame the Peruvians? After all, the moon rocks the sea in an endless lullaby, and don't women resemble those oceans, what with the amniotic ocean in which they bathe their own babes-to-be and their menstrual cycles which often follow the full moon as faithfully as do the tides?

What about epilepsy, which for centuries was often diagnosed as the result of phlegm on the brain, too much water on the brain, or too much moisture in the brain's hollows?[3] Then there was the Babylonian practice of naming the element water (as opposed to earth, air, and fire) Ishtar (or Astarte), in honor of the moon goddess.[4]

No matter. The question is academic. More interesting is the diversity of ways that this moisture theme was expressed. Early Moslems certainly thought the moon was all wet. They believed the moon was a star full of water, an idea still common in India.[5] In the Chinese Yin-Yang, Yin represents the moon and is the source of all water.[6] In Western lore, the relationship between moon and water is reflected by the fairy tale, "Jack and Jill." The fact that Jack and Jill are carrying water is a metaphor for the moon's causal influence on rain (which, as we'll see in chapter 15, is fact as well as folklore).[7]

The moon has also been blamed for a behind-the-scenes role in diseases which are supposed to be caused by "moisture." Besides inflicting epilepsy, for instance, brains of the Latin and Greek worlds decided it was the moon which made dead things rot.[8] Plutarch taught that the full moon sweated so much moisture that it made timber, wheat, and other grains cut then soft and likely to become worm-infested and rotten. The same conditions were supposed to make bread rise and leaven better.[9] On the other hand, some grains would be too dry and hard if gathered or cut around the new moon.[10]

One French medical writer described the most propitious time to bleed certain categories of medical and psychiatric patients according to lunar phases and their own unique moisture ratios.[11] After all, it wouldn't do to have a patient bleed too quickly—or at a distressingly slow pace.

Many people have even believed that a person's strength to resist death ebbs and flows like the tides, and for the same reasons. There was Mr. Peggotty's prediction to David Copperfield. Henri Charriere, the Frenchman whose escape from Devil's Island is described in the book *Papillon,* thought he noticed that men who died of dysentery at the prison all went at low tide in the afternoon or evening.[12] This belief goes back at least to days of ancient Greek glory when Aristotle wrote that animals died during an ebbing tide. Where this had been observed in France, he said, it applied only to humans.[13]

The Romans thought something else ebbed and flowed like the tides: the amount of blood in a man's veins. When a friend took ill with some moisture affliction, Romans prayed to the goddess of moisture and the moon, Diana.

And, for reasons that time has washed away, the Romans were convinced that differences in moisture content among phases of the moon would increase or decrease the medicinal effects of remedies containing . . . mice.[14]

7

Lycanthropy

Pity the werewolf:

A forty-nine-year-old woman we shall call "Maria" (because her physician has not disclosed her real name) had been married for twenty years, and all during that time she had suffered from unspeakable sexual urges. Her physician described it simply and discreetly as a compulsive longing for "bestiality." Undoubtedly, that meant she could barely control her desire to have dogs and other aggressive animals mount her, and that she actually longed to fondle and excite these animals. She told her doctor that she wanted to make love to women as well; lie with a woman, touch her, and feel that woman's hands caress and probe her own body, feel that woman's mouth on her flesh, and share herself with a woman as she would with her own husband. And she confessed to lust for adultery—often, consumingly.

Nor could she stop thinking about wolves. She imagined them by day, she dreamt of them at night. She even began to think of herself as one. She described "feeling like an animal with claws." Finally, Maria could withstand temptation no longer. At a family gathering, dinner perhaps, she undressed and approached her mother on hands and knees. She raised her buttocks and thrust her hips back, so that she had "assumed the female sexual posture of a wolf, and offered herself to her mother." The episode lasted some twenty minutes, and was probably punctuated by much grunting and moaning.

The following night, after making love with her husband, she lapsed into a wolverine state for two hours. She growled, scratched, and gnawed at the bed like a beast driven wild by desire. The devil had come into her and she had become an animal, she said.

Similar compulsions would grip her during the weeks that followed. She would suddenly feel herself becoming a wolf that yearned to kill, and at the same time she would become unbearably aroused sexually. The heat of desire would rise inside her and burn rationality from her mind. She felt tortured. She wanted women. She wanted to masturbate constantly. The craving to roll in the dust with a red-tipped animal was almost irresistible. She nearly yielded many times.

When she felt herself turning into a wolf and positively intoxicated with lust like this, she would gaze into the mirror and see "the head of a wolf in place of a face on my body—just a long-nosed wolf with teeth, groaning, snarling, growling . . . with fangs and claws, calling out, 'I am the devil.' " And she did more than imagine this; people nearby could hear her bestial moans and howls. It was as if she wanted to be as uninhibited as she imagined animals must be in their wanton mating. She must have wanted to scream and scratch, to be pinched and pawed and drooled upon, to feel herself erect and wet with her own excitement and not feel ashamed.

Moreover, the last time anyone knew of this happening to her, it was the night of a full moon.

Quite appropriately, Maria's story is described in a medical report titled "A Case of Lycanthropy."[1] But what makes her story remarkable is that it did not happen in antiquity or even the Middle Ages, but *now,* apparently in the 1970s. And it illustrates the fact that "[l]ycanthropy is a rare phenomenon, but it does exist," according to psychiatrist Harvey A. Rosenstock and psychologist Kenneth R. Vincent, who in the *American Journal of Psychiatry* discuss several cases reported in modern medical literature.[2] They consider the victims of lycanthropy psychotics whose behavior at full moons is real but whose physical transformation is a delusion. There is another medical interpretation of lycanthropy, however, which concedes that very real physical changes do take place. It is a diagnosis that concludes that leathery skin, red teeth, and long hair are the real effects of a real disease, and not just fictions which exist only in the "werewolf's" mind.

Werewolfism gets its medical name, lycanthropy, from the name of Lycaon, a king of Arcadia, a mountainous region of Greece. The story goes that Lycaon foolishly set out to test the omniscience of Zeus by offering the god a meal of human flesh, which he told Zeus was just some common hash. Zeus, of course, knew very well what the dinner was, and he was not amused. As punishment, Zeus transformed Lycaon into a wolf. Ovid describes the king's predicament:

> In vain he attempted to speak; from that very instant
> His jaws were besplattered with foam, and only he thirsted
> For blood, as he raged amongst flocks and panted for slaughter.
> His vesture was changed into hair, his limbs became crooked;
> A wolf,—he retains yet large trace of his ancient expression,
> Hoary he is as afore, his countenance rabid,
> His eyes glitter savagely still, picture of fury.[3]

The classic legend of lycanthropy, however, is the tale told by Petronius in his *Satyricon,* in which transformation into a werewolf is blamed on the full moon rather than a spiteful god.[4] One of the characters, a slave named Niceros, is describing what had started out as a five-mile walk to the farm house of his girlfriend, an attractive widow.[5,6] Niceros's own master is away on business, so Niceros has the night to himself and he leaves with a soldier, who is a guest in his master's house and a real strapping stud. Walton Brooks McDaniel's summary is excellent:

> They had come to a point on the thoroughfare where it was bordered with the tombs of the dead, as the roads beyond the gates of any Roman city were likely to be. The hour was sometime around cockcrow, but the light of the moon was almost as bright as of the midday sun, when his mate stepped aside among the monuments. Niceros sat down to wait for him, singing and amusing himself by counting the tombstones. Looking

> back at his comrade, he saw that he stripped himself and put all his garments at the side of the road. An awful terror seized the slave as he gazed at the strange performance. The last breath of life all but left his nose. He stood like a dead man. But the soldier urinated so as to circle his clothes completely with water and then suddenly turned into a wolf. The circummicturition safeguarded the clothes. Without these he could not hope to regain his human form when he came back. Niceros assures his listeners that he is not joking, that the gift of no fortune in the world would tempt him to tell a lie. After the soldier had become a wolf, he began to howl like one and fled into the woods. Niceros at first scarcely knew where he was, but then went to pick up the man's clothes only to find that they had all turned to stone. Although he was in mortal alarm, he drew his sword and kept slashing shadows with it all the way until he reached his sweetheart's villa. As he entered he looked like a spectre and all but gave up the ghost. Sweat ran down his legs. His eyes were dead. Only with difficulty could he be brought back. His dear Melissa expressed surprise that he was out walking so late and said, "If you had come earlier, you might at least have been of some assistance. A wolf entered our place, worried all our sheep, and bled them like a butcher. But he didn't get the laugh on us even if he did escape; for our slave pierced his neck with a spear." Niceros left for home at daybreak, and on his way passed the place where the garments had been turned to stone. He now found nothing there but a pool of blood. When he reached the house, the soldier was lying in bed "like an ox" (however that may be), and a doctor was attending to a wound in his neck. Then he realized that the man was a turnskin, a *versipellis,* or werewolf, and he could never bring himself to taste bread with him afterwards, even, he said, should it cost him his life if he didn't.[7]

In fact, lycanthropy has crept into every culture, past and present. The Navaho Indians, for example, believed werewolves were nocturnal ghouls who got their thrills by rustling sheep, exhuming the dead and robbing them of jewelry, and cannibalizing ambush victims—preferably female.[8] The Book of Daniel describes King Nebuchadnezzar, the Babylonian monarch who conquered Jerusalem,[9] as suffering from a depression that deteriorated over seven years until the king was convinced he was a wolf.[10] During the Roman Empire's sunset, Paulus Aegineta authored a medical description of lycanthropy which acknowledged the legend of Lycaon.[11] In the centuries since then, explanations have revolved around everything from hallucinogenic drugs to diabolical possession. Jean Bodin, a sixteenth-century French physician, wrote that "the devil can really and materially metamorphose the body of a man into that of an animal and thereby cause the sickness."[12] Jean de Nynauld and Giovanni Battista Porta blamed werewolfism on dope and poisons like opium, peyote, hashish, belladonna, and strychnine.[13] In our own century, psychoanalysts have tried to take the fangs out of lycanthropy by interpreting it as *merely* a manifestation of sexual, sadistic, cannibalistic, and necrophilic perversions.[14] Whatever the cause, it still rears its head everywhere from the most advanced industrial nations to China, Africa, Central and South America, Indonesia, Assam, and Malaysia,[15,16] although in some locales its victims are believed to be transformed into snakes, elephants, sharks, leopards, lions, crocodiles, buffalo, or eagles instead of (or in addition to) wolves.[17]

The one thing consistent through all cultures is the impact of full moons. Whatever other conditions may be required, a full moon is almost always necessary. Take sixteenth-century Europe, where werewolves were pursued with a vigor apparently unequaled before or since. The entire continent believed that people were most likely to succumb to the affliction of werewolfery during a full moon.[18]

In France, where belief in werewolves has been especially strong, the full moon plays a critical role in transformation. Sabine Baring-Gould (the nineteenth-century English clergyman, archeologist, folklorist, novelist, and composer of the hymn *Onward Christian Soldiers*) elaborated:

> If traditions of were-wolves are scanty in England, it is quite the reverse if we cross the water.
>
> In the south of France, it is still believed that fate has destined certain men to be lycanthropists—that they are transformed into wolves at full moon. The desire to run comes upon them at night. They leave their beds, jump out of a window,

> and plunge into a fountain. After the bath, they come out covered with dense fur, walking on all fours, and commence a raid over fields and meadows, through woods and villages, biting all beasts and human beings that come in their way. At the approach of dawn, they return to the spring, plunge into it, lose their furry skins, and regain their deserted beds. . . .
>
> In the Perigoard, the were-wolf is called louleerou [*sic*]. Certain men, especially bastards, are obliged at each full moon to transform themselves into these diabolic beasts.[19]

The only exception to this full-moon rule seems to be in Sicily. There, according to one writer, tradition has it that "a child conceived at the new moon will become a werewolf, as will the man who on a certain Wednesday or Friday in summer sleeps at night in the open with the moon shining full on his face. In Palermo they say that as the moon waxes to her round the werewolf begins to feel the craving; his eyes sink deep and are glazed . . . he falls to the earth wallowing in the dust or mud, and is seized with fearful writhings and pangs, after which his limbs quiver and contract horribly, he howls and rushes off on all fours, shunning the light, especially (they say at Menfi) torches, candles, or lanthorns [*sic*]."[20]

Necessary as they are, full (or new) moons often cannot turn the trick themselves. A list of other requirements can read like the script to a nightmare. For example, Petrus Salius, who wrote a medical text published in Venice in 1682, warned that anyone who eats a werewolf's roasted flesh will become one himself.[21] In parts of Germany, people have believed that a simple belt, three inches or finger-breadths wide, would do the job. The belt must be worn to impose its weird influence . . . and it must be made of human flesh. German folklore is rife with stories about fathers who fail to remember they have left such a girdle lying around the house until it's too late and a son has tried it on for size, only to be transmogrified into a werewolf.[22] Germans have also believed that the seventh of seven consecutive daughters will become a werewolf, and nothing can remedy her predicament. Sabine Baring-Gould observed that this stranded many a seventh daughter in spinsterhood.[23]

There are also theological theories which suggest divine or

satanic intervention. The Romans, for instance, assumed that Diana could turn anyone who offended her into a werewolf.[24] Their reasoning was impeccable, if circuitous: since Diana was the goddess of intellect and light, the greatest punishment she could dish out would be transformation into a witless animal like the wolf, a creature whose mental "light," so to speak, was permanently dimmed. Or consider the sixteenth-century Europeans, who seem so obsessed with werewolves. Their clerics spent much energy debating whether the devil can transform himself into a werewolf or is limited to transforming men into wolves or merely driving wolves themselves to demonic fury.[25] The physician Jean Bodin wrote in 1580 that Satan could metamorphose the body of a man into a wolf but could not alter the man's mind. He even cited Thomas Aquinas for support.[26]

At any rate, a werewolf was rarely difficult to recognize even when it had reverted temporarily to human form. In Europe, many people believed that any werewolf is identifiable by the devil's mark on his or her buttocks,[27] or the fact that a werewolf cannot disguise its bushy tail.[28] The Danes believed that anyone whose eyebrows meet and cross over his nose is liable to be a werewolf.[29] And any wound inflicted upon a werewolf would still be visible when it returns to human shape.[30] Moreover, people knew that no wolf which displayed demonic ferocity or super strength should be mistaken for a natural wolf.[31]

Tracking one down was always a relatively straightforward matter, too. Werewolves could be easily ambushed where they preferred to stage their own sneak attacks, at secluded but well-traveled spots like cemeteries, pastures, cow paths, and lonely water wells or at the werewolf's own lair near such a location.[32]

Of course, not all werewolves could be caught with blood-reddened hands. When all a suspicious citizen had to go on was circumstantial evidence, the standard investigation consisted of peeling back the suspect's skin to see if the underside is actually fur, hidden there, waiting for a full moon to bring it out. Checking the feet for blisters caused by hours of running barefoot was another typical bit of detection. And tracking the suspect by a trail of blood left by its victim or its own wound was a third investigative procedure.[33] That can be especially useful if it leads the hunters back to the werewolf's pile of human clothes, for there, people in the Abruzzi region of Italy still believe, the werewolf will restore itself to human form by wallowing in the mud it made by pouring water on the ground or urinating as Niceros's soldier-companion did.[34]

In any case, a werewolf should never be mistaken for a vampire, because the distinction is easy to recognize. Basically, *anyone* can become a werewolf. All that's needed is a full moon . . . and perhaps an appropriate curse or potion. In contrast, only a person who happens to cross paths with one of the few vampires at large in the world—and is bitten by it—can become a vampire.[35] As Montague Summers (the prolific British author, literary and drama critic, and folklorist) wrote, "A vampire, then, is altogether another thing from a werewolf. The former is dead; the latter is fearfully alive . . ."[36]

Nowhere was any of this taken more seriously than in sixteenth-century Europe. Some 30,000 cases of lycanthropy were reported to secular and church officials between 1520 and 1630.[37] Fear of these creatures grew so great that anyone the least bit eccentric or anyone with lupine features, like a narrow face or long canines, risked being accused, tortured, and executed during the periodic panics about werewolves.[38] In such an age polluted by ignorance and superstitution, it took little for neighbor to suspect neighbor of making a pact with the devil; once denounced, few defendants were able to prove themselves innocent.[39] In fact, confessions were quite common. Fire on flesh, red-hot pokers, the rack, and hacking off fingers were only some of the ways tongues were loosened. In contrast, the eventual execution was a reprieve. Death by hanging, beheading, and being burned alive were common, although some executioners preferred to take no chances whatsoever. They resorted to execution by gunfire; the ammunition, a bullet of silver, that special metal the moon's own color.[40]

When three people suspected of lycanthropy were caught in the town of Poligny, France, in 1521, their alleged deeds were widely publicized and they were publicly put to death. There is no evidence that they received a trial.[41] Fifty years later, the situation in at least one part of France was still serious enough to warrant special criminal legislation. The parliament of Dole, in 1573, ordered citizens to make a special effort "with kitchen-spits, halberds, spears, arquebuses, and sticks to hunt, capture, bind, and kill the werewolf who infests the district."[42,43,44]

The authorities dealt a brutal death to a man named Peter Stump, accused of werewolfish mayhem in parts of Germany and the Netherlands. A chronicler named Richard Rowlands in 1605 used these words to describe Stump's fate:

> Of such sundry have bin taken and executed in sundry partes of *Germanie,* and the *Netherlands.* One *Peter Stump* for being a *were-wolf,* and having killed thirteen children, two women, and one man; was at *Bedbur* not far from *Cullen* in the year 1589 put unto a very terrible death. The flesh of divers partes of his body was pulled out with hot iron tongs, his armes thighes and legges broke on a wheel, & his body lastly burnt. He dyed with very great remorce, desyring that his body might not be spared from any torment, so his soule might be sauved. The *were-wolf* (so called in *Germanie*) is in *France,* called Loupgarov.[45]

A Frenchman named Jean Peyral was tortured and executed in 1518 for his lycanthropic activities in the Jura Mountains on the Swiss border.[46] When brought before judges, it seems that Peyral boasted that he had had sexual intercourse with wolves and had been turned into the shape of a wolf by the devil. He also confessed to a number of murders while in his wolfish condition. Many church thinkers considered werewolves a type of witch, and Peyral probably confirmed many suspicions when he admitted taking part in sabbats after consummating his pact with the devil.

He also fascinated witnesses at his trial with some of his more unusual claims. He said, for example, that he could transform himself into a wolf only at night and that all of his murderous raids had been conducted at night. Moreover, each time he transformed himself he needed the assistance of a particular magic ointment. Apparently, the ingredients and recipe for this salve were so nauseating that people in his courtroom fainted when he began to demonstrate its preparation. But even that could not drive all the spectators from his trial; contemporary accounts of his day in court reveal clearly that people would not miss Peyral's description of rutting with she-wolves for anything.

When this entertainment was finished, Peyral was tortured in a variety of ways, *then* sentenced, and finally burned. His ashes were scattered to the wind.

Another Frenchman, Gilles Garnier, had to endure a similarly sensational trial for lycanthropy in 1573.[47] Of course, his accusers felt entirely justified. Garnier had confessed to attacking and devouring more than a dozen young children, using his teeth and "claw-like hands" to rip them apart. He also claimed to have eaten several of his victims, but apparently was careless enough to leave remnants behind as evidence. Dozens of witnesses testified against him at his trial, and he was sentenced to the stake where he could get a preview of the hellish flames surely awaiting him in the next world.

One of the best-known trials for lycanthropy resulted from macabre events in the Auvergne district of south-central France. The tragedy revolved around a wealthy gentleman named Sanroche, who, Montague Summers said, lived in an impressive chateau near a village not far from Apchon.[48] The land all around was richly wooded and mountainous, fine game country, according to Basil Copper, the journalist, author, and screenwriter, who has described what happened: One day in 1580 Sanroche was sitting by a window when a friend, Monsieur Fayrolle, dropped by to invite Sanroche out for an afternoon of hunting. With regrets, Sanroche declined. He had to attend to some business with his attorney, who would be arriving within the hour. Fayrolle left, and Sanroche, finished with his lawyer several hours later, decided to see if he could catch up with Fayrolle outside.

Sanroche had been hiking about twenty minutes when he finally heard Fayrolle calling to him from a hillside ahead. The sun was starting to set when the two men reached each other, but Sanroche could see that Fayrolle's clothes were torn, dusty, and stained with blood. Fayrolle himself didn't look very good either. He was out of breath, nervous, and covered with dirt. Sanroche took Fayrolle's musket and game-bag, and asked his friend what the hell had happened.

For several long minutes the tired and frightened Fayrolle said nothing while they walked back towards Sanroche's chateau. Finally, Fayrolle began his story. Deep in the forest, he had spotted several deer. As he began to creep towards them, he heard ominous growling from a gully overgrown with ferns. Fayrolle forgot the deer and started to retreat, but before he could get far an enormous wolf leaped from the gully and sprinted toward him. Fayrolle raised his rifle to shoot, but tripping over a tree root, he shot wildly. The wolf simply swerved in its rush, then jumped at Fayrolle's throat. Incredibly, Fayrolle managed to swing his rifle like a baseball bat and send the wolf sprawling, but in an instant it was up and attacking again.

Now Fayrolle bundled his cloak around his left forearm and thrust this into the wolf's jaws. He also had his hunting knife out, a massive thing with the heft and honed edge of a butcher knife.[49] Fayrolle slashed at the beast's throat, and the two of them fell to the ground, where they struggled. When they finally rolled against a fallen tree, Fayrolle chopped his knife into the wolf's right forearm, which was pressed against the tree trunk. The heavy steel cut clear through the wolf's limb and even creased the wood beneath it. The beast had lost its paw. There was no way Fayrolle could keep his grip on the howling beast, which ran off, limping and clutching its wound.

Fayrolle lay on the ground, stunned and splattered with the beast's blood. The cloak wrapped around his arm was nearly shredded, but his arm was barely scratched.

Fayrolle and Sanroche talked as they walked and soon found themselves back in Sanroche's yard. But Fayrolle had saved the best part of his story for last. He pointed to his game bag and said he had the wolf's paw. Then he bent to untie the bag and reach inside, but when he saw what was there he gasped and dropped the thing onto the grass. Sanroche, too, was shocked when he saw a human hand there on the lawn.

Fear began to squeeze Sanroche's heart as he allowed himself to realize that he recognized one of the rings adorning the slender fingers of that hand. It was a blue topaz set in an elaborate spiral pattern. It was his wife's ring!

Sanroche wrapped the hand in a cloth and hurried inside his house. His wife was home, but in bed and not to be disturbed, according to a butler. Sanroche rushed passed the servant and, finding his wife's chamber locked, broke the door down. There was his wife in bed, pale as marble, nearly unconscious, with blood on the sheets all around her. Her right hand had indeed been severed at the wrist, and a doctor was barely able to save her life.

Sanroche said nothing more about all of this for several weeks. He gave his wife that much time to recuperate undisturbed. When he finally did bring the matter up, she broke down, cried, and confessed to being a werewolf. This elicited no sympathy from her husband, though. Sanroche turned her over to the authorities, who soon brought her to trial, tortured a detailed confession from her, then burned her at the stake. Once again, the Auvergne district was safe.

Whether out of fear of such swift punishment or from self-revulsion, many werewolves are said to be unhappy about their predicament and willing to go to any extreme to conceal or remedy the curse. One cure is supposed to be a knife wound on the werewolf's forehead or scalp severe enough to draw blood,[50] and quite accidentally this was used to rescue a wealthy man in Palermo, Italy, from his lupine dilemma.[51] The story goes that only the rich man's servant knew about his employer's double life. When the gentleman turned wild and woolly at every full moon, his servant let him out of his opulent townhouse through a secret door opening onto a back alley.

During one of these rampages he happened to run across a young man who was out carousing and, by whatever hour they met, considerably drunk. The kid was simply too stewed to flee, and instead pulled a long knife "and slashed the foul grinning monster, whose white fangs had already snapped to bite, criss-cross over the slanting forehead." Dark, thick blood began to bleed from the wound, and the werewolf let out a long howl of agony. His limbs convulsed, and as the drunken young man tried to retrieve his own wits the werewolf turned back into human form. He never was transformed into the wolverine beast again.

Some werewolves tried to imprison themselves at home to avoid discovery. Copper described how a lycanthrope might lock himself into his own room at full moons and toss the key into a corner, where he couldn't find it in his madness. Some werewolves would have themselves strapped to bed by a friend or parent. Others would build a refuge in a remote spot in their home. Copper wrote that a place beneath the eaves was commonly used because noise would be muffled there. Bars could cover the windows and a stout grill, the door. Elaborate bolts and locks, which would stymie the beast's simple mind but not the recovered man's normal intellect, were used to lock the door from the inside.[52]

There are even several time-honored remedies for lycanthropy, according to Montague Summers. One is to accuse the werewolf of being one, another is to address a werewolf three times by his given or "Christian" name, or somehow to draw precisely three drops of blood from him. Each of those solutions entails the problem, however, of getting the werewolf to stand still long enough. If a person has become a werewolf by wearing one of those three-inch wide belts of human flesh, you might try shifting the buckle to the ninth hole. If he or she has become a werewolf by conniving with the devil, tradition recommends forcing the werewolf to "cut the nail of his left thumb which grew long, horny, and hard as the talon of a beast," because that forces the monster to violate its oath to Satan.[53]

And, of course, there's that old standby of confronting the monster with the Sign of the Cross.[54] Never fails.

* * *

The temptation is to dismiss all of this as superstitious bull, merely the pathetic product of an age when wolves roamed the streets of Paris by night and people would have thought nothing of declaring Halloween a legal holiday. The truth is, much of it was based more on fear than fact. But only *much*, not *all,* and perhaps not even *most.* For one thing, the fear of werewolves still stalks men's minds today. Take Italy. Walton Brooks McDaniel found that many people of modern Italy believe lycanthropy can be induced by a full moon, witchcraft, or birth at precisely midnight on particular holy days, including Christmas and the Anniversary of Saint Paul. The only antidote parents have is to brand the Sign of the Cross with a hot coal on the nape of their darling newborn's neck or sole of his foot.[55]

And what are we to make of "Mr. W.," the subject of a modern medical case report, who displayed the symptoms of a werewolf? The report, published in the *Canadian Psychiatric Association Journal,* said Mr. W. (whose identity was withheld to protect his privacy) was a thirty-seven-year-old unmarried farmer from Appalachia.[56] He had been a member of the United States Navy, which had determined that his IQ was normal and average. Apparently his behavior while in the Navy was ordinary and ship-shape because he was in the service for a full four-year hitch. After his discharge, however, something went sickeningly wrong.

His attention to farm chores and mundane daily activities began to flag, growing worse as time passed. Even more alarming, he allowed his facial hair to grow as if it were fur, and took to sleeping in cemeteries and lying down on the road in front of oncoming traffic. "There is also," the psychiatrists filing this case report wrote, "history of the patient howling at the moon." He did these things "episodically," the psychiatrists wrote, indicating later in their report that these episodes were in fact at the time of the full moon.

As for the exact cause of Mr. W.'s bizarre behavior, the doctors could only say, "[A]n altered state of consciousness existed . . . caused by irreversible brain disease, although the periodicity of his psychosis, occurring during the full moon, remains unexplained on an organic level."[57] Mr. W.'s own explanation was much more confident. He claimed to be a werewolf.[58]

A similar situation was discovered in Rome in 1949. According to Robert Eisler, who had recently lectured on lycanthropy, sadism, and masochism before the Psychiatric Section of Britain's Royal Society of Medicine, the Rome correspondent of the London *Daily Telegraph* cabled this report on July 15:

> Howls coming from the bushes in gardens in the centre of Rome last night brought a police patrol to what seemed a "werewolf." Under the full moon they found a young man, Pasquale Rosini, covered in mud, digging in the ground with his finger-nails and howling. On being taken to hospital Rosini said that for three years he had regularly lost consciousness at periods of the full moon and had found himself wandering the streets at night, driven by uncontrollable instincts. He was sent to a clinic for observation.[59]

A third report about a modern werewolf emanates from Zimbabwe. The eyewitness was a Dr. Gerald Kirkland, a thirty-seven-year-old physician from Trellwis, Glamorganshire, England, who was then a government medical officer. The date was March 23, 1933. The report is narrated by Nandor Fodor, who discussed the incident along with several others in an article dealing with cultural and psychological aspects of lycanthropy.[60] Fodor says Dr. Kirkland observed a ritualistic "jackal dance" performed by an unidentified tribe or clan of natives. Kirkland made his observation without revealing his presence to the natives, which enabled him to maintain some detachment and objectivity. This also permitted the participants to remain uninhibited. And uninhibited they were, for what Kirkland saw was a number of male natives eating partially rotted meat and drinking themselves into a frenzy with liquor, then repeatedly mounting one or more women as if they were all jackals in heat.

Fodor is circumspect, but reading between the lines it is clear Kirkland was witness to quite a party. Even Fodor describes it as an "orgy." It's easy to imagine the racket of singing, clapping, drumming of gourds and hollow logs, the women crouching in the dust, and the men leaping around the roaring campfires. The actual acts of intercourse must have been frenzied and long; Fodor describes the men "as potent as only dogs can be." Still, if you can believe it, this carnal gluttony was not what impressed Kirkland most.

What did astound the good doctor more than anything else he saw was the transformation of two of the natives into jackals. Nandor concedes that Kirkland may well have been wrong, but he emphasizes that Kirkland was a trained medical observer, confident enough about what he saw to "almost swear to it." Moreover, Kirkland was willing to talk about it in print and risk public reaction. Fodor says that Kirkland described what he saw first in a letter to him, then in a professional publication. "His account . . . is not only vivid and detailed," says Fodor, "but exposes the psychological motive behind the lycanthropic ceremonial he witnessed." In other words, the doctor was not distracted from scientific considerations by the sexual spectacle.

Yet another modern case of lycanthropy is cited by several sources.[61,62,63] This one was originally reported by a Dr. Morel and published by Dr. Daniel Jack Tuke in his *Dictionary of Psychological Medicine, II.* The subject was a man residing in the asylum of Mareville, France, who was firmly convinced he was a werewolf. " 'See this mouth,' he could exclaim, separating his lips with his fingers, 'it is the mouth of a wolf; these are the teeth of a wolf. I have cloven feet; see the long hairs which cover my body; let me run into the woods, and you shall shoot me!' "[64]

Still, Summers says that the man was allowed to see children, "whom he tenderly embraced, and of whom he was very fond." Later, however, he would pity the children for having hugged a wolf. Summers also says the man hungered for raw meat. He would yell that he was a wolf and needed raw meat, then "he would greedily devour some part, and reject the rest saying that it was not putrid enough." Nevertheless, the man learned to live with it. Morel's "patient" lived out his days right there at Mareville.

Finally, there is the case of a twenty-year-old man whose lycanthropy was triggered by drug use.[65] The man, who was a soldier on duty with the United States Army in Europe, had hiked into the woods and ingested LSD, the potent hallucinogenic drug. The doctors reporting his case indicate that he felt fur growing on his face and saw it sprouting on his hands. He was sure he was turning into a werewolf, and he had "a sudden uncontrollable urge to chase and devour rabbits." He tripped like this for two days before rejoining his Army unit.

Back in camp, he remained convinced he was a werewolf. He "believed that the mess hall sign 'feeding time' proved that other people knew that he was a wolf." He entered psychiatric treatment, and six months later he was returned Stateside on medical evacuation to a drug rehab program. Doctors found that he had a long history of using such drugs as grass, mescalin, heroin, amphetamines, psilocybin, and acid, but during the next few months he quit all the dope except marijuana. He continued to believe he was a werewolf, though.

The soldier was an unmarried, previously unemployed kid from Appalachia. He eventually found himself hospitalized, and there his mental state deteriorated. He began hallucinating freely, both visually and auditorily—thinking he could hear his own thoughts aloud or hearing his name being called. Inside the hospital, he would "see" goats and Black Mass paraphernalia on the floor. He'd look in a mirror and see a devil's claw over his eyes. And he thought others could read his mind. He felt powerful enough to stare down dogs with his demonic gaze, but he was afraid doctors were putting drugs in the hospital food to make patients crazy. He had "bizarre sexual preoccupations and fears regarding homosexuality," according to psychiatrists Frida Surawicz and Richard Banta. He fancied himself a genius and omnipotent, but he wondered whether the hospital staff was controlled by the devil.

Thirty-two days after being admitted to the hospital, he was discharged. He no longer believed he was a werewolf, but he stopped taking his prescribed medication because he didn't trust it. For comfort, he turned to satanism; for the same reason, he broke all contact with the hospital.

Perhaps he's your neighbor now.

The question is, can anything that has generated so much publicity in the past and present be merely an illusion? Can werewolves be only a figment of our collective imagination? Are werewolves simply one of those myths with no basis in fact, like those about a Great Flood, which crop up in practically every culture? The answers, naturally, are yes, maybe, and no. And, if you enjoy riddles, try this: the explanation is in the physical description of werewolves.

Take the description immortalized in a medical text by Pierre van Foreest, an eminent sixteenth-century Dutch physician. One werewolf, he wrote, was spotted roaming through churchyards, clubbing local pet dogs, and leaping madly over sidewalk benches. The doctor, according to Montague Summers, also gleaned these details from witnesses: "It was remarked that his bare legs, unwashed and filthy, were scarred with the bites of dogs and old ulcerated sores. His body was gaunt, his limbs squalid and foul with neglect, his face ghastly pale, the eyes deep-sunken, dry, and blazing."[66]

Basil Copper was even more specific.[67] He listed the features that crop up again and again in eyewitness descriptions of werewolves through the ages and then made a remarkable observation about these characteristics. The victim of lycanthropy, he wrote, grows hair on the palms of his or her hands. His or her hands curve like talons, and the nails lengthen and thicken like claws. A male werewolf's untamed beard eventually seems to merge with his hair and eyebrows so that it looks like a lion's mane. Werewolves' eyes redden and glow like a cat's at night. Their entire bodies become furry, although a rash often appears on their chests. In addition, lycanthropes are likely to go without shoes, because their feet become cramped and the toes distorted and nearly prehensile. Eventually, the lycanthrope's feet become so callused that she or he can run over rocky terrain a normal person would never trespass barefoot.

Copper also noted certain disease-like features. The lycanthrope suffers headaches and a profound thirst. He often perspires heavily, has trouble breathing, and suffers from a running nose and uncontrollable salivation that foams his mouth. As if all this were not bad enough, Copper said, the diagnosis includes swelling and elongation of the hands and a coarsening and fraying of the skin on all the extremities, as if the person had leprosy. What with this and the apparent distortion of hands and feet, Copper said, it is only natural that the lycanthrope would prefer to wear as little clothing as possible.

Inevitably, this sense of restriction would have mental as well as physical reverberations; the lycanthrope would yearn for the freedom of outdoors . . . with or without clothes.

Copper's description is meant to do more than shock us and fill us with pity, though. What he was getting at is the theory that lycanthropy is merely a disease, a disease that could be analyzed and cured but, instead, has been misunderstood and feared as an incurable curse. It is the theory, Copper wrote, of a Dr. Lee Illis, of Hampshire, England, who points out that the symptoms of lycanthropy are remarkably similar to the symptoms of an extremely rare but medically recognized disease, porphyria. Illis suspects that many people burned at the stake, tracked down and shot, or otherwise persecuted as werewolves over the centuries have actually been victims of this malady.

Dr. Illis's thesis was made public when he presented a paper to the Royal Society of Medicine in October 1963, titled, "On Porphyria and the Aetiology of Werewolves."[68] If the document's contents and pertinence to lycanthropy are not well known, it is only because porphyria is so rare. Illis himself pointed out that only eighty cases had been described in all the vast body of medical literature. Compare that to something like, say, smallpox. Besides, what Illis had done was make a glamorous thing into something ordinary. By explaining how people become "werewolves," he removed the shroud of mystery and occultism from it. He transformed a dramatic event into a mundane medical mechanism as surely as the full moon had turned people into werewolves. And ordinary, mundane things that are rarely a matter of practical concern simply are not newsworthy.

Dr. Illis pointed out that the "symptoms" of lycanthropy match the symptoms of porphyria: skin rashes and lesions, discoloration of the skin, progressive mutilation of such cartilaginous structures as the nose and ears as well as the fingers and eyelids, and a gradual reddening of the teeth. As the flesh sores break out, a person's skin becomes extremely sensitive to any type of contact, so any porphyria sufferer is likely to prefer to let his facial hair grow rather than shave it. Illis scarcely needed to remark that it takes no daring leap of imagination to see how scared people might easily mistake a man's unshaven face for the furry visage of a beast.

As for the ranting and raving that witnesses so often ascribe to werewolves, Illis indicated that a wide range of mental disorders including epilepsy is frequently a part of porphyria. Such disturbances can result either directly from the incredible metabolic distortions taking place or hereditary factors, or indirectly as a result of persecution or the depression which a victim might well develop as his or her appearance becomes increasingly grotesque and puzzling. (In any case, we shall see in other chapters how the manifestations of mental disorders so often follows daily and monthly lunar patterns.)

Dr. Illis explained that there are several types of porphyria. Basil Copper, whose discussion of Illis's work is thorough and lucid, made it clear that the form of porphyria which corresponds to the signs of lycanthropy is only the congenital form, which is rare. It is an hereditary disease brought on by a recessive gene that makes a person's skin extremely sensitive to light. Copper quoted Illis, then commented on what the doctor had to say:

> Illis observes, " . . . There is a tendency for the skin lesions to ulcerate and these ulcers may attack cartilage and bone. Over a period of years structures such as nose, ears, eyelids and fingers undergo progressive mutilation."
>
> Other effects of porphyria are pigmentation of the skin; and the teeth may be red or reddish-brown due to the deposit of porphyrins. As the reader may have noted, some of these medical symptoms are the classical signs by which the lycanthrope has been identified throughout the ages.
>
> The wandering about at night, which the victim of porphyria would find more bearable than exposure to daylight; the excoriations and lesions to the skin of the face and hands, typical of the werewolf who had been bitten by wild animals; and possible nervous manifestations; all would have been enough, in medieval times, to condemn such a poor wretch to the execution block as a proven werewolf.
>
> Significantly, Dr [*sic*] Illis postulates, "The nervous manifes-

> tations may be referable to any part of the nervous system, and include mental disorders, ranging from mild hysteria to manic-depressive psychoses and delirium. Epilepsy may occur. . . ."
>
> The disturbance in the body metabolism also results in severe photo-sensitivity in which the victim is unable to bear the action of light upon his skin and for this reason prefers to wander about in the dark.[69]

Illis neglected to mention that whatever effect sunlight has on porphyria may be augmented by moonlight, which, of course, is greatest at the full moon. At any rate, Dr. Illis did point out the greatest tragedy about the disease. Although its effects are astounding and traumatic and the disease may be found in many parts of the world, its development can be arrested by treatment with modern drugs.

8

Hungry Dragons

Two Chinese astronomers died 4,000 years ago when a dragon ate the sun. And it was their own fault.

Ancient Chinese peasants and noblemen alike understood perfectly well that solar eclipses were caused by pesky dragons, who were always trying to make a snack of the sun.[1] Fortunately, these attacks could be accurately predicted by astronomers of the Imperial Court, who would alert the people to mount the defense that had always saved the sun: a vigorous counterattack with arrows and a frightful cacophony of loud shouts, drum beats, hammered gongs, and angry clapping. It was a simple but sufficient solution to a dire threat. You can imagine then the vexation of Emperor Chung K'ang, fourth emperor of the Hsia Dynasty, when he found the sun of his realm being unceremoniously swallowed on October 22, 2137 B.C., without so much as a peep of warning from Hsi and Ho, the chief Imperial astronomers.[2]

Panic reigned among the people as the sun shrank into a dim crescent and seemed about to disappear forever, but Chung K'ang's hastily mobilized defense saved the day—literally and figuratively—and the dragon was forced to retreat to the infernal region from which it came.[3] The nation was saved and K'ang could thank his lucky stars, but Hsi and Ho were not so lucky. They had chosen the wrong day to indulge in a blind drunk. Their doom was sealed. At their trial, they were caught in a Catch 22, a legal heads-K'ang-wins-tails-you-lose. The law clearly required the death penalty "without respite" for an erroneously early prediction of an eclipse and the death penalty "without reprieve" for predictions which were late.[4]

Unlike their attention to the eclipse, their execution was right on time.

Next to the moon's regular waxing and waning, eclipses are its most obvious action. They are certainly its most terrifying. The sun may disappear each day with nightfall, and the moon may vanish once a lunar month predictably, but what could be more frightening for primitive peoples than the disappearance of either in the middle of the day, in the middle of the month, in a matter of seconds? No wonder eclipses have held a death-grip on the imagination of men and women for millenia. Their attempts to explain eclipses have been space shots of imaginative beauty; nevertheless, the fear of eclipses has affected the outcome of war, altered the course of history, lent a hand to Christopher Columbus's success, and helped Aristotle prove the world is not flat.

The explanations of pre-technological societies were (and, in some primitive locations, still are) elegently simple if not accurate. There was that dragon eating the sun. Farther south, in Southeast Asia, China's neighbors blamed a ravenous frog for eclipses of the moon.[5] The first written record of a lunar eclipse, however, is Chinese and dated almost exactly 1,000 years—January 2, 1136 B.C.—after Hsi and Ho's fateful blunder with booze.[6] Yet eclipses are among the simplest celestial events for modern science to explain.

A solar eclipse occurs whenever the moon passes directly between the earth and sun. That's the same general position the moon is in once a lunar month, every month, when it is new. The moon does not eclipse the sun every month, though, because the plane of its orbit around earth is at an angle to the earth's orbit around the sun. In fact, the moon's orbit is tilted by more than five degrees relative to earth's orbit.[7] So, when the moon is new, sometimes it passes above or below the sun's position in our sky. Then there is either no eclipse at all or only a partial one. When a solar eclipse does take place, it can be at any time of day, meaning that the sun might be high in the sky or near the horizon. Whatever the alignment of moon, sun, and earth, it will be 6,585 days and eight hours—or eighteen years, eleven days, eight hours—before the three are aligned in exactly the same part of the sky again (although solar eclipses in other parts of the sky will happen in the meantime).[8,9] That eighteen-year process is known as the Saros cycle.

Basically, the same dynamics apply to eclipses of the moon, which occur when the sun, earth, and full moon are aligned.

Neither type of eclipse is especially rare, however. In a typical century, there are 237 partial and total solar eclipses, and 154 lunar eclipses.[10] Most, though, occur over remote spots on earth's surface, unseen by people, so many people never see an eclipse in their entire lives. Moreover, the shadow of a total eclipse is only about 100 miles wide on earth's surface, which limits the number of people who can see it, and, even though the moon, sun, and earth align in exactly the same way every eighteen-plus years, the same spot *on earth's surface* may be privy to a total solar eclipse only once every 360 years[11] because of the earth's daily spin.

This sounds like pretty straightforward stuff, but you can imagine how much more difficult it would be to understand an eclipse if you did not know that the earth, moon, and sun are all round and all are satellites in orbit (the sun is in orbit around the center of our galaxy). In fact, after centuries of intellectual fumbling, it was a lunar eclipse that finally helped man understand that the earth is indeed round and moving freely in space. Man's conception of reality was still cloudy the day Thales of Miletus (624–547 B.C.), the Greek philosopher, happened to walk into a deep well and found that he could gaze heavenward and see stars even during the middle of day. Thales became fascinated by astronomy and soon revealed his conviction that the earth must be floating on water like a log.[12] Anaximander, a young contemporary of Thales, figured that earth floated in space but is shaped like a cylinder. The earth is one flat end, he thought, and the sky is the other.[13] Pythagoras had a hunch earth was round, but either he wrote no proof or it has been lost to time.[14] The ancient

Chinese and Hebrews believed the earth stood on pillars.[15] The people of India also believed the earth was standing on something: the shoulders of hefty elephants, which in turn were carried about by a giant turtle swimming through an endless sea.[16] Perhaps earthquakes were the result of seasick pachyderms.

It was left to Aristotle, in the fourth century B.C., to use more than wild imagination on this puzzle of the earth's shape.[17] First, he expounded a crude theory of gravity in his observation that "the shape that a body naturally assumes when all parts of it tend toward the centre" is a sphere. Second, he noticed that stars like Polaris, the North Star, are higher in the sky above the horizon the farther north you go; for example, Polaris is higher in the skies of Greece than in Egypt. On the other hand, Canopus, the Southern Star, can be seen from Alexandria, Egypt, but not from Athens. That, Aristotle said, is possible only if the earth's surface is curved and Canopus is always below the horizon and invisible from Athens. Aristotle's clincher came during an eclipse of the moon. He pointed out what was momentarily obvious. When the moon entered the earth's shadow, the shadow seen on the moon's surface was round.

Christopher Columbus once used a lunar eclipse to avoid starvation. It was in 1503, during his fourth voyage to the New World, when he had run aground at Jamaica. He and his crew had no way to leave, and when Columbus's crewmen grew rowdy and offensive to the natives of the island the Jamaicans began withholding supplies from them.[18] The situation was critical when Columbus, with his navigator's knowledge of the skies, remembered that an eclipse was due—which gave him an idea. Columbus approached the Indians and once again asked for food, but now he threatened to make the moon change color and go dark if the Indians would not provide his men with something to eat. The Jamaicans called the Italian's bluff, and were petrified into generosity when Columbus's dark prediction was fulfilled.[19,20]

In contrast, an eclipse of the sun some 2,000 years earlier served the cause of peace. The Medes and Lydians of Asia Minor were in the sixth year of warfare on May 28, 585 B.C.

when their armies once again were engaged in a deadly dance on a blood-soaked field. Then it happened. The historian Herodotus described the scene: "Just as the battle was growing warm, day was suddenly changed into night." The moon had blotted out the sun. Both armies saw this as an ominous omen against continuing the fight, and by nightfall a truce had been made.[21,22,23]

The power of Athens itself went into eclipse because of a solar eclipse in 413 B.C., changing the course of Western civilization. The waning glory of Athens eventually created a vacuum that Rome would fill. The Peloponnesian War between Athens, the center of scholarship and art, and militaristic Sparta was underway. An Athenian army on Sicily had been meeting only defeat, and the time to withdraw had arrived. Unfortunately, so did an eclipse, and the Athenian commander, Nicias, delayed evacuation of the island for several days because he feared embarking on any enterprise in the face of such a portent. The Spartans however, were more interested in sitting ducks than celestial shadows, and they soon had slaughtered all but a few of Nicias's men.[24,25]

One author has observed that the Sicilian debacle was the turning point of the war. Within a decade Athens succumbed, but victorious Sparta could not replace her sister city-state as the leader of Greece.[26] Ironically, the Athenians should have known better. At least fifty years earlier, the brilliant philosopher Anaxagoras had explained to his fellow Athenians the cause of eclipses, and a prominent citizen like Nicias certainly should have known about that.[27]

Nearly 500 years later, the Roman emperor Claudius used an eclipse for political advantage. Unlike Nicias, Claudius had a sound knowledge of science and he knew that the eclipse of A.D. 45 would coincide with his own birthday. He was also a student of human nature, and he knew the populace might be quite displeased with a ruler whose birthday was marred by an eclipse. He did the wisest thing: he publicly predicted the eclipse and issued an explanation for the event.[28] As a result, his biggest worry that day was blowing out some candles.

Not so for Emperor Louis of Bavaria in A.D. 840. The

eclipse that year frightened him so much that he died of terror, after which his sons fought over succession to the throne, which hastened the collapse of the great empire that had been founded by Charlemagne.[29] More stalwart leaders withstood similar crises. The Roman general Drusus appeased a rebellion in his army by predicting a lunar eclipse. Sulpicius Gallus, during war against Persia, did the same thing. And Alexander the Great, near Arabella, was called upon to calm the terror of his troops when an unexpected eclipse suddenly loomed overhead.[30] The total eclipse of 1706, however, did spread panic and fear through the French army besieging Barcelona, Spain.[31]

An American medical journal once reported the disastrous effect eclipses had in several European medical cases between the sixteenth and nineteenth centuries.[32] The ensuing fear proved too much for several patients in one hospital; they died. Several Parisian physicians who had rushed to the bedside of an outrageously wealthy woman momentarily left the room to watch a solar eclipse in progress. When they stepped back inside, their patient had been frightened into a coma. One German nobleman flew into such a panic during an eclipse that he ran from his house and began slaughtering pedestrians with his sword. Peasants outside Paris besieged the homes of clergymen to make confession during one early eclipse. And England's Francis Bacon simply fainted during one lunar eclipse. If Bacon really was Shakespeare's ghostwriter, as some scholars claim, you can bet he didn't pen a single sonnet while the earth's shadow crossed the moon.

Then again, Bacon may have been in Mother Nature's majority. During the solar eclipse over parts of North America on February 26, 1979, wolves in Washington Park Zoo in Portland, Oregon, paced nervously when the sunlight began to fade, then laid their ears back in an obvious pose of submission. Crows flocked to their nighttime nesting places, ducks quacked, and birds in flight became confused. Chickens started laying eggs as if it were night.[33]

Eskimos of Greenland regard eclipses with a similar wariness. They know the moon as a frequent ne'er-do-well, whose only productive activity is a monthly seal hunt. More ominously, the moon is a fellow who rejoices in the death of women; the sun, in the mortality of men. Thus, the Eskimos teach that men should stay indoors during an eclipse of the sun when the sun has left the sky and may be prowling the earth, and women during an eclipse of the moon.[34]

Ditto for Indians of South America and South Pacific islanders, who held noisy rituals to fend off the evil blackness of a lunar eclipse in 1971.[35] Peruvian Indians shoot arrows at the sun during a solar eclipse to scare away the monster munching it, and Indians along the Orinoco River in Venezuela bury lighted sticks of wood for safekeeping during lunar eclipses so that even if the moon were to be extinguished all fire on earth would not also vanish.[36]

Nor are modern soldiers any different from the old. Whereas Emperor Chung K'ang's militia resorted to bows and arrows to save the sun, twentieth-century soldiers in his backyard use the contemporary equivalent. In 1969, at the height of the war in Vietnam, Lon Nol's troops in Cambodia could be found firing their automatic rifles at the darkening sun during an eclipse.[37]

Then, victorious in that battle, they returned to their previous one.[38]

9

Epilepsy

In the Bible is the story of a man whose son is afflicted by seizures. When the disciples of Jesus are unable to cure the boy, his father brings him to the Master. Jesus diagnoses the boy's condition as possession by an evil spirit, which he rebukes and banishes from the boy. The apparent origin of that evil spirit is just as interesting as the remedy. The Latin Vulgate Bible describes the lad as *lunaticus,* which meant "moonstruck" and was used in reference to epileptics.[1]

In other words, Jesus cured the boy of epilepsy, a lunar affliction.

This Biblical passage was nothing unusual for its day or, for that matter, many centuries thereafter. The moon has long been considered the cause of epilepsy. Many people have believed a special relationship exists between the two. Just as some of our words for insanity, for instance, have their roots in the Latin word meaning "moon," the word "epilepsy" is also derived from the word for "moon" in Greek.[2] And there is that double application of the Latin *lunaticus,* illustrated by the Bible and many early Latin and Greek authors.[3,4] This connection between the moon and epilepsy arose early—and stuck.

It is not just any old moon that people have had in mind, though. People have almost always believed that epileptic attacks grow more severe as the moon waxes and are most violent during the full moon.[5] There's less agreement over *how* the moon causes the disease. One of the most popular old theories is that it has to do with sex. Hippocrates' great admirer, the Greek physician Galen, was convinced that it was women who could not menstruate who suffered from epilepsy, and that a restoration of menses would cure them.[6] Galen even suggested a way to bring about this remedy: wear the root of a peony as a neck pendant. A Greek naturalist scribbled this warning onto Galen's prescription, however: no doctor should *ever* try to pull a peony from the ground himself because the exposed roots will immediately kill the careless harvester. Instead, the cold-hearted author recommended that physicians use an expendable dog to extract peonies.[7] Another prominent author who was a contemporary of Galen wrote that if medication does not cure epilepsy, he could tell you what would: a toss in the hay. The "commencement of sexual intercourse" will do it every time, he promised.[8]

That passage from Matthew in the Bible illustrated another old theory, that epilepsy is the result of demonic possession or is the punishment of a god.[9] How else could men explain someone acting so out of character, as if the personality they knew had been replaced in the victim's body? And when the epileptic claimed afterwards that he could not remember his or her fit, wasn't that more proof that something had temporarily replaced his or her very soul? Unfortunately for epileptics, though, this affliction was usually interpreted as divine punishment for having sinned,[10] probably against the moon. That was why epilepsy was often referred to as the "sacred disease," and epileptics were held in disgrace.[11]

A third theory was that epilepsy was caused by excessive moisture on the brain, moisture brought about by the moon.[12] This seemed perfectly natural to people because the moon was also blamed for heavy deposits of dew on cloudless nights[13] and, in general, associated with water, flood, and rain. This is an especially intriguing theory because, as we shall see in subsequent chapters, not only has recent science vindicated many "myths" about the moon's influence over rain, assorted odd weather, menstruation, and bleeding, but now cerebral edema (which is the deadly accumulation of pressure from fluids around the brain) is suspected of causing epilepsy.[14]

Then there was the theory of Richard Mead, an eighteenth-century English physician, who said that in the previous war with France he had seen young naval officers succumb to epilepsy during battles that occurred just before a full or new moon.[15] American physicians have observed that other neurological disorders, whose symptoms also involve convulsions, follow the same lunar clock.[16,17]

One theory, however, sounds more like something from a Woody Allen movie than anything else. It was recounted by an article in the *Psychoanalytic Review,* which said that somewhere in the otherwise erudite Hebrew Talmud is the warning that anyone who stands nude in front of a shining light, like the full moon, risks contracting epilepsy . . . and, epilepsy is liable to strike the children conceived during sexual intercourse in a lighted room.[18]

Part Two

The Moon and Its Effects

The moon is a unique satellite in the solar system, and we know much about it. Here, a description of the moon and the body of evidence about its effect on earth and earth's living inhabitants . . . a body of evidence which grows like the waxing moon itself.

10

Selenology

In the beginning, earth and moon were one, a single planet. In its infancy, this primitive planet was molten and plastic, very different from the cool, crusted world we know today. Before long, the sun's enormous gravitational pull had raised a bulge on this malleable earth's side. The earth's spin, much faster than it is today, helped throw the bulge farther and farther out until it formed one end of a lopsided dumbbell, stretching out like taffy. When this bulge finally broke away, like a babe severing its umbilical, the moon was born. Its womb would some day be the Pacific Ocean.

Or . . . the moon was an independent planet captured by the earth's gravity. Just as Pluto appears to be an escaped moon of Saturn or Neptune captured by the sun's gravity, so our moon may have been a tenth planet whose eccentric orbit carried it within earth's gravitational grip.

Or . . . earth and moon are a double planet, twins born from the same swirling cloud of gases and dust, which refused to condense into one, larger planet.

Three theories for the moon's origin, contradictory and strange. None is any more firmly established than theories about the earth's own creation. We know much more about the anatomy of this compelling companion of earth, this goddess of love, which has fascinated mankind for tens of millenia; indeed, for as long as beautiful women have fascinated men and women have stared in wonder at a body which seems to share the secret of gestation.

We know its diameter is 2,160 miles—not quite the distance between San Francisco and Cleveland[1]—compared to the earth's 7,910-mile girth.[2] Or, put another way, if earth were the size of a basketball, the moon would be as small as a tennis ball.[3] Its weight is 81 quintillion tons; that's 81 followed by 18 zeros, or 8.10 multiplied by 10-to-the-nineteenth power.[4] The earth is an even more hefty six sextillion, 588 quintillion (6,588 followed by 18 zeros) tons.[5]

The moon's surface area is comparable to Africa's. Its gravity is only one-sixth the earth's.[6] It holds little or no atmosphere.[7] It is, in fact, far from being the largest moon in the solar system. Four of the thirty-four or more natural satellites are larger.[8,9,10] Jupiter alone has three of those. One, Ganymede, is even larger than Mercury.[11] Neptune's giant moon Triton is bigger than both Mercury and Pluto.[12] Still, our moon is the largest satellite in proportion to its parent planet.[13]

When Galileo Galilei and the Englishman Thomas Harriot first gazed upon the moon through telescopes in 1609, they saw a planet at least 4.6 billion years old, pock-marked by craters. It was Galileo, the next year at the university in Padua, Italy, who began naming the moon's smooth plains *maria* (a Latin word for "seas") because they resembled earth's placid oceans.[14,15] Galileo's modern successors believe the maria are plains formed by lava floods billions of years ago. The lava followed gravity into low places on the lunar surface, and since many of these low places are giant craters, the lava filling those craters formed round maria.[16] Curiously, most maria are on the near side of the moon, which faces the earth.[17] On the moon's far side, the impact craters of meteorites are unobscured by such seas of hardened lava.

The favorite explanation for this is that the moon's crust is thicker on her far side,[18] and this thicker crust forms a more effective barrier against fissures which in the distant past could have bled lava onto the moon's surface. In addition, the moon is pear-shaped, with the pointed end pulled toward earth by earth's gravity. Astronaut James Erwin observed and marveled at this visible distortion from his space craft floating between moon and earth.[19] It causes the moon's center of gravity to be 1.2 miles away from the moon's physical center, closer to the side facing earth.[20]

As for temperature, it's just what you would expect from a passionate but fickle goddess of love: *hot*! . . . then *cold*. Noon temperature at the equator reaches 260° F. while midnight can be a chilling −280° F.

One other intriguing aspect of the moon's anatomy is the content of its crust. This is the outer layer of the moon, 36 to 62 miles thick. It covers the moon's inner mantle (over 1,000 miles thick) and core (which has a radius of about 135 miles).[21] James Burke, of Cal Tech's Jet Propulsion Laboratory, describes this crust as "rigid, cold, and composed of the lighter elements and minerals that floated to the surface in an early global episode of melting and sorting out of the chemical elements."[22] But what makes this crust so interesting is that it contains lumps of dense rock, called "mascons," or lunar mass concentrations, below the prominent, circular maria of the earth-face side. These *mascons* appear to be either huge reservoirs of hardened lava which have sunk beneath the moon's surface under their own weight, or large accumulations of the rocky remains of comets and meteorites which have settled into the moon after smashing into its surface, or a combination of both.[23,24]

Whichever, the dense *mascons* are suspended in the moon's lighter, rigid crust like so many raisins floating in stale sponge cake, and whenever one of man's sensitive space probes passes overhead there is no mistaking that their gravitational tug is greater than the less densely packed lunar crust around them.[25] They might even explain why the same lunar surface always faces earth. This side of the moon may have faced away from the earth before the maria had formed. But once lava and, perhaps, meteorites had created the weighty *mascons*, "the resulting imbalance in . . . the moon's mass might have allowed the earth's gravitational attraction to turn the moon around and forever lock the side with the maria toward the earth."[26] Thus, moon and earth are like lovers, embracing for eons in gravity's relentless kiss.

Theirs is certainly a long-distance romance. The closest they ever come is 221,456 miles at perigee; the farthest, 252,-711 miles at apogee.[27] Those are roughly 110 times the moon's diameter.

It takes the moon 27 days, 7 hours, and 43.2 minutes to complete a 360-degree orbit around the earth. That orbit, and that amount of time, are the "sidereal" month. That is not the amount of time between full moons, however. Full moons are an average of 29 days, 12 hours, and 44.1 minutes apart.[28] That period is called the "synodic" month and is sometimes referred to as the "lunar month." For us, it is the more important of the two orbital periods. But how can there be "two" months? The explanation is this: in the time it takes the moon to travel 360 degrees around the earth, the earth has moved forward in its own orbit around the sun; the moon must orbit another 53 hours before it is in the same position relative to both the earth and sun. Here's one way to visualize it. Imagine the sun, earth, and moon forming a 90-degree angle in space. One sidereal month later the moon has traveled 360 degrees, completing one whole circle around the earth. But because the earth has moved, that angle between the sun, earth, and moon is larger than 90 degrees; it won't close to exactly 90 degrees for another 53 hours.

The new moon is generally considered the start of the lunar month. Full moons are the halfway point in each lunar month. The moon moves from new moon to waxing crescent, then first quarter, waxing gibbous, full moon, waning gibbous, last (or third) quarter, and waning crescent. The four phases which come up most often in folklore and scientific study are the full and new moons, first and last quarters. They're known as "the four quarters."

These phases are simply a matter of light reflected by the moon. The moon, of course, has no light of its own; it reflects the sun's light, and it's the amount of that light visible on earth that determines the phase. Half the moon is always illuminated by the sun (except at lunar eclipses). At the full moon, we can see that entire half because it is facing the earth; moon, earth, and sun form a single line. At the first and last quarters, though, we see only half the illuminated side because the moon is "beside" the earth. At the new moon, the moon is between the earth and sun. The moon's dark side is facing earth while its illuminated half is facing the sun.

Then there is the matter of the lunar "day." Since the same side of the moon always faces earth, it takes the moon the same amount of time to turn once on its axis as it takes it to orbit earth once. A lunar day, then, takes one sidereal month. However, unless we specify that *that* is the lunar day we mean, when we write about the "lunar day" we will be referring to the amount of time between moonrises on earth, 24 hours and 50 minutes. That's how long it takes the earth to turn so that any spot on earth finds itself directly beneath the moon again.

Bringing up the rear in this parade of jargon is the word "selenology." The word means the study of lunar astronomy, and often includes the concept of "selenography," or the study of lunar "geo"-logy. And like so many things in science, it comes from fantasy—the name of Selene, the Greek goddess of the moon and love.

11

Ocean Tides

The most visible, least debated, and best understood influence of the moon is upon the ocean tides. There isn't a youngster in your neighborhood who can't tell you the difference between high and low tides. We assume this has been as evident to people of every era as it is now, and, sure enough, ancient scrolls and books prove that long ago the Chinese, Arabic, and Icelandic people, to name just a few, were familiar with tides.[1] Yet, incredibly, tides practically escaped notice by the thinkers and writers of classical Greece and Rome.[2]

The reason was simple but puzzling: the Mediterranean Sea is nearly tideless.[3]

A few Greek writers took stabs at explaining what little tidal motion they had observed as early as the fourth century B.C.[4] During the first century A.D., the Roman naturalist Pliny speculated that the moon might have something to do with it.[5] But for the most part mankind around the Mediterranean and beyond remained ignorant. After Johann Kepler, early in the seventeenth century, tried to point out that tides did indeed seem to follow the sun and moon,[6] it was no one less than Galileo who accused him of being a chucklehead. Any theory based on lunar influence, Galileo sneered, smacked of astrology and superstition.[7] Tides, he argued, obviously were created by the rotation and orbital motion of the earth,[8,9] similar to the way in which nudging a pail of water causes the liquid to splash. High tide was merely so much water splashing over the terrestrial pail's edge.

It wasn't until Isaac Newton scratched out his monumental *Principia* in 1687 that an explanation existed which was based on solar and lunar influence and backed by convincing mathematics.[10]

What we know today is that the moon, with only one-sixth the earth's gravity, manhandles the earth's oceans. It does this despite the fact that, on earth, the earth's gravitational pull is 280,000 times stronger than the pull of the moon overhead.[11] It even has more than twice the tidal tug of the sun.[12] That's because it is so much closer to earth than the sun.[13]

As the moon passes over any point on earth, it pulls up the water directly beneath, forming a high tide there. High tide also occurs at the same time on the opposite side of the earth because the moon actually pulls the solid earth away from the water.[14] Earth thus has two high (and two low) tides every day, about half a day apart. In theory, these high tides should occur when the moon is directly overhead, but they don't; they occur after the moon has passed because friction delays the oceans' motion, causing them to lag behind the moon.[15]

Tides are highest when the gravitational pull on them is strongest. That happens approximately twice each month, at full and new moons. That's when the sun and moon are aligned, pulling together. At full moon, they are in line on opposite sides of the earth, and at new moon they are aligned on the same side of the earth. At first and third quarters, though, the moon and sun are at right angles to each other relative to the earth, and pulling literally at cross purposes. High tides are not as great as they are at full and new moons, and this is when there's the least difference between high and low tides. The higher tides at full and new moon are known as "spring tides," even though they occur throughout the year. The tides at quarter-moon are called "neap tides."[16,17]

At any time of the month, high tides occur about twice a day, usually 12 hours and 25 minutes apart.[18] That corresponds to the length of the lunar day, 24 hours, 50 minutes, which is actually the amount of time it takes the earth to rotate so that any point on earth is again beneath the moon. That's 50 minutes longer than the earth's day because in the 24 hours it takes the earth to rotate once, the moon in its orbit has moved farther around the earth. The earth must spin another 50 minutes before it has completed one rotation relative to the moon.

Think about that a moment. If you divide the length of the earth's equator (nearly 25,000 miles) by the length of the lunar day, you get the speed at which tides travel: nearly 1,000 miles an hour.[19] Like two watery bulges racing around the earth on opposite sides, that's how fast tides travel at the equator.

When Sir Isaac Newton finally explained how lunar and solar gravity cause tides, he predicted that the range between high and low tides on the open oceans of the world should be 2.95 feet, which is amazingly close to the true tidal range of 2.5 feet.[20] His mathematical models, however, could not explain why the height or time of tides varied from one English harbor to another, or from English to Continental harbors, for that matter. Here was a puzzle which stumped the British genius: Why should tides at London Bridge have a range of 21 feet at one time of the month, but only 15 feet during the rest of the month? And why only range some 2 feet in the Mediterranean and at certain islands in the Pacific?[21]

In fact, some Pacific islands have two high tides daily, with only a slight ebb in between, then a very low tide. Shrimp boaters in the Gulf of Mexico see only one high and one low tide a day, and the same happens at Saint Michel, Alaska,[22] and Do-Son in the Tonkin Gulf.[23] In Tahiti, high and low tide occur at the same time every day.[24]

What Newton, laboring alone and in an age prior to electronic pocket calculators, did not grasp was that the sun and moon are merely the motors that propel tides; where they go, how high, and with what frequency, are affected by the tides' roadways. The depth of oceans, earth's tilt on its axis, continents forming roadblocks . . . those affect the regularity of tides.[25] And when the size, shape and depth of a body of water are such that a tide always "bounces" from one shore to another at the same time the moon's pull takes hold every day, then that tide will be a lot higher than the worldwide average of two and a half feet.[26]

That's exactly what happens in the Bay of Fundy, on Canada's southeast coast. The Bay forms a veritable bowling alley, perfectly lined up with the direction that the North Atlantic Ocean's tides regularly surge toward shore. Moreover, the Bay's "resonance period" (the time it takes high tide to bounce from one end to the other and start back) is approximately 11½ hours, which nearly matches the 12½-hour rhythm between lunar-caused high tides in the Atlantic.[27] The result is a tidal range of 70 feet, according to one source;[28] more than 50 feet, according to others.[29,30] Whichever it is, the Bay of Fundy's tides are the world's highest[31] and come barreling up the Bay behind a "bore," or wall of water, three to six feet tall.[32] Large ships are often left high and dry at low tide and must be lashed to their docks by stout cables,[33] a nuisance the ancient Greeks and Romans never knew.

12

Atmospheric Tides

The French meteorologist D'Alembert was the first scientist to record lunar tides in the earth's atmosphere. He reported his observations in 1746 in Latin, as any reputable scholar of his day would do. In response, the Academy of Berlin hailed him. The French rushed a translation into print before another year passed.[1] Several French academicians expanded on D'Alembert's theory in the years that followed. British contributions were made in the next century.[2]

Tides in the atmosphere follow daily and monthly lunar patterns similar to those of ocean tides. High tide is when the moon is directly overhead ("upper transit") or on the opposite side of the earth ("lower transit").[3] Tide is measured as air pressure, and highest tide is at lower transit every day. Daily high tides peak two times every lunar month, at the full and new moons.[4] The daily tide is higher still when a new or full moon occurs while the moon is at perigee, and even higher than that when those conditions occur as the moon crosses the "ecliptic," the geometrical plane formed by the path of earth's orbit.[5]

The difficulty with proving the existence of atmospheric tides (and the reason most people today don't realize they exist) was that they are so small. Basically, it is hard to distinguish between periodic undulations in air pressure caused by lunar gravity and those caused by the sun's heating of the atmosphere, which also affects air tides.[6] In fact, one modern study of lunar daily air tides had to continue twelve years before the researchers felt they had results worth reporting,[7] and another involved observations made over a sixty-two-year period.[8]

But the moon's influence is there, as surely as the moon rises every 24 hours and 50 minutes. The moon's gravity is enough to push the barometer up .001 inches a day.[9] Its influence is not the same everywhere, though. It causes the barometer to rise about three times as much in the tropics as it does in middle latitudes.[10] Scientists have even measured the speed of the lunar wind along the earth's surface. It comes along at about 1/20 mile per hour.[11] Hardly breathtaking. More like a lover's soft whisper. Which may explain why it was a Frenchman who first proved it was there.

13

The Eiffel Effect

When an exploration party led by Hans Jelstrup, a Norwegian, arrived at Sabine Island off the west coast of Greenland in 1932, they dutifully set about determining their precise location. Sextants in hand, the fur-coat clad explorers began lining up stars and earth's horizon from the most prominent local landmark, a pier which had been used by another expedition for the same purpose sixty-two years earlier. But something was wrong.

They surveyed their position several times, but each time their own measurements put the pier nearly 1,030 feet west of where the 1870 party had calculated its position to be. Jelstrup's men knew that their predecessors could not possibly have made an error of that size.[1] Or could they?

Halfway around the world at nearly the same time, a radio station in Shanghai, China, was keeping in regular radio contact with stations in Berlin and Bordeaux, France. Careful records were kept, indicating the precise time messages were transmitted, then received. No one at the observatory, however, could explain why the signals took longer to complete their journey on some occasions than others. It was as if the radio stations were 60 feet farther apart during some transmissions than during others.[2]

In 1931 scientists conducted what was supposed to be a routine measurement of the distance between the astronomical observatory at Córdoba, Argentina, and the Royal Observatory at Greenwich, England. They were startled to find that their observations placed the Córdoba observatory some 1,200 feet farther away from Greenwich than the prior special measurement, in 1871, had indicated it was.

Incompetence could not explain the discrepancy. The 1931 group, working with modern electronic timing devices, knew that the earlier observations had been conducted by Dr. Benjamin A. Gould, one of the most respected and painstaking mathematicians of his time, whose calculations had been supplemented by reliable data supplied by the U.S. Naval Astronomical Expeditions. Nor could continental drift account for the difference. If anything, the two stations should have been closer together.[3]

And when astronomers working for the U.S. Naval Observatory calculated the distance between San Diego and Washington, D.C., in 1933, they found their figure differing from the one calculated only seven years before by 55 feet, a colossal distance in the hair-splitting world of geodesic surveys. Even when they recomputed the 1926 data using more recent analytical methods, the astronomers still found an unexplainable discrepancy of 37 feet.[4]

Each of these groups had encountered the same riddle: either trained scientists were making calculation errors far too large to explain, or the vantage points for the observations—the astronomical observatories themselves—were moving. Since the distances would mean errors that were just too big to be plausible, scientists considered the alternative. But how could it be any more plausible for observatories (or a boat pier) to move? Many astronomers felt the explanation had to be with the well-known "wobble" in the earth's daily rotation about its axis.[5] This would explain how the position of stars used for celestial navigation seemed to change, relative to various observatories, from one observation to another. One astronomer, however, didn't buy this theory.

Dr. Harlan T. Stetson, working at a special laboratory in Needham, outside Boston, argued that the earth's wobble could account only for a small part of the mixed-up measurements. Most of the discrepancies, he said, corresponded neatly to the moon's motion above.[6] Stetson pointed out that in Greenland, in Argentina, in Shanghai, and in Washington, D.C., the first and second location calculations had been based on celestial observations made at different times of the lunar day. The moon was not at the same place in its orbit during the later observations as it had been during the first. And when he adjusted each surveyor's raw data to compensate for the time of lunar day, sure enough, each pair of observations became a match. The moon was actually pulling the "solid" earth a quarter of a million miles beneath it, stretching the ground just as it stretches the ocean and air to form tidal bulges.

Other researchers, like A.A. Michelson, America's first Nobel laureate in science,[7] had argued the same thing earlier. But it was Stetson who went on to add persuasive corroborating evidence. On a visit to colleagues working in the Gulf Research building in Pittsburgh, Stetson found a way to show exactly how much the earth rises under the moon's attraction. There, on the floor of a basement laboratory, he worked with a gravimeter, a device sensitive enough to measure decreases in earth's surface gravity occurring when that surface—and any gravimeter on it—moved farther away from the center of earth's mass. And that's exactly what the device described. Day after day, for months, this gravimeter had recorded a rise and fall of two feet in the earth's surface.[8] It even indicated that this terrestrial tidal bulge built up enough momentum each lunar day to keep rising for 50 minutes after the moon had passed overhead.[9]

Today these earth tides are well known and accepted by the science community.[10] But, like atmospheric tides, terrestrial tides remain unknown to most of the lay public.

The first evidence of such tides was actually recorded well before the twentieth century. It was some 2,000 years ago, and again Pliny the Elder was the investigative reporter. Pliny was a gentleman and aristocrat, a sort of Roman jet-setter, who traveled through much of the then-known Western World. On at least one occasion, these travels took him to Spain, where he noticed the same peculiar phenomenon at widely separated places. It was at Seville, then Cadiz near the temple of Hercules, and then at a spot on the banks of the Guadalquivir, that he found springs of water similar to wells that sometimes rose and fell with the nearest ocean tides, but other times did just the opposite.[11] Pliny, who recognized a freak event when he saw one, knew these weird wells were worth mentioning in his encyclopedic *Historia Naturalis.* It remained for physicists much later to interpret them.

What Pliny had observed was the earth acting like a giant sponge, having water squeezed out of it. When he saw the spring water fall while the ocean rose, it was because the moon was overhead, lifting both ocean tides and the solid earth. As the earth rose, more space opened in the porous ground below for spring water to retreat into. When the moon was not above and ocean tides were low, the moon's gravitational grip relaxed on the land, too. The terrain would settle and compress itself, forcing subterranean water to ooze up through fissures and wells.[12] When Pliny saw well water and ocean tides rise simultaneously, it was because in that place rising, twisting land was wringing water up and out of itself, rather than letting water in by opening its pores like so many underground bellows.

Were he around today, even the worldly Pliny might find it hard to believe that the same forces which propelled his well water make the city of Moscow rise and fall an estimated 20 inches twice daily.[13] And what would he think if someone told him that the moon plays the earth's surface like an accordion, pushing and pulling Europe and North America together and apart so that sometimes the Empire State Building is 63 feet closer to the Eiffel Tower than usual?[14]

14

Earthquakes

Dawn would bring terror that July morning in 1952. The citizens of tiny Tehachapi, California, could not know they had only a few remaining minutes of peaceful sleep. As day was about to break, long cracks suddenly appeared in the walls of the women's prison just outside town. In the center of town the ground shook as if a giant fist had slugged the earth. A wall on a hotel dropped to the ground like a rag, and beds rolled over the edge of exposed floors and hung there, halfway in the air, halfway in the hotel. Other buildings collapsed completely, crushing eleven townspeople, nine of them children. The highway from nearby Bakersfield moaned and slowly buckled like a black rug. At the Paloma oil refinery outside Bakersfield, the shifting earth twisted buildings and rubbed metal beams against each other like matchsticks until their sparks ignited a terrible fire. Even in Los Angeles, 100 miles to the south, buildings swayed and household pets paced nervously. Movie stars and other Beautiful People inhabiting the swank San Fernando Valley complained that precious water had sloshed out of their swimming pools.[1,2]

It was the earthquake of July 21, 1952, at that time California's most severe since the San Francisco shock of 1906. It was the explosive climax to weeks of tremors, but it was not the finale. One month later, on August 20, a vicious quake rattled the Oregon seashore just above the California border.[3]

Two days later a quake centered in Bakersfield rumbled the Golden State.

More recently, there was the San Francisco quake of August 7, 1979, worse than the '52 episode. Buildings are more quake-proof now, but there was still damage to water and gas pipes, electric power lines, and roads. Trailers in a mobile-home park were knocked from their foundations. A stock-broker in the city's financial district could only wish stocks rose as well as his desk, which jumped a foot. And a tourist from France sitting in the lobby of the Hilton Hotel decided she had had her fill of the New World when she saw chandeliers shake and felt her chair move.[4,5]

Anyone who has experienced one of these rock-and-roll shows can tell you they're exciting. But what excites seismologists about these five in particular is that they took place on the exact day of a full or new moon (August 22, 1952 was barely two days after the new moon), the two times each lunar month when the moon causes the highest tides in the ocean, atmosphere, and solid land.

Coincidence? Not at all, says Dr. Harlan Stetson, the terrestrial tides expert. In fact, it was Stetson who first explained the lunar connection to earthquakes, which is now the conventional wisdom among scientists: "deep-focus" earthquakes—earthquakes whose main motion is centered well underground—can be triggered by tides in the land.[6] If geologic stress is building up to an earthquake, Stetson wrote in 1944 in *Science* magazine, "there is a better chance of [its] occurrence during a time when the horizontal tidal component of the moon's gravitational force is at maximum" twice a day.[7] In other words, at terrestrial high tide. And, by implication, it should happen especially often at full and new moons, the two times each lunar month when daily tides are highest.

That's exactly what an American team of scientists recently documented in Turkey and California. Dr. M. Nafi Toksoz, an M.I.T. geophysicist, and his colleagues first poked through the rubble of 2,670 earthquakes in Turkey that had occurred between 1913 and 1970. Then they focused on sixty that had wracked the western end of the well-recognized North Anatolian Fault during the last decade. What they found was that temblors took place twice as frequently "when the moon exerts its greatest pull on the surfaces of an earthquake fault,"[8] either during the two daily high terrestrial tides caused by the moon, or at full and new moons.[9]

Toksoz's Turkish temblors, however, were all of the sizes classified as "intermediate" or "large" by seismologists, so he took the precaution of examining another group of smaller quakes. These were some 2,400 earthquakes with a Richter scale magnitude of three or less along central California's San Andreas Fault, south of Bear Valley, and sure enough Toksoz found a small correlation between the largest of those California quakes and lunar phases.[10] He cautioned his colleagues at the spring, 1979, meeting of the American Geophysical Union that final conclusions would have to await additional research.

Similar studies have done nothing but confirm Toksoz and Stetson's findings. In 1937 Sir Gerald Lenox-Conyngham reported in *Nature,* that Bible of the scientific community, that the land tides caused by the moon seemed to have triggered volcanic explosions in the West Indies.[11] It has also long been gospel among campers that Old Faithful's high- and low-water cycle is exactly the same as the moon's 18-year, 11⅓-day Saros cycle—the amount of time it takes the moon to return to precisely the same alignment with the sun and earth for an eclipse in any given spot in the sky.[12] And, more recently, T.R. Visvanathan, a geologist at the University of South Carolina, reported finding a relationship between earthquakes in the Charleston-Summerville region and new moons as well as lunar perigee.[13]

Both Visvanathan and Toksoz emphasized the importance of their findings for predicting future quakes and evacuating threatened people and livestock. Amateur seismologists, however, have been making successful predictions of this sort for years. In 1935, a gentleman named Reuben Greenspan began pestering New York newspapers and professional scientists with claims that he could foretell the time and place of earthquakes and volcanic eruptions. Editors throughout the Big

Apple dismissed him as just another crank until one newsman, growing weary of Greenspan, decided the best way to get rid of him was by exposing his presumably absurd claims.

The journalist's leg-work turned up just the opposite, though. He found that Greenspan had accurately predicted the time and place of every important seismic disturbance over a period of six months.[14] Other reporters reacted to this revelation like starving men to the sight of food. All of them suddenly were desperate for Greenspan's story. But Greenspan's secret sounded simple enough. All he had done was anticipate Toksoz's and Visvanathan's more detailed work, correlating times when seismic faults on the earth's surface would be aligned with the highest-tide-producing positions of the moon and other planets.

Greenspan's impact? Like an earthquake! One publication appearing soon afterwards described the scientific world as "greatly shaken."[15]

15

Moon Weather

More than 15,000 years ago Atlantis and its mid-Pacific counterpart Lemuria[1] did indeed exist and were home to flourishing societies. Moreover, the entire basin of what is now the Mediterranean Sea was dry land populated by a robust civilization dominated by Atlantis in the Atlantic Ocean, according to Plato,[2] and the heart of the emerging Western world. What turned history in the direction we are more familiar with was resolution of a conflict far from Earth.

Beyond the Earth, inside the orbit of Mars, was the Solar System's original fourth planet. It had been born with the other planets billions of years before. It was a charter member of the sun's family and had circled Sol uneventfully for ages. Yet this planet was a cosmic mistake. There was no room for it between Earth and Mars. There was not enough space for a mass that size to orbit the Sun undisturbed. First it would wander into the Earth's gravitational grip, then Mars'. Each time, its orbit became more eccentric and less stable. Each time, it became more vulnerable to the next approaching planet's attraction. This was an astronomical imbalance which could not continue forever, and the odds were that sooner or later Earth and Mars would pull it apart or, like the prongs of a sling-shot, hurl it toward the sun. Then, something else happened.

The planet rolled so close to Earth that Mars' grip was broken and its own orbit ended. Rather than shatter as the planet beyond Mars once had, or fall from orbit into the sun, this fourth planet, called "Luna" by the people of Earth, fell into place around the Earth. Thus, the moonless third planet from the sun gained a satellite.

Traumatic as this was for Luna, its effect on the inhabited Earth was even more disastrous. According to one commentator, Atlantis, Lemuria, the whole Mediterranean for that matter, and other "major parts of the earth sank during the generalized seismic activity resulting from the moon's sudden gravitational pull, and new island blocks were pushed above the surface of the waters, which were also redistributed to their present configurations."[3]

Civilizations were destroyed. Cities drowned upon grassy plains which suddenly became ocean bottoms. Gibraltar cracked away from the Pillars of Hercules and allowed an immense wave from the Atlantic to flood the land between Europe and Africa, creating the Mediterranean Sea. It was a scene repeated around the world. Like the Greeks with their myths speaking of a moonless age, the Chibcha Indians have religious stories which tell of a time before any moon, followed by flood and the moon's appearance.[4] The Choctaws of Oklahoma, the Ami of Formosa, and the Kalits of Australia's Pellew Islands also have legends relating a great flood to the full moon.[5]

This story of "Luna's" capture is the theory of H.S. Bellamy, which Douglas Kelley analyzes in *The Psychoanalytic Review.*[6] And although Kelley makes it clear that science has its doubts about Bellamy's scenario, one reason he presents it is to remind us just how strong and how old are ideas connecting the moon—the full moon in particular—with that meteorological paradigm, The Flood.

The notion that the moon influences the weather is nothing new. It is at least as ancient as the verse inscribed by Aratus, a Greek physician and poet of the third century B.C., in which he explains how to forecast weather by the phase and apparent color of the moon.[7] If the lunar crescent has sharp, red tips for three nights running, for example, "look out for great squalls. . . ." In contrast, a full moon which shines clear and bright is a sure sign of fair weather, whereas a full moon "stained with dark spots . . . announces rain." And when the moon is surrounded by a single halo, calm or slightly windy weather is due; more halos are a warning of rude breezes on their way.

In the Middle Ages, recognition of the moon's influence on weather was incorporated into a nursery rhyme. We've already seen that "Jack and Jill" is an allegory about the moon's waxing and waning (e.g., the name Jack is derived from a verb meaning "to increase," and Jill from a verb meaning "to break up or dissolve.")[8] But the water they carry is also a symbol of the moon's control over weather and rainfall in particular.[9]

Similarly, what contemporary fisherman, sailor, or schoolboy on summer vacation isn't familiar with the maxim that a ring around the moon is a sign of rain the next day?[10] (That's a change from Aratus's day.)

Serious scientific verification of this lunar connection was attempted as far back as 1830 by the German, G. Schubler.[11] Early in this century meteorological records for France and Germany were compiled in an attempt to show that more rain falls during a waxing than a waning moon.[12] But it was during the 1950s that a torrent of convincing, thorough evidence began to be published.[13,14] Now the causal connection between the moon and earth's weather is irrefutable.

Consider two of the most dramatic and destructive forms of weather, hurricanes and typhoons. Thomas H. Carpenter and his colleagues have demonstrated that statistically significant clusters of these storms occur around full and new moons. After examining 1,013 such blow-ups, which had occurred over a 78-year period (1891–1968), they found that an incredible 20 percent more of them had formed just before and after new moons and within a day or two after full moons than near the first and third quarters,[15] a ratio which mathematical analysis says is most unlikely to occur simply by chance. Moreover, Carpenter and his associates had made a very cautious examination. They used data from only the North Atlantic and northwest Pacific, whose hurricanes and typhoons respectively are the best documented in the world. Those oceans, of course, are the locations of prime shipping lanes for the United States and Japan, two data-hungry nations with the technological ability for thoroughly documenting the weather events that affect their maritime trade and, in America's case, naval activities as well.

Exactly the same lunar pattern to hurricanes was found by an American government analysis of hurricanes. Using computers, the National Center for Atmospheric Research (NCAR) reviewed the dates of sixty years' worth of North American hurricanes and found that they form more frequently at new and full moons.[16]

Carpenter's group also found related patterns for "severe tropical storms" (that is, storms whose winds are not quite up to typhoon-hurricane speed) in the southwest Indian Ocean, Bay of Bengal, and Arabian Sea. Over a 75-year period, these storms showed a clear tendency to form more frequently several days after "syzygy" (i.e., when the moon, earth, and sun are aligned; either a full or new moon) and, to a lesser extent, a few days after the first and third quarters than any other time of the lunar month.[17] They also found that severe North Atlantic storms over a 78-year span which did not evolve into full-fledged hurricanes followed an equally consistent lunar timetable: they usually started around the quarters, rather than at new or full moons.[18]

Less violent weather is also affected by the moon. That NCAR study found that the heaviest rainstorms across the United States usually form one to three days after new moons and from three to five days after full moons.[19] A trio of scientists from New York University and the U.S. Weather Bureau (U.S.W.B.) found the same thing; the worst rainstorms in the continental United States occur in the week after new moons and the week after full moons. Their survey was splendidly comprehensive. They focused on the dates of heaviest rainfall each month over the fifty years from 1900 to 1949. What they came up with was 16,057 downpours on 6,710 individual dates, reported by 1,544 weather stations from sea to cloudy sea. To that they added the 91-year-old precipitation histories of important individual stations like New York, Boston, the

District of Columbia, and even Toronto, for another 1,000 dates of heavy rainfall. The pattern which emerged was a lot clearer than the weather had been.

Heavy rainfall had happened most often "near the middle of the first and third weeks of the synodical month, especially on the third to fifth days after the configurations of both new and full moon. The second and fourth quarters of the lunation cycle are correspondingly deficient in heavy precipitation . . ."[20] Without doubt, they concluded, "There is a demonstrable persistence of this lunisolar effect in U.S. weather records throughout the history of official meteorological observation."[21]

Nor does that reflect some peculiarity in America's weather or the analytical procedures of the N.Y.U.–U.S.W.B. trio. A Texas meteorologist who found that flash floods in the Lone Star State generally follow full moons also found that rainstorms in San Salvador occur most often right after full and new moon.[22] Two Australian radiophysicists, E.E. Adderley and E.G. Bowen, found this pattern on the other side of the world. Using data from fifty weather stations, they found that large rainstorms took place most frequently during the full and new moon phases, with the highest peak of frequency being in the full-moon phase.[23] (Ironically, their curiosity had been provoked when they happened to read a 1937 meteorological paper that found a different rainfall pattern in the Iberian peninsula. There, the correlation was between storms and lunar perigee and apogee rather than lunar phases.)

Similar lunar rain dates have been reported by Glenn Brier, a member of that N.Y.U.–U.S.W.B. team. Brier found that the average amount of precipitation each lunar month over the United States was 20 percent higher whenever a full or new moon occurred while the moon was at perigee and near the plane of the ecliptic (the imaginary line between earth and sun). Brier had deduced this after examining weather reports filed at 150 U.S. stations from 1900 to 1962, when there were sixty-one such syzygies.[24] On the basis of what he found in those reports, he also confirmed an earlier study he had authored with Donald Bradley, in which they concluded that there are two peaks each lunar month in heavy rainfall, just after full and new moons.

Furthermore, Brier discovered a pattern of rainfall which corresponds to the lunar day. Now, meteorologists know that rain is most likely to begin in the United States just before 3 A.M. and shortly before 5 P.M.,[25] and Brier's research showed that the heaviest rainfalls tend to start at lunar zenith when that "high moon" occurs either shortly before 3 A.M. or 5 P.M.[26]

All this adds up to a lot more than a bunch of rained-out baseball games. Lives and considerable property are at stake, and the ability to predict calamitous weather is the key to protecting both. And what have we seen such weather correspond to? Over and over, it is to the full and new moon, when the moon's ability to raise tides in the oceans, atmosphere, and solid earth is mightiest. Hurricanes, typhoons, and the worst rainstorms—the most furious forms of weather—tend to start near the spring tides. In contrast, nasty weather which fails to get worse—aborted typhoons and "mere" gales—can erupt any time of month, although even some of these show a preference for certain lunar phases. Weather is a complicated phenomenon; the moon's motion around the earth is only one influence. There are the interaction of ocean and air, collisions between masses of air, the egg-beater effect of earth's rotation, and bursts of atomic particles from the sun to be considered, as well. Full and new moons may not *start* storms, but something about them apparently is all it takes to trigger the worst kinds when all the other meteorological chemistry is right.

Moreover, as Glenn Brier found, lunar perigee during syzygy makes this storm trigger click more strongly. Skeptics need think back only as far as the blizzard of 1978, when Old Man Winter buried the Northeast alive beneath ice and snow. Some 7,000 homes along the New England and Middle Atlantic shore were demolished or badly damaged during that one storm, according to Francis Wylie, a student of lunar tides.[27] And that "fateful combination" of lunar conditions has happened before and will again.

In an article in *The New York Times,* Wylie explained that

historical records of unusually vicious storms were compared to a list of dates when these "fateful" astronomical conditions had prevailed. Sure enough, "there was a remarkably frequent coincidence of extreme tides and of high onshore winds that would drive them higher" during storms at syzygy during lunar perigee.[28]

But how predictable is this? Wylie's analysis in the *Times* appeared in December 1978, and he warned "[e]veryone who lives on the shore, either Atlantic or Pacific . . . to mark 'Watch for storm!'" over the dates on their calendars for the next syzygy at perigee. That would be the new moon of January 28, 1979; like the attack on Pearl Harbor, which also wreaked havoc, a Sunday. By the 24th, Nature was already growing wild. Winds in Boston reached 55 mph, the tide rose a foot above normal, seas were two to three feet, and there was flooding. In the Midwest there was knee-high snow. Chicago was buried under the white stuff only one week after a record blizzard. In Florida, winds and small tornadoes damaged 100 homes and trailer houses on the Gulf shore and ripped down trees and electrical power lines.

The next day, record rains began falling on eastern Massachusetts. At least one major earthen dam collapsed. A foot of snow fell in New Hampshire and Maine, and 100 people had to be evacuated from flood-threatened homes in Revere, a Boston suburb ravaged by the Blizzard of '78. On January 28, four days of the worst flooding from rain in New England history finally ended. High tide was a foot above normal at Boston, and National Guard troops had to be mobilized.[29]

The February new moon was more of the same, with emphasis on rain and ice and a solar eclipse thrown in for dramatic visual effect. Homes along the Connecticut, New Jersey, and New York shorelines were evacuated by National Guardsmen. In Sea Bright, New Jersey, the chief of police compared the ocean's surge over a sea wall to Niagara Falls. In New York City, the Highway Department mobilized 120 pothole-filling crews to contend with some ten thousand potholes rapidly turning into swimming pools, and schools were forced to open later than usual, if at all.[30]

Several trucks peppering New Hampshire highways with

salt had to travel in reverse on steep roads to get traction. Boston's Logan International Airport was temporarily shut down. And the Boston Edison Company had to activate extra crews to cope with burning power lines pushed together by tree limbs sagging beneath the weight of ice.[31] The storm was the principal source of that month's record 17.74 inches of precipitation, prompting one newspaper to dub it, "The Great Sleet Storm."[32]

Such was the accuracy of Wylie's lunar weather forecast. Or, as he himself had concluded, "In other words, folklore about the moon's affecting the weather may be right, after all."[33]

16

The Aquatic World

King Thakombau had rung up enormous debts, so he decided to do the only sensible thing: sell everything he owned. Most of all, that meant the Fiji islands, but when he offered to cede his sovereignty over that Pacific archipelago to the United States, President Abraham Lincoln was preoccupied by more pressing concerns. The British government, however, with nothing better to do, accepted the good monarch's offer about a decade later, in 1874, and that's how William Burrows some seventy years later found himself "high commissioner for the Western Pacific" and His Majesty's governor of paradise.[1]

That's also how Burrows became a witness to one of the most spectacular displays in all of nature, something he would describe as "an unforgettable event," the spawning spectacle of the Palolo worm, *Eunice viridis.* This mass mating occurred twice a year, in October and November.[2] To find out the exact date, Burrows and other eager spectators would consult an aged Fijian living in the village of Tokou on the island of Ovalau. The night before the predicted day, the Fijians would leave their boats ready at the shore, equipped with dip-nets. Everyone would sleep until about four the next morning, then rally and carry lanterns, torches and other gear to the waiting boats. Before the first light of day, crews would push their boats through the powerful surf and begin paddling out to sea. The only illumination at first would come from the burning torches on board. Everyone was sky-high with excitement by the time of sunrise. In a report to *Nature,* Burrows described the scene:

> To attend a "rising" is an unforgettable event. With the necessary preparations made, I have boarded my boat at 04.30 [4:30 A.M.] after a sleep in the village and paddled out to a position about half-way out to the main reef, which skirts the shore at this spot at a distance of about a mile. Then torches are shone into the water vertically from the boat's side to see if there are any indications. If it is the right day, small stray bits of the worm make their appearance, and nets are got ready. Then, when the first light of dawn appears, great funnels of worms burst to the surface and spread out until the whole area is a wriggling mass of them, brown and green in colour.
>
> When the tropical sun rises perpendicularly from the sea the catch is in full swing, and hundreds of boats, canoes and punts are filling up kerosene tins and jars by the simple process of dipping them out with nets.
>
> The worms also provide an annual feast for the fish; for all round and between the boats big fish and sharks cruise quietly along, gulping them in, and take no notice whatever of the boats or their occupants.
>
> As the sun makes itself felt, a change begins to occur in the length of the worms. They begin to break up into shorter and shorter bits, until some three hours after sunrise the entire surface of the sea shows nothing more than patches of scum.

The marine harvest tastes considerably better than it looks, Burrows added, and like the shellfish it resembles is even rated as quite an aphrodisiac:

> Mbalolo [the Palolo] is rightly prized as very good eating and, if one can forget what it looks like before being cooked, is delicious. Fijians—and I have known Europeans to do likewise—eat some raw, when perhaps it may resemble oyster; I could never bring myself to try. In its raw state it is said to have a stimulating effect on fecundity. The Fijians also say that a dish of it eaten in any form will protect a person from all sickness until the Christmas Day following.
>
> A curious fact is that all fish caught in the neighbourhood of

the rising are poisonous to human beings for about ten days or a fortnight after the event.[3]

One thing governor Burrows apparently did not realize is something many trained marine biologists have successfully observed: anyone can foretell the date for this water-borne wedding dance as accurately as the elderly Fijian sage. The reason is that the worms follow a strict lunar calendar for their biannual oceanic orgy. They unfailingly spawn precisely at the last quarter of the moon in October and November.[4,5] At dawn of the appointed days (the day before and the exact day of last quarter), the worms back out of their burrows in rock and coral crevices on the sea bottom. The posterior part of each worm, 10 to 15 inches long and containing sperm or eggs (depending of course on sex), breaks off from the head, or anterior part, and floats to the surface, where it wriggles about until it has consummated its maritime marriage. The head, meanwhile, slinks back into its hole where it must bide its time until next year.

This memorable display is only one of many regular activities by marine animals (and plants) which occur according to a lunar rhythm. In fact, it seems that lunar cycles have been documented for more inhabitants of earth's oceans, lakes, and rivers than for denizens of earth's dry land or skies. Lunar patterns for so many water dwellers have been demonstrated that even the most strident skeptics about the moon's power over man concede their obedience to the lunar clock. The fish market is one place where men of science do not debate the moon's influence. And the most persistent power is that of the full moon.

As long ago as the fourth century B.C. Aristotle observed that the ovaries of sea urchins are biggest (and tastiest) at each full moon.[6] Cicero wrote the same thing about oysters and other shellfish, and so did Pliny.[7] Both believed the muscles or gonads of such animals grew as the moon waxed and shrunk as the moon waned.[8] Meanwhile, half a world away, the Chinese scholar Lu Pu-Wei was duplicating Aristotle's observation in the third century B.C.[9]

The renowned British biologist H. Munro Fox found that

belief in this concept of lunar sympathy was widespread throughout the ancient Greek and Latin worlds.[10] He also found that Saint Augustine had this faith in full moons, and that Francis Bacon had once cheerily predicted that controlled experiments would confirm "the opinion . . . that . . . brains in rabbits, woodcocks, calves, etc., are fullest in the full of the moon . . . and so of oysters and cockles, which of all the rest are the easiest tried, if you have them in pits."[11]

In his brilliant "Lunar Periodicity in Reproduction," Fox noted that even that august science association, the Royal Society, had asked readers of its *Philosophical Transactions* in 1667 whether in their travels to the East Indies any of them had noticed that "shell-fishes, that are in these parts [i.e., around Europe] plump and in season at the full moon, and lean and out of season at the new, are found to have contrary constitutions in the East Indies?"[12]

Fox went on: "This belief that the size of certain marine invertebrates, chiefly molluscs and echinoderms [e.g., starfish and sea urchins], varies with the phases of the moon is found in the literature of classical Greece and Rome and of the middle ages, and is held to-day in the fish markets around the Mediterranean and in the Red Sea. At Suez sea-urchins and crabs are said to be 'full' at full moon and 'empty' at new moon, at Alexandria the same thing is said of mussels and of sea-urchins, the Tarentines believe that oysters are fattest at full moon, while at Nice, Naples, Alexandria, and in Greece . . . urchins are said to be fullest at full moon. The part of the sea-urchin which is eaten is the gonad, while in the crab it is the muscles, so that these tissues are supposed to vary in bulk with the phases of the moon."[13]

When Fox set out to determine whether any of this was true, he found that it certainly is as far as the sea urchins at Suez are concerned. "In the last-mentioned form the gonads undergo a cycle of growth and development corresponding with each lunation throughout the breeding season. Just before full moon ovaries and testes are at their greatest bulk, filled with spermatozoa or eggs which are spawned into the sea at the time of full moon. The shrunken gonads then gradually fill again with ripening sexual products to be shed at the next full moon."[14]

Fox left nothing to chance. He went to the eastern stone jetty at the entrance to the Docks of Port Taufiq in Suez, got down on his hands and knees, and scooped up sea urchins with a hand net. Back at the Quarantine Laboratory he examined his samples by microscope and confirmed, "There is a periodic reproductive cycle correlated with the lunar month, the genital products being spawned round about each full moon until the breeding season closes in September. . . ."[15] Fox examined those sea urchins in 1920 and 1921. In the second year, he took a larger sample of swimming subjects and subjected them to more rigorous observations. Still he found the full-moon breeding cycle.

Fox also reported that a fellow scientist, D.H. Tennent, had documented the same thing in another part of the world. At the Tortugas islands in the Caribbean, Tennent had found that the sea urchins there spawn at the full moon, discharging their spermatazoa and eggs. "During the three summers preceding 1908 and again in 1908," Tennent said, "I noticed that the gonads of sea-urchins taken after a night of full moonlight were empty, while those obtained a week later gave abundance of eggs and spermatazoa."[16]

In addition, Fox said that researchers had demonstrated that the reproductive "swarms" (as the mass spawning congregations are known) of another marine worm, *Nereis limbata,* occur after sunset from June to September, beginning near full moons.[17] That's at Woods Hole, Massachusetts, a center for oceanographic study. Scientists there had also observed the worm *Platynereis magalops* swarm each summer night after the full moon until a new moon, but not during the waxing moon, according to Fox and biologist A.G. Huntsman.[18,19]

Other ocean creatures follow this full-moon lure as well. Adult eels start "their migration from European rivers . . . back to the spawning grounds in the Sargasso Sea—3,000 miles away—where they first came to life" after a full moon.[20] North Atlantic fishermen are well aware that the "biggest catches of herring . . . are usually made at full moon. . . ."[21] In the balmier clime of Bermuda, "the surface of the sea becomes brilliantly luminous with the swarming and breeding of the Atlantic fireworm" at each full moon during the spring, according to one report out of New York.[22] Further, scientist Huntsman, who lived briefly on the island, reported that the worms not only swarm in the spring but all year round.[23] In midwinter months they simply arrive in fewer numbers.

When Huntsman was staying at the Grasmere Hotel in Pembroke Parish in 1926, he got a chance to watch it for himself. Standing on a boat landing below his hotel or sitting quietly in a boat in Bermuda's Great Sound, he saw the worms, *Odontosyllis enopla,* rise to the water's surface and glow each night just after sunset for several days following every full moon. Just as the lunar day is 55 minutes longer than the solar day, so this display began 55 minutes later each night. The worms would emerge from crevices on the bottom of the shallow bay where they live and swim upward. The females glow for three to eight seconds once they reach the surface; they do this every 10 to 50 seconds. This display of love lights really turns on the males, in more ways than one. They swim to the females, giving quick bursts of their own lights. When two worms mate, they form a circle some six inches in diameter and swim round and round. The lucky couples live to do it again next full moon. The unlucky ones constitute dinner for feeding fish.

Huntsman's report in the *Journal of the Fisheries Research Board of Canada* also indicated that the marine worm *Odontosyllis hyalina* swarms all year round after sunset for three nights after each full moon at the bay of Batavia, Java, Indonesia.[24]

Further east in Indonesia, at Amboina island, the worm commonly known as the "Wawo" swarms on the second and third nights after the full moons of March and April.[25] Elsewhere, the prawn (tiny shrimplike crustaceans, upon which innumerable types of fish feed) *Anchistioides antiguensis* spawn for about a week before and after full moons.[26]

The sex life of crabs is of more direct culinary concern to humans. One correspondent recently told *Science News* that while growing up on the New Jersey shore he frequently saw blue crabs that had shed their shells at the full moon. "[I]n Barnegat Bay (N.J.) where I grew up, the general belief held that the blue crab shedding was by far the heaviest around the time of the full moon. Science or not, all my data from hundreds of hours a season hunting soft-shell crabs (that remain soft only a matter of hours after a molt) as a boy tended to substantiate this idea. . . . The soft-shelled crab, lobster, or crayfish is unarmed and unarmored, incapable of fast flight, and just about one hundred percent edible."[27] Mature blue crabs, lobsters, and assorted crayfish do breed when they molt; that's the only time females can lay their eggs. And this New Jersey native only needed to consult an almanac to see whether a molting had indeed corresponded to a full moon.

Dr. Clark Timmins made a similar report in his book on farming and gardening, based on a letter from a colleague, who said that many crab and lobster fishermen on Long Island had confirmed his own observation that hard-shell crabs become soft at full moons.[28]

Another favorite sea food, scallops, is typical of many water dwellers, insofar as it spawns at both full and new moons. James Mason, a Scottish marine biologist, found that the two annual breeding periods of *Pecten maximus* at Port Erin on Britain's Isle of Man coincided with just those lunar phases. "All three spawnings in 1952 and that in August 1951 occurred shortly after full moon, while the 1951 spring spawning occurred at about (though possibly just after) new moon," he wrote in *Annals and Magazine of Natural History.*[29]

The scallop's clammy cousin, the oyster, also gets it on twice every lunar month. J.L. Cloudsley-Thompson, in his comprehensive text, *Rhythmic Activity in Animal Physiology and Behavior,* credits P. Korringa with charting the boudoir behavior of these mollusks. What Korringa found was that oyster larvae in the Basin of Oosterschelde, Holland, appear in greatest numbers about ten days after full and new moon. Korringa pointed out, though, that since this particular species, *Ostrea edulis,* is incubatory, the actual spawning would occur many days earlier; right at the full and new moon, to be exact.[30] The same goes for a second species, *Littorina ner-*

oides, whose egg capsules are found far more often in plankton tows made during spring tides at Plymouth, England, than at other times during the breeding season.[31,32] And George Sarton, another student of physiological cycles, wrote in a science periodical, "It has been shown that our common oyster has a tendency to 'spat' in much greater numbers during the week following the full and new Moon than at any other time."[33]

The most familiar sexual "two-timer" is the grunion, *Leuresthes tenuis,* a fish that spawns twice each lunar month, at full and new moon, from March through August along Southern California beaches. Thousands of people have been able to watch this fish's breeding ritual, which, like so many other things in California related to sex, is peculiar. Boyd W. Walker provided an excellent description of these nautical nuptials in the *California Fish and Game* journal.[34]

The main attraction, Walker wrote, is on the second, third, and fourth nights after the full and new moons, along the grunion's principal range, which is between Point Conception in southern California and Punta Abreojos in Baja California. There, beginning within half an hour after the night's high tide, these fish assault the beaches. The first fish ashore is usually a male. Like a true Californian, he surfs in on a wave. Then he beaches and waits for the next wave to carry him higher. Within twenty minutes of his arrival, the rest of the grunion begin to land.

Each female may be escorted by as many as eight males. But if none ride ashore with her, she leaves on the next receding wave; it's tempting to think she has left in a huff, like a lady stood up for an important date. If she is accompanied by any hot suitor, the scene that follows is torrid enough to make Burt Lancaster and Deborah Kerr's famous beach scene in *From Here to Eternity* pale in comparison. The female desperately digs herself into the sand by arching her body, head up, and wriggling her tail back and forth until she has sunk into the wet sand. She tunnels at least up to her pectoral fins, sometimes higher, sometimes burying herself completely. At the same time, the males curl around her, their sex vents close to or touching her, and when the twisting female discharges eggs two or three inches below the mud's surface, the males release their sperm-laden milt, which oozes down the female's body to the eggs below.

This seashore spectacle peaks about an hour after that first male ventured from the safety of water onto the alien, sandy environment. It continues for another hour or two. The fish are slender and about six inches long, with bluish-green backs and bright silver sides and bellies. At the height of their spawning run, they turn the wet beach into a shimmering silver sheet. This is the moment when human spectators zig-zag across the mudflats, trying to grab the slippery fish, which often flip-flop free.

Meanwhile, the males act like selfish human adolescents. Once they've had their fun they wriggle back toward the sea, abandoning the females, who must free themselves from their muddy love nests, then hope they can find a wave on which to return home. Walker described them as "spent and obviously tired."

The tide covers the eggs with several additional inches of sand. At the next spring tide they are exposed and sucked back into the sea. Only two or three minutes out of the sand they hatch. Eggs not exposed this first time may make it at the next high tides about two weeks later. The largest runs are in April, May, and June, and Walker said the runs occasionally start as early as late February and continue into early September.

A related species, *Hubbsiella sardina,* also makes its spawning runs at the full and new moons during the same season as the grunion's runs, although Walker witnessed runs as early as January at Guaymas, Sonora, Mexico, in 1950. Its range is the upper Gulf of California, not that distant from the grunion's preferred beaches. It also runs at the same time relative to high tide. The main difference between these two fish is that *Hubbsiella,* unlike *Leuresthes,* runs during daylight as well as night hours.[35]

An Australian fish, *Galaxias attenuatus,* more closely resembles the grunion in choice of time of day of spawning, as well as lunar phases. Walker pointed out, though, that this fish spawns at sea rather than on a beach.[36]

Japanese fishermen pursue a worm they call "Bachi,"

which is like the Palolo of Fiji, except that it is the front end of this worm which breaks from the rest and rises to the water's surface, according to George Sarton. "The swarming occurs during the nights immediately after new and full Moon in October and November," Sarton wrote, "and the fishermen catch them by means of lights to which the worms are attracted; they use them then as bait."[37]

Yet another creature that must be added to this "score" card is the so-called "fire worm," *Odontosyllis phosphorea,* which spawns most abundantly just after sunset at Departure Bay on the coast of Canada's British Columbia for eight days after full moons and in slightly smaller numbers for ten days before new moons, July through December.[38]

Interested students and scholars of marine biology (or lunar phenomena, for that matter) can find the balance of Korringa's long list of fish, worms, and shellfish whose hearts turn to thoughts of fancy at each full and new moon on page 89 of Cloudsley-Thompson's text.

Then there is the relatively exclusive club of critters that reproduce or, in the case of one, perform a characteristic activity only at new moons. Shrimp swarm in the waters off Bermuda, according to surgeon Edson J. Andrews, "just before midnight on the day of the new moon, once a year, and are then seen no more."[39] *Conchophthirius lamellidens* is a one-celled animal that reproduces by conjugation dramatically more often the day after new moons than at any other time.[40] It is a ciliate protozoan, which means a single-cell animal that propels itself by means of its cilia, hair-like oars with which it rows through water. Study samples were taken from a pond in Calcutta, India, where they were living on the gills of a particular fresh-water mussel.

The animal whose nonsexual activity coincides with new moons is the flatworm, *Dugesis dorotocephala,* known to most every high school biology student as the "planarian." The planarian's tendency to creep away from light was already well known when Frank A. Brown, Jr., of Northwestern University, demonstrated that this aversion becomes strongest exactly once every lunar month.

Brown placed forty-five planarians on a circular grid one at a time each morning and watched what would happen. The grid was a circle measuring a meager two inches in diameter, and each worm was placed in the center. The semicircle in front of the worm was marked off by 180 degrees for the points of the compass. If the worm turned directly to its left, it would be making a 90-degree turn. If it crawled straight ahead, its angle relative to its original direction would be zero degrees, or no change at all in direction. Both the grid and each planarian were started off facing directly north. A light was illuminated directly behind each worm and directly to its right, and the worm was off and creeping.

Brown did this for four years. Invariably, the worms crawled forward and to the left, away from both lights. But the astonishing thing was that each lunar month, at the new moon, the worms turned sharpest toward the left. At full moons, they turned least dramatically. The closer it was each month to a new moon, the more they turned. The closer to a full moon, the less.[41]

* * *

What almost all of those aquatic animals have in common is sex. Most breed at full and/or new moons. (Planarians, which want to bore forward at full moons, at least show the appropriate spirit.) Such nonreproductive functions as eating, color change, growth—even breathing—appear to follow lunar rhythms other than the full and/or new moon, rhythms like the lunar day, first and third quarters, or some arbitrary time in the lunar month. There are even a few organisms whose sexual cycles follow those lunar patterns. Two of these are plants, not animals, however. Another is an animal, one that, as we'll see, may have saved Christopher Columbus's life.

Daily rhythms usually involve feeding. One of the most important and best-known discoveries about the moon's influence over life on earth involved an experiment with this feeding cycle conducted by Frank A. Brown, Jr.[42] Brown's subjects were common oysters. Oysters are most active every 12½ hours. That's approximately twice every solar day. It's precisely twice every lunar day, and it is when oysters feed.

In 1953, Brown gathered a dozen specimens of *Ostrea vir-*

ginica from Long Island Sound near New Haven. The oysters were packed in opaque containers in a way that would assure their survival, and shipped to Evanston, Illinois. There they were kept in salt-water trays under unvarying low illumination and constant temperature, attached to delicate spring devices which measured every movement of their shells.

For two weeks the oysters opened their shells most frequently by far when they always had, the time of day that was high tide near New Haven, 1,000 miles away. Then they began to change so that in a few days' time they were most active at the time of lunar zenith over Evanston, the time that would be high tide at landlocked Evanston. More remarkable, though, was that it was the moon and unquestionably not tides signaling the oysters. Brown had placed the oysters in barely enough water to cover their shells, pans of water whose lack of tidal action could be proven. The lunch call had come from above, not below.

Similar lunar rhythms abound. J. Bruce Guyselman has found a type of crayfish, *Cambarus virilis,* whose walking activity peaks twice each lunar day.[43] Guyselman collected thirty crayfish from a stream in Morristown, Minnesota, and placed them in tanks in three groups of ten, half male, half female. The water tanks contained running wheels, like those placed in a pet hamster's cage, which were used to measure the time and amount of the crayfish's activity. The first group was most active every 12.4 hours, while the second and third groups were least active at those intervals. When Guyselman kept air pressure inside the airtight chambers constant, it made no difference in the crayfish's activity. Neither did normally fluctuating barometric pressure.

Biologist Audrey M. Stutz has shown that the striped shore crab, *Pachygrapsus crassipes,* the most common intertidal crab along southern California's rocky coast, are most active every 12.4 hours.[44] Their scurrying about peaks two hours after each high tide. Most of her samples were collected just north of Birdrock in San Diego. She was able to measure their motion precisely by placing each one in an "actograph," a circular dish mounted on a pinpoint so that every time its occupant moves the dish will totter like a seesaw. Its bottom rim touches a metal strip beneath the dish, completing an electric current which is mechanically recorded.

Muriel Sandeen and Grover Stephens, working with Frank Brown, Jr., have found that *Littorina littorea,* a periwinkle or small snail, breathes according to a lunar schedule, with two daily peaks in oxygen consumption.[45] This group gathered specimens on a rocky beach just below Nobska lighthouse near Woods Hole on Cape Cod. By placing the periwinkles in plastic bags submerged in water and attaching the bags to air flasks, the crawlers' respiration could be measured. The more they breathed, the lower each bag sank.

Sandeen and Brown had collaborated earlier with H.M. Webb and Milton Fingerman to demonstrate that the daily color change of fiddler crabs follows a lunar pattern. Specifically, the spread of pigment through the shell is slowest every 12.4 hours, or twice every lunar day.[46] That means the crabs are darkest 50 minutes later every 24 hours. They're darkest at the same hour of the solar day twice every lunar month.

Fingerman has found a similar pattern in the blue crab.[47] Another researcher has found an activity cycle in the common European shore crab, *Carcinus maenas,* similar to the 12.4-hour lunar cycle Guyselman found in his crayfish.[48] Daily lunar patterns have also been found for crab locomotive activity, the opening and closing of the valve of the common quahog, oxygen consumption and color change in several invertebrates, and the geographic orientation of "sand-hopper" fleas.[49]

Similar cycles are shown by two types of marine worms, including the intervals at which they emerge from beach mud as well as the proliferation on the mud of algae that live in the digestive tract of one of those worms (*Convoluta roscoffensis*); the rhythms of expansion and contraction in the sea anemone; of light sensitivity in the hermit crab; of locomotive activity in the mud snail *Ilyanassa obsoleta;* and of propulsion by squirting water in two types of mussels.[50] Again, Cloudsley-Thompson's summary is comprehensive, as is Fingerman's in "Lunar Rhythmicity in Marine Organisms."[51]

Finally, there are non-syzygy lunar monthly rhythms. One of the most extraordinary is also one of the most recently documented. Peter G.K. Kahn, of Princeton University, and Stephen Pompea, of Colorado State University, reported in *Nature* late in 1978 that they had found that the chambered nautilus (which resembles a snail and is a cousin of the octopus) forms a new chamber in its spiral shell once every lunar month, and each chamber is marked by growth lines corresponding to solar days.[52]

What makes the nautilus's shell growth doubly interesting is that it appears to be a reaction to some geophysical lunar effect, perhaps even moonlight, but almost certainly not ocean tides. Dwelling 400 meters down, and away from land in the southwestern Pacific Ocean,[53] the nautilus simply lives too deep. Where it lives, agree the experts, there is virtually no tidal action to adapt to.[54]

A second fascinating aspect of the nautilus's growth is that it helps prove the theory that eons ago the moon was closer to earth and revolved around it much more rapidly, which means that there were fewer days in a month.[55] Records of ancient observations of eclipses, studies of the friction exerted on earth by ocean tides, and the daily and annual growth bands in coral are some of the other evidence.[56] In fact, the reason that Kahn, a paleontologist, and Pompea, an astronomer, had been studying the nautilus (*Nautilus pomilius* Linnaeus) was to learn more about "past dynamics of the Earth-Moon system" and formation of earth's continents. What they noticed was that contemporary nautilus shells have more growth lines per chamber than their fossilized ancestors do. Since the nautilus forms one growth line every solar day, that means each chamber—each month—has more days now. Four hundred and twenty million years ago, for example, it apparently took the moon only about nine days to circle the earth because 420-million-year-old fossil nautilus shells have only 8 to 9.5 growth lines per chamber. One hundred ninety million years ago, nautiloids still had only 17 growth lines per chamber. The average number today is 30, corresponding neatly to the 29.53 days in a synodic month.

The New York Times reported their deduction this way: "They found a gradual decrease in the number of growth lines in each chamber as the shells got older, a finding consistent with scientific data showing that, eons ago, the moon was closer to the earth and revolving around it more rapidly than it is now.

"The researchers . . . concluded that the moon was receding from the earth at a variable rate that for millions of years had averaged 94.5 centimeters annually."[57]

Non-syzygy monthly rhythms even exist on a cellular level. When a single nerve cell from the sea hare *Apylysia californica* (a mollusk without a shell whose arched body and earlike anterior tentacles make it resemble a hare) is surgically extracted, specific chemical reactions continue to occur in it twice every lunar month.[58]

Some rudimentary aquatic plants have monthly sexual rhythms. "Among plants the sole authentic case of a lunar rhythm in reproduction seems to be among the algae," H.M. Fox wrote in "Lunar Periodicity in Reproduction." "The marine *Dictyota dichotema* at Beaufort, North Carolina, produces one crop of sexual cells in each lunar month. . . .

"Kofoid found a lunar periodicity in the frequencies of plankton organisms in the Illinois River. W.E. Allen found indications of the same thing in the San Joaquin River, California. The maximum frequency of algae occurred at full moon, that of crustacea, a little later."[59]

Then there are the life rhythms among animals that are locked into step with the moon at the first and third quarters rather than at syzygy. There's the worm, *Nereis dumerilii,*[60] which swarms only at those quarters, and the Fijian Palolo, and the Fijian's Caribbean cousin. This is the so-called "Atlantic Palolo," *Eunice fucata,* which swarms within three days of the last quarter between June 29 and July 28 at the Tortugas. George Sarton reported, "The sexual portions begin to rise to the surface at least two hours before sunrise; by sunrise they are present in countless numbers and when the first rays of the sun strike the water they break up and discharge the eggs. The dying bodies sink to the bottom where they are eagerly devoured by waiting fish and by three hours after sunrise none are to be seen. . . .

" . . . It has been thought that the stimulus for spawning might be found in the state of the tides. Experiments have shown, however, that probably the tide can have no influence, for worms placed in floating tanks spawn naturally at the usual times, and in this case the worms could have had no means of telling the state of tide either by the pressure of the water or the speed of its movement."[61]

The common quahog, *Venus mercenaria,* which opens and closes its valve according to a daily lunar or tidal rhythm, also follows a monthly lunar pattern. The number of openings each lunar day increases during the course of a lunar month, so that the number peaks once a month; there's also a minor peak midway through this synodic cycle.[62]

A British researcher has shown that a certain lugworm, *Arenicola marina,* spawns but once a year—during a two-week period in the autumn—always avoiding both the full and new moon by answering the call of the wild precisely between spring tides.[63]

And, of course, in any discussion of romance (no matter how remote), the French eventually enter; marine biology is no exception. Thus, Milton Fingerman doffs his lab cap to the Frenchmen Fage and Legendre for documenting the romantic rhythms of the worm *Platynereis dumerilii,* which "breeds from May to September between sunset and midnight during the first and third quarters of the moon."[64]

Without a doubt, though, the most intriguing non-syzygy lunar rhythm is one that occurs at the third quarter and may have saved Christopher Columbus from being thrown to the sharks by a panicky crew only hours before he did make landfall on his fateful voyage of discovery. It also sheds light on the controversy about exactly where Columbus did first land in the Americas.

The Admiral weighed anchor at Palos de la Frontera half an hour before dawn[65] on Friday, August 3, 1492, with forty men aboard the 117-foot *Santa Maria,* twenty-six men aboard the roughly 50-foot *Pinta,* and another twenty-four men aboard the *Niña,* also about 50 feet.[66,67] No sooner was Columbus's convoy underway, however, than it encountered the first of several obstacles that would nearly defeat the expedition and cost Columbus his life. The *Pinta* lost her rudder and *Niña's* lateen rig began causing trouble, so the trio of ships put in at the Canary Islands, off northwest Africa. Repairs made, the ships set to sea again on the sixth. Columbus was especially eager to be underway because he had been informed that three Portuguese caravels were out to waylay him.[68]

The crew received its second jolt on September 13 when it saw the compass needle waver to the west of true north.[69,70] What on earth, they wondered, could cause this? Then, two days later the men were dumbfounded to see a meteorite sizzle into the sea some twelve to fifteen miles away.[71] Next, they sailed into that eerie oceanic plain of seaweed called the Sargasso Sea.[72] What aberration would follow? Pulitzer Prize–winning biographer of Columbus and naval historian Samuel Eliot Morison has said "there is no evidence" that the men feared falling off the edge of the earth. "But they were afraid they would be unable to beat back against the wind which always seemed to blow from the east. After three weeks of sailing, the longest anyone had ever sailed in one direction out of sight of land, it was hard for Columbus to persuade them to carry on."[73]

"Hard" is putting it mildly. Columbus had already turned to psychological ploys to win their cooperation. Shortly after leaving the Canaries he had instructed the crew that after sailing 700 "leagues" they must not navigate at night because land surely would be near.[74] Soon, he resorted to subterfuge. Columbus began to keep two records of the ships' progress. One was an honest reckoning, which Columbus kept to himself. The other was a counterfeit, which reassured the crew by telling them they had traveled less than Columbus believed they had. (Ironically, what with the primitive navigational tools of the day, the "phony" was closer to the truth.)[75] Nevertheless, on September 17 frightened whispering among crewmen grew into a demand for an explanation for the errant compass.[76] Columbus managed to offer an interpretation and pep-talk that calmed their fears, for the moment at least. The next day they were further encouraged by the sight of birds and a ridge of low-lying clouds, which meant land must be near.[77] On the twentieth, boobies and other birds were spotted flying nearby.[78] Hopes rose more. But when the men's expectations weren't fulfilled in the next few days, their talk turned bitter again.[79]

Now Columbus may have feared for his own life as well as the expedition's. Like deadly whirlpools, mutinous plots swirled around him. On September 25, Columbus himself began to doubt, and he sought the advice of Martin Alonso Pinson, captain of the *Pinta.*[80] That night Pinson thought he saw land, but was mistaken.[81] Disappointment nearly degenerated into mutiny, but Pinson talked the men out of it.[82] On October 7, another false alarm was sounded, this aboard the *Niña.*[83] During the next two days, the men were on the verge of rebellion.[84] Finally, Columbus had to agree to turn back if no land was found within three days.[85]

It was on October 11 that someone aboard the *Pinta* fished a cane, a board, a pole, and a stick which seemed to have been made by tools from the Atlantic, while one of the *Niña's* crewmen spotted a branch laden with berries float by.[86,87] Joy rippled through the crews, but if this latest encouragement led only to disappointment rather than land, Columbus might have found himself the next thing floating in the sea.

Time was running short. At ten o'clock that night, though, Columbus and others saw a light dancing ahead of their frail fleet. In his journal, Columbus described it as the "flame of a small candle alternately raised and lowered."[88] Four hours later, Rodrigo de Triana, a sailor aboard the *Niña,* sighted the New World. It was an island called Guanahani by the Indians and named San Salvador by Columbus. After the sun came up, Columbus went ashore with a large party. He was splendidly clad, as befit the occasion. His officers carried banners and crosses. When they reached the beach, the party knelt upon the sand; several men kissed the ground and cried, and all gave prayers of thanks. Columbus claimed the land on behalf of his Spanish patrons. The men who had considered mutiny prostrated themselves at the Admiral's feet and, weeping, begged for his forgiveness.[89,90]

Now, the question is, where did this scene take place? Which Caribbean island is Columbus's "San Salvador"? Many scholars believe that Columbus made landfall on Watling's Island in the Bahamian chain, but one amateur historian, intrigued by a puzzling clue, has offered evidence in support of an alternative theory that the landing was at nearby Cat Island.

In a report to *Nature,* marine biologist L.R. Crawshay, of the Marine Biological Association Laboratory in Plymouth, England, said that a clue is the mysterious light seen by Columbus and several crew members. He pointed out that according to Columbus's journal or log the light was spotted at 10 P.M. on October 11, "i.e., about four hours before making the landfall, and an hour before moonrise."[91] Crawshay then cited the straightforward calculation of historian R.T. Gould: Given Columbus's estimation of his own speed, those four hours mean that Columbus was still about 35 miles to the east of wherever he did eventually touch land.[92]

Then Crawshay played detective. If those ships were 35 miles east of Watling Island, the lights would be "well out into the Atlantic, . . . where the presence of a native canoe accounting for it, as suggested by [the historian] Markham seems inconceivable." That spot is also above 3,000 fathoms of water, nowhere near a beach on which any man could have been holding a torch. Crawshay also dismissed the suggestion by some historians that the light was a figment of Columbus and company's imagination.

What that light could have been, Crawshay said, is the luminous glow of the marine worm, *Odontosyllis enopla,* during its breeding. Crawshay's studies over several years had demonstrated that *Odontosyllis,* which is native to these Bahamian waters, swarms to breed within twenty-four hours of the moon's last quarter. Only once had he observed the breeding as much as three and a half days away from the actual quarter, and that was on the occasion of disturbed weather. As for 10 o'clock on the night of October 11, 1492, that was indeed within twenty-four hours of the last quarter, which would occur the next day. The worm's behavior also matches the description of Columbus's light, which rose and fell and remained illuminated only briefly. "[T]he illuminating display of a single *Odontosyllis* female," Crawshay wrote, "will at such times usually show this feature of separate short periods of excessive and declining brilliance, repeated two or three times over, or more. From the poop of the Santa Maria, it is easy to believe that this light would be visible on a dark night up to 200 yards, or even farther, away. As probably as not, the strange and unaccountable light would disappear almost as soon as there was time to report it."[93]

But could these worms be about 35 miles east of where Columbus landed? Yes, wrote Crawshay, if he landed at Cat Island, which is 43 miles in the right direction, and if we can accept the idea that small ships sailing at night in uncharted waters could travel 43 miles *thinking* it was 35. (Remember that unintentionally erroneous book of reckoning Columbus kept.) Moreover, everything *Odontosyllis* would need is right at Watling, and Crawshay knows why Columbus did not spot Watling itself.

The worm "ordinarily frequents grounds of shallow water . . . up to about 2 fathoms in depth," Crawshay wrote. That is exactly what exists as "a large shallow bank, with rocky heads, extending out for some 3½ miles from the present low-lying northern shore of [Watling]; a position near the northern point of this bank, as shown in the chart of [the historian] Mackenzie with indication of the position of the light, would leave little difficulty in explaining not only the presence of the [worm] as the source of the light, but also the passing of the island unobserved in the darkness at such a distance."[94]

So if Columbus sighted the luminous worms off Watling and sailed on to Cat Island, Crawshay reasoned. But if another day had gone by . . . who knows what would have happened to Columbus, his crew, and the course of history. Columbus should have thanked his lucky stars. Or, more appropriately, the moon.

17

Aboard Noah's Ark

For land animals, every full moon is springtime. It is a time for mating and a time when life blossoms; births are more common and the very pace of life surges. The metabolism of many animals seems to shift into overdrive.

Four Yale University zoologists got a startling look at this in the early 1960s. They had been studying a large group of lemurs, monkeylike tree-dwellers with foxlike faces, and lorisoids, cousins of the lemurs, when they noticed some unexpected types of cyclical behavior. The zoologists began to pay closer attention.

The cyclical behavior was mating. The lemurs were being housed on the fifth floor of Yale's zoological laboratory tower. The two females under closest scrutiny, Sal and Calo, could reach windows facing north and east and see out other windows facing south and west. When these lemurs went into heat, they usually became more aggressive, more active in general, and marked by the characteristic symptoms of swelling and reddening of external genitalia. The scientists kept watch on a rotating basis, so there was almost always someone keeping an eye on this main group of animals under observation. Some of the mating was observed by dim white light, but even without any artificial light the zoologists could tell whether the long-tailed mammals were mating by the lemurs' equivalent of pillow talk.

What made this mating so interesting was *when* it happened. The lemur ladies would go into heat for five or six days, as lemurs are wont to do, and these periods would always end just before full moons every other lunar month. The males generally were blasé for the first day or so of the females' heat, but once mating got underway it clustered right around the full moon, sometimes even extending a few days beyond oestrus.[1] As for the lorisoids, their amorous activity was more ambiguous. Some appeared to exhibit a lunar cycle to sexual activity, but not one as distinct as the lemurs'.[2]

A Dutch army surgeon apparently trying to make the most of his time during a hitch in Surinam, once a colony of the Netherlands in South America, made a similar observation. This surgeon, a fellow named Hill, noticed that the local guenon monkeys menstruated for three days at every new moon and also seemed to go into heat then.[3] Edmond Dewan (whose study of lunar cycles to human sexuality is discussed in chapters 19 and 26) pointed out that this means Hill's monkeys ovulated two weeks earlier, at the full moon.[4]

Buffalo cows in India have similar romantic preferences. An animal husbandry expert made this discovery after putting two intriguing pieces of information together. Mr. O. Ramanthan had been stationed for some time at a government agricultural research station at Kovilpatti, in the Madras district near the southernmost tip of India, when he read an article in *Nature* about rhythmic breeding patterns of birds. What impressed Ramanthan was that birds in tropical Cameroons would breed all year round, apparently because the climate is as consistent as the Madras region's. Ramanthan's curiosity was further piqued when local cattlemen began telling him stories about buffalo mating with exceptional frequency "during periods of dark nights"; that is, around the new moon.

That prompted Ramanthan to begin a decade-long examination of the buffalo's breeding habits. When he was finished, he had recorded the dates that 2,457 buffalo cows had mated with the research station's own stud bulls. What he found was a crystal-clear pattern: the cows came into heat three times more frequently than usual during the new moon, and twice as often at the full moon.[5] "This clearly indicated that the position of the moon would . . . influence the onset of oestrus [heat] in Buffalo," he wrote in his own report to *Nature.*[6]

Another animal whose thoughts, so to speak, turn erotic at the full moon is the mayfly, *Povilla adusta.* J.L. Cloudsley-Thompson, in his superb survey, *Rhythmic Activity in Animal Physiology and Behavior,* discusses the research by another hyphenated scientist, Hartland-Rowe, in Africa during the mid-1950s. Over a two-year period, Hartland-Rowe observed twenty-two of that insect's breeding swarms at Kaazi, which is near Kampala in Uganda, and at Jinja, which is also on Lake Victoria. The swarms were always within five days of a full moon, and the greatest number were regularly on the second night after the full moon.[7] Moreover, lunar sexual rhythms in insects are hardly unusual. Zoologist John D. Palmer says many insects have one sort or another. "For example, certain insects hatch out of their pupal cases into adults at the times of full moon."[8]

Like the Ugandan mayfly, at least four species of giant Malayan forest rats mate most often at the full moon. Biologist J.L. Harrison was studying the breeding patterns of disease-carrying animals around the capital, Kuala Lumpur, when he discovered one pattern he had not anticipated. One hundred forty-four of the jumbo rodents, all members of the four most common species, showed a clearly statistically significant tendency to mate right before the night of a full moon. Almost every single one mated right then, and only then. Squirrels followed a similar pattern although somewhat less faithfully. One species of giant rat also gave birth most frequently at full moons.[9,10]

Furthermore, Harrison observed nearly 300 domestic rats which regularly turned human homes into rodent brothels at full moons. These smaller rats, however, conceived their young less consistently at the full moon than their forest relatives. Harrison concluded it was because they had access to so much food, water, and indoor light that they were simply less attuned to nature's forces.[11,12] Shortly after publishing these findings, Harrison was advised by Dr. W. van der Biji of the Royal Netherlands Meteorological Institute that his statistical methodology was amiss although the bottom line itself was not necessarily wrong. Harrison recalculated his data, including more recent information, and confirmed his original conclusions.[13]

Halfway around the world, scientists have confirmed the eagerness of a much more popular animal to breed according to timetables dictated by the full and new moons. Again, it is J.L. Cloudsley-Thompson who describes the research, this time by Swedish investigators studying a species of large European grouse near Soderhamm, Sweden. The Scandinavians found that these birds blithely mate and make whoopee until their breeding cycle happens to coincide with a new moon. For some reason, the grouse grouse about that particular lunar phase, and they won't start breeding anew until the next full moon.[14] After that, they're regular lovebirds again.

Even a species of bat found in the New Hebrides, between Fiji and Australia, has a breeding season synchronized to lunar phases.[15] But the most dramatic example of the moon's influence on the sex life of animals may be witnessed in the Arctic. There, the sizes of populations of at least three very different animals fluctuate over cycles which last many years and follow certain long-term lunar cycles.

According to those Swedes who discovered the large European grouse's lunar love life, the "varying hare" (that's its name) in Canada reaches its largest numbers every ten years; Norwegian lemmings and several game birds in Finland peak in population over three to four years. Cloudsley-Thompson explained the complicated lunar cycle to which these population tides correspond: the interval between each population peak is equal to the interval between years when a full moon (or any other phase) starts on nearly the same date, and a given phase returns to within six days of the same date every three to four years and to within one day every 9.6 years.[16] That's because a lunar month is 29.53 days long. Twelve lunar months amount to 354.4 days, or 10.9 days less than a solar calendar year. "Thus each moon occurs 10.9 days earlier than its equivalent in the previous year. After a certain number of years, a given phase of the moon must return to the same date as at the beginning of the period."[17] Nine and six-tenths years and three-to-four years are the lengths of those periods.

Cloudsley-Thompson believes the moon may be creating these cycles through some effect on the foods these animals depend on, although he does not rule out some direct effect. He is sure of one thing, however; it is the moon, and nothing else, that is responsible for the cycles. "All attempts have failed to find a cause for these rhythms by correlating them with weather conditions, sun-spots and other cosmic factors."[18]

Birth and mating cycles, however, are not the only ones affected by the full moon. The very engine of life itself picks up more steam in many animals at that time of month. Consider hamsters, one of the most widely observed experimental creatures. Frank Brown, Jr., and Young H. Park have demonstrated that the standard metabolic rate of hamsters is as much as 15 percent higher at full moons than at other times of the lunar month.[19] What Brown and Park did was place male hamsters in compartments measuring 48 inches by 25 inches by 16 inches. Each compartment contained a six-watt bulb lit from six A.M. to six P.M., a running wheel, and more than enough food. Each hamster's activity could be precisely measured because the number of revolutions for the wheel was counted automatically. Food was overabundant so that activity would reflect only the hamster's get-up-and-go, and not its attempts to "earn" food.

The hamsters did indeed run when they felt like it. That was mostly at night, in the dark, and mostly not long after a full moon. They ran nearly as much shortly after each new moon, as well.

In earlier experiments, Brown working on his own found several other lunar rhythms to hamster activity.[20] One was a daily lunar rhythm to wheel running. The amount each hamster ran peaked every 24.8 hours, which is the length of the lunar day. Another was the rhythm to groups of these daily runs. Each hamster did not peak at the same time each day; nor did each run every day. Instead, each hamster took a few days' or so vacation between long period of daily running. But each hamster would commence its running period on a day when the starting hour of its own lunar day (those 24.8-hour cycles of running) coincided with a full moon.

The third lunar rhythm occurred when the hamsters began to adopt daily cycles longer than a lunar day. One began peaking every 25.7 hours, for example. All of Brown's hamsters maintained these longer "days" for two to six weeks, but each returned to a lunar-day rhythm when the hour that activity began during one of these long-days coincided with the start of a new moon!

In 1970 and 1972, Brown's work was corroborated in a roundabout way. Margaret Klinowska set about to confirm Brown's report of a lunar monthly cycle to hamsters' metabolic activity.[21] Male hamsters were placed in cages not unlike the compartments Brown and Park had used. Instead of running wheels, Klinowska used a device somewhat like a seesaw. The floor of each cage was set on a pivot so that each time the hamster moved, the floor teetered. Movement was automatically recorded. In addition, Klinowska carefully measured the daily amount and pH level of each hamster's urine.

But, whereas Brown had found the monthly peak around full moons, Klinowska found it at new moons; and while his minor peak had been at new moons, hers was at full moons. A lunar rhythm, to be sure, but not the one expected. Something —or someone—was wrong.

Klinowska was too good a scientist to accept the discrepancy, and by 1972 she was able to report the explanation.[22] The difference in results had simply been caused by a difference in methods. Brown had exposed his hamsters to steady artificial light: 12 hours light, 12 hours dark. But Klinowska had relied on variable natural lighting. There was something even more interesting in Klinowska's new data, though.

What she found was that each hamster's monthly activity peak occurred on whatever day after the full moon the moon happened to rise after solar twilight. That would always happen from two to nine days after a full moon, during the experimental period. And this corresponded to the peaks Brown and Park had found. But this was clear only when Klinowska examined each hamster's pattern individually. In contrast, her original results had been based on averaging together several months' activity cycles for more than one hamster. That had inadvertently obscured the full moon peak in her statistics. By chance, Brown and Park's artificial lighting regimen (6 P.M. lights out) had usually not interferred with this moonrise effect, so the full-moon peak had showed. Klinowska not only resolved the discrepancy between her conclusions and Brown and Park's, she refined those conclusions as well.

One of the earliest experiments with which Brown was involved led to the discovery that several of these lunar rhythms are followed by a less popular rodent, the rat.[23] Brown and his colleagues, J. Shriner and C.L. Ralph, showed that a full-grown male white rat in a cage with a running wheel has a single-day peak of marathoning once a synodic month, every 29.5 days. They also found an unmistakable daily pattern: the rat would be busiest at lunar "midnight"; that is, when the moon is at its lowest point beneath the horizon. The rat would be least active at lunar zenith. And when activity during three-day clusters was studied, Brown and company realized that activity peaked just about every 27.3 days, which is the length of the sidereal month. (A sidereal month is how long it takes the moon to orbit 360 degrees around the earth. A synodic month is the time from one full moon to another—or one new moon to another—and requires an orbit of more than 360 degrees.)

Brown and yet another colleague, Emma D. Terracini, discovered nearly identical activity patterns in white mice.[24] Mice were placed alone in small cages continuously restocked with ample food and water. As with Margaret Klinowska's hamsters, the mice's cages stood on seesaw brackets which allowed each cage to rock whenever its inhabitant moved; any movement was automatically recorded and counted. Light and temperature were kept constant and at comfortable levels. The mice wanted for nothing, and any time one moved it had to be simply because it wanted to.

The results were clear and showed three basic life rhythms. The first was a simple solar-day (24-hour) pattern to activity. Underlying this, however, was a lunar-day pattern. The *time* of day when the mice were most active was later each solar day. It was, in fact, always shortly after moonset; a secondary peak in activity often occurred around moonrise. The third rhythm involved a time of day when the mice were usually inactive, 6 A.M. Terracini and Brown found that the mice's activity at this time of day actually fluctuated over the course of a lunar month, so that the mice were most active for this time of day just before each full moon and least active then right before the third lunar quarter. And the difference between those two times of month was statistically huge: 34 percent, clearly statistically significant (as ranges in activity were for the first two patterns discovered by the experiment).

Terracini and Brown even noticed a bonus correlation. The mice had a typical, or "mean," amount of activity for each hour of the day, but the amount of activity on any given day could vary from that mean. Now, the difference for any given day could be expressed as a percentage. For example, say the mice were usually active for 90 seconds every day from 6 to 7 A.M., but on July 4 they scurried about for 120 seconds between 6 and 7 A.M. That's a 33⅓ percent increase or difference. Terracini and Brown found that that percentage difference for the period of 2 to 6 A.M. was almost always exactly equal to the percent change in barometric pressure during those hours for half the lunar month, six days before a full moon to six days before new moon. The rest of the month the mice's activity change was the mirror image of barometric change, rising by as much as the air pressure fell, and vice versa. Just chance? Not likely! Terracini and Brown pointed out that the exact same correlation to barometric pressure and time of month is shown by the rate that potatoes, carrots, crabs, and snails consume oxygen.

Repulsive rodents aren't the only land animals that obey the full moon as if it were a guru. Certain birds do, too. There's the nightjar, for one, which starts its normal night activity later at the time of full moons.[25] Those ubiquitous children's pets, gerbils, also show lunar rhythms. Audrey M. Stutz, of California State University at San Diego, has shown that the daily activity of Mongolian gerbils peaks right after full and new moons.[26] Stutz showed that the furry creatures do that in the spring, summer, and fall, but in the winter their daily pattern of activity flip-flops. It's highest around the last lunar quarter and several days before full moons, and lowest right after full and new moons. Stutz measured her subjects' daily activity by housing them in cages balanced on a fulcrum. Each time a gerbil moved, its cage tottered, movement which was mechanically toted.

Stutz made a couple other interesting points, as well. For one, the California biologist noted that Brown and Park's hamsters had very nearly the same lunar pattern in their daily activity as her gerbils. For another, she pointed out that mealworms have a metabolic rhythm which is basically the contrary of gerbils' activity cycle. That is, oxygen consumption by mealworms (*Tenebrio molitor*) declines each month at the new and full moons, which is when gerbils usually have activity peaks, except in the winter. So, mealworms' cycle closely resembles gerbils' winter cycle.[27]

Earthworms also breathe to a lunar beat. This was demonstrated by Charles L. Ralph, of Northwestern University, where Brown worked.[28,29,30] What Ralph did was place worms in airtight containers. As a container of reserve air suspended in water was depleted by the worms' breathing, it became less buoyant and sank. That vertical motion—as well as the date and hour it occurred—could be measured by a simple lab device, which is how Ralph found daily and monthly lunar patterns.

Over the course of a month, the daily rate of oxygen consumption was lowest around the first lunar quarter and highest around the new moon. It was generally highest between full and new moons, and generally lowest from new and full moons. During individual days, consumption peaked about three hours before lunar nadir and some two hours after zenith. In addition, each of the two groups Ralph tested showed subtle daily peculiarities. But one thing was certain for all the worms. The time of greatest oxygen consumption did not correspond to times when the worms wiggled around most. Respiration seemed influenced only by the moon, not physical exertion.

Finally, there are numerous lunar cycles followed by various nocturnal insects.[31]

The most impressive thing about these lunar rhythms is that

they happen in land animals. How do they know when the moon is full or new? What tells them the moon is at its daily nadir? It is easy to imagine marine creatures responding to the unmistakable message of tides, although scientists have demonstrated that most by far are responding to the moon itself. At any rate, land animals of course don't have any ocean tides to respond to. It must be something else controlled by the moon that moves them. Moonlight, terrestrial tides, atmospheric tides, tides in an animal's own body, even tides in the earth's magnetic field . . . these are some of the possible explanations we'll examine in Part Three.

18

Diana's Green Thumb

The moon has always been an ally of man's effort to work the soil. Stonehenge was as much an agricultural tool as any primitive plow was. In the same way that the Druids and others used alignments of Stonehenge's pillars and lintels to gauge movements of the sun and moon, the Hohokam Indians of Arizona used windows and decorated walls in a four-story adobe temple they built between what are now Tucson and Phoenix.[1] Then there is that stone structure built by the Anasazi Indians high above the New Mexican desert, which they used in a similar way for farming. And, of course, farmers throughout the ancient Mediterranean closely followed the doctrine of lunar sympathy in their agricultural and animal husbandry chores. Like modern, college-educated American farmers, all of these ancient tillers thought of themselves as prudent agriculturalists paying attention to the laws of nature —as expressed by the moon.

People today use the moon in the same ways. Instead of stone structures using the moon to indicate precise moments of the planting seasons, however, people in the twentieth century use printed tables of the lunar zodiac. Most such charts explain the lunar zodiac as a record of the moon's passage through a different part of the sky, day by day and season by season. The sky is divided into twelve such parts, which are called "signs." Those, in turn, can all be categorized into one of four "elements": earth, air, fire, and water. Some signs are said to be better for planting, some for harvesting. Some plants—or even *parts* of plants—should be sown or weeded or harvested or fertilized in one sign; other plants, in other signs.

Nancy Passmore's 1980 lunar calendar includes one such chart.[2] *The Old Farmer's Almanac* does, too.[3] There's also an interesting summary of such charts in Dr. Clark Timmins's *Planting by the Moon*:

> Fish are said to respond to the lure more readily when the Moon is changing phases and in a watery sign (Cancer, Scorpio, or Pisces); and that the best period during any month is within three days, before or after the new Moon. It is also said that crabs and mushrooms are best and most plentiful at the time of the full Moon. As the author is no Nimrod, he cannot confirm the above suggestions.
>
> Preserves and jellies made while the Moon is waning and in fixed sign (Taurus, Scorpio, or Aquarius) will be found to possess exceptional flavor and good keeping qualities. Perhaps Scorpio is the best of these, being both fixed and watery. Fruits or vegetables should be canned while the Moon is waning and in a watery sign (Cancer, Scorpio, or Pisces) for best results. These suggestions have been completely verified by personal observation and experience covering many years.[4]

The principles of lunar sympathy are followed today as they've always been. Some farmers in Italy still plant and reap according to the doctrine.[5] There are French lumberyards where wood felled during a waning moon is still marked "preferred."[6] And *The Old Farmer's Almanac* includes several charts which show how to apply the doctrine to any number of plants. One lists forty-six varieties of plants and the best time to plant each for each of sixteen geographical regions around the United States.[7] In general, modern adherents believe—as the ancients did—that plants which produce a desired fruit or flower above ground should be planted during a waxing moon, and plants which yield below ground (e.g., carrots) should be planted during a waning moon.[8]

Moreover, if the proliferation of the *Almanac* and various zodiac books and lunar calendars is any indication, these lunar laws are used all over the country by individual gardeners and farmers, as well as groups like Circle Wicca in Madison, Wisconsin (see "The Moon is God"), and the Kimberton Hill community in Kimberton, Pennsylvania.[9]

What makes all of this especially interesting is that modern science has proven the moon's influence over plants. For one thing, there is Clark Timmins's home-grown evidence. During the waxing moon, he planted a number of things which are supposed to thrive only if they are in fact planted at that time of the lunar month: tomatoes, sweet peas, carrots, cosmos, turnips, sunflowers, beets, calendula, and veronica. They all came up roses, so to speak. But when seeds for the same types of plants were planted at the wrong time, i.e., during a waning moon, they germinated much less successfully. Some did not germinate at all. Those that did were often abnormally small and weak. Tomato vines yielded less fruit, and the flowering plants took longer to blossom and did so less impressively. Furthermore, out of ten plants which should be grown during a waxing moon, all ten died when transplanted during a waning moon.[10]

Nor are these just the ravings of a man who has been working in a field beneath the hot sun too long. Other hard-nosed scientists who probably have nothing but contempt for talk of astrology and the zodiac have discovered lunar rhythms in plants which are remarkably similar to those that Timmins and *The Old Farmer's Almanac* tout.

Frank Brown, Jr., for example, found an increase in the metabolism of potatoes over the course of every lunar month. The average metabolic rate was lowest at every new moon, then increased steadily past the full moon until it peaked each month at the third quarter. At that point, it would be 20 percent higher than it had been at new moon.[11] That's loosely comparable to the difference between a groggy sailor and Popeye after he's swallowed some spinach. And the cause was definitely the moon, nothing else. Brown had hermetically sealed the potatoes in containers, in which light, heat, humidity, and air pressure never changed. He did this with several types of plants and animals and got the same results.[12]

In another experiment, Brown and Emma D. Terracini

found lunar cycles of oxygen consumption in both potatoes and carrots. What they found was that the percentage change in the amount of oxygen consumed by those plants between 2 and 6 A.M. equals the percentage change in outdoor barometric pressure during those same hours. That happens every day, from six days before the full moon to six days before the new moon. But during the rest of the month, those changes are the mirror image of each other. By whatever percentage one of them increases, the other decreases; and vice versa.[13]

Beans were next for Brown. In this experiment, Brown and Carol S. Chow demonstrated that pinto beans absorb water fastest four times a month: at each lunar quarter.[14] The pattern was clear and pronounced; at full and new moons and the first and third quarters, the amount of water absorbed by baskets of beans rose dramatically. In between those quarters, the amount absorbed plunged.

Brown and Chow started their study by obtaining several 100-pound bags of pinto beans, which they stored in a biology laboratory at Northwestern University. The lab was air-conditioned and kept at a constant temperature. Every day, twenty undamaged beans were taken from a bag and placed in a shallow aluminum basket. They were weighed, submerged in tap water, then immediately removed from the water and blotted dry before being weighed again. Four hours later the beans were again dunked and weighed. The difference between the first and second weights indicated the amount of water absorbed, and the weight of that absorbed water was recorded as a percentage of the beans' initial dry weight. The twenty-bean samples, which weighed between 7 and 9 grams dry, usually gained about 16.8 percent in weight.

That was their basic experiment. When Brown and Chow changed particular environmental conditions, some plants would absorb even more water at particular times of the lunar month. One of those environmental changes was location; some groups of beans were close to other groups, some were not. When compared to "control" groups spaced widely apart, pinto beans in containers only 20 inches apart showed the largest differences in water absorption four to five days after full moons and the smallest differences four to five days after new moons. That's when they were compared only to each other. When both adjacent groups were compared to "control" groups spaced widely apart, they had the biggest differences in water absorption four to five days after new moons and the least four to five days after full moons.[15] The explanation? Plants can sense the electromagnetic fields generated by nearby plants, something we'll deal with more in the final chapter.

Another researcher, who studied corn and peas for nine years, found that corn planted two days before the full moon grew larger than corn planted two days after, and peas planted at the new moon withered more quickly than is normal.[16] The French government and the U.S. Department of Agriculture have sent scientists in search of similar results.[17] And let's not forget those lunar rhythms in the growth of algae, which we discussed in "The Aquatic World."

Rounding out this lunar cornucopia are tomatoes, those gastronomical delights whose reactions to phases of the moon were discovered by a researcher from an appropriate place, the culinary capital of the world, France. Dr. E. Gravious, of the University of Lyon, found that seeds from at least one species of tomato consumed less oxygen in the morning than in the afternoon. But, according to Bernard Dixon in *Omni,* a science-oriented magazine, "uptake of oxygen was significantly greater on mornings . . . coinciding with the new and full moon. Sunflower seeds behaved in a similar way."[18]

Only the moon could be responsible for this variation since Gravious had kept the seeds in otherwise unchanging conditions: total darkness and a constant temperature. In Dixon's words, "[W]e now have to accept that heat, light, and nutrients are by no means the only factors regulating plant behavior."[19]

We must consider the moon, too.

19

Reproduction

The primitive Papuans of New Guinea have an explanation for the onset of womanhood that is earthy and innocent. The moon takes the shape of a man and sneaks into bed with the sleeping girl, with whom he makes love. His penetration is what causes her first menstrual bleeding, but she is oblivious. She merely dreams that a real man is embracing her.[1]

The Maori, who are aborigines of New Zealand, have a less poetic explanation for menstruation. It is simply an illness caused by the moon. When the moon is new and cannot be seen, women are safe. But any other time of the lunar month it can inflict its harm. The Maori even have a special name for menstruation: "mata marama." Its literal translation is "moon sickness."[2]

Menstruation and the moon; for millennia they have been associated with one another in man's mind. How could they fail to be? There was the moon, an ominous spirit in the sky. And there was menstruation, often preceded by pain; unnerving for men and women alike. What could be more impressive than these formidable phenomena coming and going with identical regularity?[3] It was only natural that early in its history humankind would decide that something so strange connected to things so important could not be mere coincidence.[4] With time, this association only became stronger and its articulation more elaborate.

The Babylonians, for example, felt assured that the moon not only causes women to menstruate, but does so because the moon itself menstruates. And why not? Was the moon not Ishtar, the *goddess* of love?[5] This explanation is so universally appealing that several American Indian nations held a similar belief, that the moon is a woman who bled, appropriately enough, during her waning period.[6] Today in India certain sects believe the same thing, and for the benefit of skeptics, priests triumphantly display bloodstained cloths after the statues of the goddess have been placed in seclusion during her "sickness."[7] The ancient Babylonians took all this one step further. They believed that Ishtar bled around the time of the full moon, and on that day all important activity was prohibited. They called that day "Shabathu" (or "sabattu"), from which we get the name of our own day of rest, the Sabbath.[8,9,10] Colloquial speech in the world today expresses the same belief. French country folk refer to the start of a woman's period as "le moment de la lune."[11] In parts of Germany menses are simply called "the moon."[12] And in India, Zaire, Mandigo, and Australia and New Guinea along the Torres Straits the same words can be used to talk about either the moon or menstruation.[13,14]

But this identification of the moon with menstruation went beyond blame for women's monthly discharge. It was an identification of the moon's monthly cycle with the entire menstrual, or reproductive, cycle. Aristotle was very specific about this. He described how the moon caused uterine tissues to swell day by day with nutrients in anticipation of an embryonic life, which would need nourishment.[15] Galen, whose stature in early medicine is second only to Hippocrates', taught that the "moon controls the monthly period in women."[16] Language that we still use reflected this. The Latin word *menses* was both the plural for "month" (itself a word derived from the word "moon") and the word for "menstruation"; one Greek word, *katamenia,* meant both "menstruation" and "by the moon."[17,18]

This belief in the moon's relationship to the menstrual, or reproductive, cycle is as strong as ever today, even in comparatively modern, industrialized corners of the world. After all, who does not know a nurse or obstetrician who will swear that births seem to cluster around full moons? The apparent trend is so clear that many medical professionals have no qualms about stating it publicly.[19,20,21] And why not? These supposedly superstitious notions about the moon's control over human menstruation are actually rather accurate reflections of reality. The menstrual cycle and the lunar month are the same length, about 29.5 days,[22,23] and the moon influences other aspects of human sexuality. For one thing, the moon is virtually a midwife. It may not be there at the bedside, but it certainly controls the time of births. The fact—not the superstition, but the *fact*—is that a statistically significant majority of births occur at full moons.

There are as many statistically sound surveys corroborating this as there are mothers in a big-city maternity ward. Take the work by Edson Andrews, a Florida surgeon, who happened to chart the number of births at Tallahassee Memorial Hospital from 1956 through 1958 while he was in the course of research on an entirely separate subject. What he found—after setting out to investigate a different matter, mind you—was that 401 babies had been born within two days (a statistically acceptable "window" period) of the full moon. Three hundred seventy-five had been born around the new moon, 320 near the moon's first quarter, and fewer still around the third quarter. In Dr. Andrews' words, "Draw your own conclusions."[24]

Then there is the exhaustive research by Walter and Abraham Menaker, of New York. Three separate studies of theirs showed that births happen significantly more often at full moons than any other time of the lunar month. First they counted births at fifty-seven hospitals in the city during thirteen lunar months, beginning January 1, 1954. They found that the smallest number of the more than 120,000 births happened at new moons, while far and away the greatest number occurred on the three days centered around each full moon.[25] Full-moon births led new-moon ones by a full seven percent,[26] more than enough to satisfy any statistician, but the Menakers wanted to be sure their numbers weren't a fluke. Suppose the difference was due to cultural reasons like the well-known preference of physicians to perform elective deliveries on weekdays rather than weekends?[27] Sure enough, more new moons than full moons were on weekends during the survey period, which the Menakers thought might have made full moons look responsible for a tendency actually initiated by doctors.

To compensate for that, they started all over again. This time they counted births only at municipal hospitals, where deliveries are usually made by staff physicians available at all times.[28] This way the dates of births would reflect only the preferences of Mother Nature, not New York's obstetricians. Over 250,000 births during nine years ending in January 1957 were tabulated this way, and again the three days around full moons were easily the time of most births, and again new moons were the lowest three-day period.[29] But the Menakers still were not through.

Now their work with numbers got a little fancy. They looked at births at ten private hospitals again, with an eye to discovering what day is the boundary between the two most dissimilar halves of the month. After reviewing a quarter of a million births, they found that one 14½-day period does indeed have more births than the other. And where was that dividing line? Why, day 13 of the lunar month—the day before the full moon.[30]

When they repeated this process for 510,000 births at both private and municipal hospitals, they found an even bigger difference between the two most dissimilar halves. They also found the divider was again day 13, and the single day of the full moon had an "extraordinary" lead in the number of births.[31]

A statistical accident? Hardly. The Menakers pointed out that by one conventional mathematical analysis the size of the difference between the two most dissimilar halves of the month would happen by chance only once in a million times. As for the exceptional number of births at full moons, that could happen by chance only once in three to four thousand times.[32] And after considering the studies which show similar full-moon birth patterns among other animals, the Menakers were convinced—finally—that luck and sociological flukes had nothing to do with their results.[33]

Eight years later Walter Menaker delivered one more survey into the world. He analyzed another half-million births that had taken place during 1961, 1962, and 1963 according to the method of dissimilar half-months. Once again, the halves with significantly more births were those clustered around full moons.[34]

Studies 'round the world echo the Menakers' findings. Researchers in Multomah County, Georgia, found an impressive rise in the number of births over a five-year span at each full moon.[35] An Emory University School of Medicine psychiatrist found births clustered around full and new moons at a small hospital in Florence, South Carolina. That pattern—for 1,907 births—existed for the entire six-year period (1957–1962) studied, as well as for each individual year.[36] The survey had, incidentally, focused on births by black parents because, according to the Emory psychiatrist, the black population's birth patterns had not been extensively studied.[37] At Methodist Hospital of Southern California, in Los Angeles, more than 11,000 births over a six-year period (1939–1944) showed two clear lunar patterns. One was that the number of births peaked once a lunar month. The other was that nearly 18 percent more births occurred during the waxing than during the waning moon.[38] The odds against such a large difference occurring by chance are astronomically large. A study in Bavaria, Germany, also found a 29.5-day cycle to births, with a clear majority of male births during the waxing phases.[39]

Some studies have dealt with the timing of births in a more general way. That Emory shrink, for instance, cited a German study published in 1938 which described a significant tendency of births to follow full and new moons at regular intervals.[40] A Dr. Albert Schnurman reported in the pages of the *Virginia Medical Monthly* that births cluster around the days that lunar phases change. He wrote that two-thirds of 2,691 births which took place during a five-year span at a hospital in Roanoke, Virginia, occurred within a three-day "window" of a phase change.[41] He described this as a clear "lunar effect."

And an early article in *The Lancet,* a prestigious medical publication, describes records kept by a young Pennsylvania physician which showed that he regularly made more deliveries during some lunar phases than others.[42]

No wonder women for centuries have invoked the moon's assistance when they are giving birth.[43]

* * *

If births do indeed occur more often at full moons, then there should be evidence that humans make love more often at full moons, too, and the reason is simple. Not only is the average menstrual cycle the same length—29.53 days—as the synodic lunar month, but the average gestation period is also nine lunar months.[44] If birth is at full moon, then conception probably was too, nine months earlier.

That's the arithmetical prediction. Professional Peeping Toms confirm it. No less reliable an authority than the *New England Journal of Medicine* was the forum for one such exciting report. In a November 1978, issue, two members of Wesleyan University's psychology department described their study of thirty-five healthy women who apparently knew exactly what they wanted in their lives—as well as how much, when, and how often. They were "college-educated white women between the ages of 21 and 37 affiliated with the college community. Some were faculty wives."[45] The rest presumably were students, wives of students, and employees of the Middletown, Connecticut, university. They all were asked to keep detailed daily records regarding all their sexual activity, and that's just what they did, recording everything from 24-karat kink to cuddly daydreams. They described all their sexual adventures, real or imagined: lovemaking, masturbation, caressing, fantasy, and turn-ons from books, films, magazines, and dreams. Rolled into one and spiced with narrative, the accumulated diaries just might read like that story about another small New England town, Peyton Place. The women even received payment of $15 for their efforts—the recordkeeping, that is.

The one crucial criterion for this survey was that only sexual activity initiated by the women could be recorded. It was *their* pattern of interest, not their partners', that had to be discovered. Previous studies elsewhere had made the mistake of recording all sexual activity, regardless of which partner started it, which works if you're trying to measure stamina and endurance, but doesn't tell you anything about the peaks and valleys of women's sexual interest.

And precisely what vital statistics did these scientists groping in the dark finally get their hands on? They found a whopping 30 percent increase in sexual activity at the time of ovulation,[46] which we have already seen is usually *at* the full moon. And probably because of it.

So, women don't just happen to become pregnant at full moons. They become pregnant because they're more turned-on then and engage in sex—all sorts of sex—more often at full moons. Thus, like other mammals that go into heat, women apparently grow randier at ovulation. Incredibly, that's something no prior study had demonstrated adequately, the investigators said.[47]

These Wesleyan findings are reinforced by an earlier article in *The Psychoanalytic Review,* which considered the possibility "that the sexual organs are more stimulated during . . . the full moon . . . than at any other time."[48] A more recent study reached precisely the same conclusions as the Wesleyan psychologists: the female desire for sexual union is greatest just before the period of ovulation,[49] during the three days around the full moon.[50] In a published discussion of this study, one prominent American zoologist described how carefully it had been conducted. "The greatest difficulty in carrying out the study was the selection of suitable subjects. All volunteers who were taking birth control pills had to be eliminated as were those who had undergone hysterectomies, those having intercourse regularly and thus often sated, those who were admittedly frigid, and those who 'always felt like sex.' The investigator finally assembled thirty women, who all had regular menstrual cycles and no regular sex life."[51]

A corollary for all this concerns menstrual bleeding. If ovulation takes place at full moon, then menstruation (which generally occurs about fourteen to fifteen days later) should be at the new moon. Sure enough, that's exactly what several studies have found. German investigators reported in 1936 that a survey of 10,000 women with regular menstrual cycles had revealed that more menses began at the full or new moon than any other time of month.[52] A Kansas biologist who has studied lunar cycles in the cardiac activity of cockroaches, mice, and men (see "Bleeding") also cited research in the 1960s that found menstruation occurring most often at the full and new moon, as well as at the first and third quarters.[53]

Three Czechoslovakian obstetricians and gynecologists have found a different lunar pattern. Eight hundred ten student nurses living in Prague were surveyed in 1962, and the Czech physicians found that their menses were more frequent at the first and third quarters than chance would predict. The exact number expected did occur at the full moon, but a below-normal frequency happened at new moons.[54] While the lunar pattern is significant, this study hardly negates the German and American ones mentioned above or the vast body of medical literature documenting the full-moon cycle's relation to births and, by implication, to conception and ovulation. The group studied was smaller than those groups above and not a random population sample. All the girls were engaged in the same occupation, and may have been merely displaying the familiar phenomenon of "sympathetic" menstruation. Furthermore, the two-year survey did not cover the summer months when the girls (they all were 14 to 18 years of age) were out of school and living back home.

Then there is the 1898 study by Svante Arrhenius, the Danish Nobel Prize winner and physiologist, who found women in a Stockholm maternity hospital menstruating on the average every 27.32 days, almost exactly the length of the sidereal month.[55,56] Again, a lunar pattern, but not the one confirmed by more modern and, presumably, more reliable inquiries.

There are several theories about how this connection between the moon and the reproductive cycle was born. One is that menstruation, like the oceans' flow of fluids, became synchronized by the moon's tidal pull and has been genetically locked into that lunar rhythm ever since (see the chapter, "Biological Tides"). Charles Darwin believed something similar.[57,58] The great naturalist felt it must be a result of mankind's ancestors' life by the sea. While humankind's predecessors were still marine creatures or animals that had evolved to an amphibious stage, they found that the month's highest tides—which would be at the full and new moons—were the best time for menstruation, ovulation, and reproduction. Only those that did so then survived. Perhaps eggs deposited in intertidal mud flats were safest from predators. Perhaps the tidal pools among the rocks above a beach's mud slope, which would be safer for spawning, became most accessible only at the highest tides.

Another theory is that it is the moon's light, rather than its tidal attraction, that synchronizes the menstrual cycle. More on this in chapter 26, "Moonlight," where we'll see how medical experimenters have helped women tame their menstrual periods. One woman, for example, whose cycles ran unpredictably for 33 to 48 days was exposed to an artificial full moon, a 100-watt light bulb, on the fourteenth through seventeenth nights after her last menstruation. Presto! This triggered her return to a typical reproductive cycle of about 29 days.

Advocates of that moonlight theory argue that the moon's light sets off a biochemical chain reaction leading to menstruation and ovulation. In contrast, Havelock Ellis, an English psychologist and pioneer in objective sex research, suggested that the influence of moonlight is much less complicated. "[I]t is perhaps not extravagant to suppose that . . . the periodically recurring full moon, not merely by its stimulation of the nervous system, but possibly by the special opportunities which it gave for the exercise of the sexual functions, served to implant a lunar rhythm on menstruation."[59]

Ellis cited one scholar's observation that "young and robust persons" grow sexually restless at full moons. Another pointed out that moonlight is simply a utilitarian aid to courting couples. Ellis illustrated these points with case studies from the *Journal of the Anthropological Institute.* These described the wild, erotic dances conducted by African Bantu tribespeople and southern Australian aborigines, which evolved into full-scale orgies. Ellis evoked images of torch-lit scenes of writhing, leaping dancers glistening with sweat, working themselves into a frenzy before retiring to secluded love nests among the bushes. For any reader who didn't get the point, the Englishman added that these "sexual festivals" were climaxed "by promiscuous intercourse."[60] All, Ellis noted with scientific meticulousness, beneath the romantic full moon.

A physician from White Plains, New York, has taken this utilitarian analysis an extraordinary step further. Not only was moonlight an aid or hindrance to romantic strategies, E.H.P. Ward wrote in *Medical Record,* but in the prehistoric past when man's genetic patterns were still being programmed, "nordic races" would be safer from predators while "in the act of mating" during full moons, whereas "brunette races" would be safer around the new moon when they would blend in best with their darkened landscape. Ward elaborated on this racial theory:

> No doubt in primitive man sexual activity—the act of mating—took place at night. Hence degrees of light or darkness affecting it would depend on the moon. . . . If so, by a process of natural selection, sexual activity in the brunette races would become periodical at intervals of a lunar month and would occur in the dark of the moon. With the blonds in northern regions, on the other hand, mating might reasonably be assumed to take place most favorably in the moonlight; absolute darkness would not be necessary for safety where lurking enemies were not numerous and moonlight might be a positive advantage in escaping from such enemies as there were, such as wolves. If so, natural selection would bring it about that sexual activity would take place at intervals of a lunar month, and at the full moon.[61]

Ward even enlists a few cultural clues in support of this theory. "I understand . . . that in the romantic literature of the blond races the full moon plays an almost unfailing part in the love scenes, apparently being inseparably associated with mating; this would bear out my hypothesis. While, on the other hand, the French, a mixed blond and brunette race for whom no particular phase of the moon would be associated with mating—least of all the full moon as they are more brunette than blond—never tire of ridiculing the German novelists whose idea of romance they consider is limited to an introduction of the full moon into the picture."[62]

All of which is of dubious value. It merely seems one scientist's way of saying: at full moons, blondes have more fun.

* * *

The ancients were firm in their faith that the moon regulated reproductive cycles, and they tried to put this knowledge to good use. Pliny advised farmers to place eggs under a hen at the new moon so they would develop as the moon approaching fullness does.[63] Hippocrates taught that human conception is much more likely to occur at full moons.[64] Now, physicians once again are hoping to use the lunar rhythm method to advantage.

The Menakers pointed out its practicality for prospective mothers in their 1959 report on the proliferation of births at full moons. Their advice was especially appropriate for women having a hard time becoming pregnant. "As to immediate application of our data," they wrote in the *American Journal of Obstetrics and Gynecology,* "one is tempted to advise that, where conception is desired, the most auspicious time seems to be a day before full moon . . . and also full-moon day (but not the day after full moon)."[65] This same lunar rhythm method was suggested by an article published fourteen years later in that same medical journal by a trio of Empire State physicians,[66] who found an increase of births at full moons similar to the trend reported by the Menakers.

In fact, one recent researcher incurred the armed wrath of the Soviet bureaucracy because of his research, which showed how this full-moon rhythm method could be used as a natural means of birth control. Not only that, but he also taught how to predict an unborn baby's sex by plotting its mother's birth date against patterns of full moons.

This medical Merlin was Dr. Eugen Jonas of Czechoslovakia, who established the Astra-Nitra Center for Planned Parenthood in south-central Czechoslovakia in the spring of 1968 with his government's blessings. When American medical investigators began looking into Jonas's work that summer, they found that the center had dispensed some 30,000 prescriptions for birth control between 1968 and 1970 without resorting to pills, surgery, or any other contraceptive device. Moreover, the 1,252 women who were participating enjoyed an extraordinary 97 percent effective rate of birth control over a one-year survey period.[67] All this without the inconvenience and unreliability of such contraceptive methods as condoms and the diaphragm with spermaticidal jelly, or the occasionally perilous side-effects of the pill. Impressive as the results were, Dr. Jonas had more to offer: a way to predict a baby's sex. The Americans later reported that Jonas tested his method by poring over records at a local maternity hospital. Basing his calculations on the principle that a fetus's sex is determined by the day of the lunar month on which its mother is born, Jonas successfully predicted in retrospect the sex of 217 out of 250 children, an 87 percent rate of accuracy. Lady Luck would have given him the correct prediction only 50 percent of the time.[68]

Jonas's seminal triumphs still weren't over. Seeking independent confirmation and wider acceptance of his theories, he sent his data to the Slovak Academy of Science. He expected a swift and impartial hearing on his work, but all he got was disappointment. The Academy protested that it had no one qualified to judge his work, and Jonas was forced to forward his documents to the Czech Academy of Science in Prague,[69] where it was received with encouragement by Dr. Jiřï Malek, head of the group that studied the lunar menstruation pattern of the Prague nursing students mentioned previously.

Around this same time, Dr. Kurt Rechnitz, a professor of gynecology and director of the Women's Clinic at the University of Budapest, caught wind of Jonas's findings. When Rechnitz tested Jonas's sex-prediction method on more than 100 births for which he had records, he achieved precisely the same rate of accuracy that Jonas had, 87 percent. Rechnitz soon became Jonas's collaborator, and their joint theories were put into successful practice at the Astra-Nitra Center.[70]

Jonas's method for preventing pregnancy was surprisingly simple. First, he determined a woman's lunar birthday; that is, the day of the lunar month she was born. Say a woman was born October 5 of a given year, but that date was six days after the previous full moon. That would make her birthday nearly twenty-one days after the previous new moon (the first day of the lunar month) so that her lunar birthday would be the twenty-first day of the month, which Jonas designated as one of her two optimal fertility dates. Next, Jonas would use ordinary gynecological procedures to determine that woman's present ovulation period, which is the conventionally recognized period of fertility, and correlate that to the woman's lunar birthday. If the woman's current menstrual cycle has her ovulating on the twenty-first day of the month, that would coincide with her lunar birthday, and Jonas felt that that would be her time of greatest fertility—the best time to try to have children, or the most important time for a woman who does not want to become pregnant to abstain from intercourse.[71]

Jonas's method for predicting sex relied upon tedious calculations based not only on the lunar phase, but also the moon's exact angle in the ecliptic.

Jonas's work came to a tragic halt in 1970,[72] two years after the Soviet Union had invaded Czechoslovakia and confronted the center with its own brand of birth control for unauthorized ideas: tanks and bayonets. After all, these were the armored minions of the state that required its own biologists and agriculturalists—on penalty of death—to practice Trofim Denisovich Lysenko's socialist science (which repudiated such bourgeois concepts as chromosomes) instead of Gregor Mendel's "revisionist" genetics—to the everlasting regret of Ukrainian wheat farmers. So, it was no surprise that the only lunar influences the Red Army believed in were the ones it believed were in Jonas's head, and he soon . . . disappeared.

Like a moon in permanent eclipse.

20

Male Periods

As the Roaring Twenties drew to an end, Dr. Rex Hersey, a University of Pennsylvania physician, began an analysis of the monthly periods of factory workers. They displayed all the familiar female symptoms. One twenty-two-year-old had a four-and-a-half-week cycle with mood variations one observer described as typical for a menstrual cycle.[1] When this survey subject was down and depressed, apathy toward homelife and work set in. Another subject with slightly longer cycles felt alternately buoyant and deflated; outgoing and confident, then apathetic about work, withdrawn, and often tired.[2]

Overall, Dr. Hersey concluded that his subjects showed the common extremes of irritability and amiability which are typical of monthly periods. In both their daily behavior and performances on standard psychological tests, they did nothing unusual for women. The only unusual thing about them, in fact, was that Dr. Hersey's subjects were not women, at all, but men—perfectly normal, heterosexual men, whose actions went a long way toward proving that men do indeed have monthly "periods." They did not, of course, menstruate, but in other biological functions and emotions they were the same as women.

Now the existence of monthly periods in men has been amply demonstrated, most recently by Alice J. Dan, of the University of Chicago, in 1977.[3] Scientists have finally welcomed men to that company of women, apes, and chimpanzees who succumb to sexual cycles with emotional[4] and physiological reverberations, swinging back and forth each month to the beat of the lunar metronome.

Preposterous? Hardly. Biologists have now catalogued a large number of biological rhythms men share with women. Dr. Estelle Ramey, for example, a professor of physiology and biophysics at Georgetown University, has described how men and women experience similar variations in body temperature and physical strength during each 24-hour period.[5] She has also reported how adrenal hormones like cortisone and sex hormones fluctuate for men and women alike. Even diseases display rhythmic activity, according to Dr. Ramey. Take the metabolic activity and growth by cell division of certain cancer cells, which peak during the very time of day when normal cells in the same organ are least active. Or intellectual acuity, which also varies over the course of a day, as any world traveler who has suffered jet lag can attest. Nor are male rhythms confined to short periods of time any more than women's are. Just as women experience menopause, Dr. Ramey points out that men experience "a gradual decrease in the secretion of testosterone, the male hormone, from youth to old age."[6] In fact, male menopause is not only now accepted by medicine as reality, it is one of the most widely studied aspects of male periods.[7]

The same goes for monthly fluctuations, and these too are strikingly similar to changes experienced by women. Sanctorius, the brilliant seventeenth-century Italian physician who pioneered in modern methods of physiological research by using precision instruments,[8] demonstrated that men undergo a monthly weight change of about one or two pounds.[9,10,11] He did this by using a fine scale to painstakingly weigh healthy men over long periods of time. What he found was a gradual increase in the men's weight each month accompanied by "feelings of heaviness and lassitude,"[12] followed by a sudden loss of body liquids which caused the men to return to normal weights. The English physician Laycock reported "monthly discharges of blood from the sexual organs and other parts of the body in men" in the mid-1800s, and attributed the phenomenon to the moon's influence.[13] Near the turn of the century, Dr. Campbell Clark reported similar discharges to the British Medical Association. "This may be in the form of a headache, or a nasal hemorrhage, or diarrhea, or abundant discharge of uric acid, or some other unusual occurrence," he wrote.[14] In addition, a recent sixteen-year Dutch and American study of the male sex hormones contained in urine revealed an "ebb and flow of hormones [which] followed a pronounced" lunar monthly rhythm.[15] Modern research has also documented a number of nonsexual brain and blood enzymes whose monthly fluctuations are triggered by cycles of sex-related hormones.[16] It was in the last century that a European zoologist proposed an explanation for these cycles which is attracting considerable interest in our own day: Males are rudimentary females, with vestigial female organs.[17]

Whether or not that's true, researchers agree that men, like women, have a greater sexual appetite once a month. One of the most noted students of human sexuality, the English psychologist Havelock Ellis, emphasized this in his landmark work, *Studies in the Psychology of Sex,* originally published in seven volumes between 1900 and 1928.[18] In addition to his own research, Ellis pointed out that physicians had been reporting male sexual periods in the professional medical literature worldwide for over a century. There was the German physician, for example, who had described a colleague's monthly "attacks of almost satyriacal sexual excitement,"[19] the Frenchman who became far more easily impassioned by a person's touch once a month and who enjoyed erotic dreams for one or two *whole days,*[20] and another Frenchman whose periods practically paralyzed him. The man hardened into such states of sexual arousal that he could think of nothing but sex and was unable to sleep.[21]

There was also a healthy, twenty-eight-year-old American whose powerful sexual impulses seem to belong less to a man than to the villainous beast in John Gardner's version of *Beowulf* named Grendel, whose dank-smelling scrotum fairly quivers at the thought of combat and bloodshed, let alone sex. Ellis's Yank periodically "had an itching feeling about the testicles; . . . felt slightly irritable; . . . [and his] penis erected with the slightest provocation." A vivid wet dream would resolve that excitement, but "so regular was the matter that he usually wore a loin garment at these times, to prevent the semen getting on the bedding." His periods lasted two or three days and were accompanied by muscular tension. About a year after these periods were first recorded, the American reported that his monthly wet dreams became less frequent but that he still had "a peculiar 'heavy' feeling about the testicles, and a marked tendency towards erection of the penis." He "often awoke to find a tense erection. Moreover, these feelings usually continued a week."[22]

Ellis also cited a study by the Dutch neurologist and psychologist L.S. von Romer, who said that men not only grow the proverbial horns once a month, but that they tend to do it at full moons and, to a lesser extent, at new moons.[23] In turn, von Romer acknowledged the earlier studies by F.H. Perry-Coste, who had discovered a nearly identical pattern. In addition to subjects following a full-moon frequency, Perry-Coste had worked with two subjects who had wet dreams with incredible regularity at both full and new moons.[24] Still one other study, this by a Rutgers biologist, described the two-year pattern of one man's wet dreams, which happened once every sidereal lunar month as predictably as Old Faithful's eruptions.[25,26]

Three of the most dramatic case studies of male periodicity were reported in the journal, *Medical Record,* by New York physician C.P. Oberndorf. All involved patients whose sexuality was synchronized by the full moon. The subject of one was a twenty-nine-year-old Englishman who had been living with a woman friend in London until his work as a musician brought him to the States, where he soon asked to be admitted to a hospital in Manhattan. The problem, he said, was his uncontrollable lust, which he was afraid would lead to a violent assault on one of New York's numerous lovely women . . . as it recently had in London. The mystery, to him, was that these compulsions occurred every full moon. Dr. Oberndorf's summary:

> Shortly after the age of six the patient manifested a desire to wander away from home into the fields, and it was not long before his mother began to notice that these wandering expeditions would occur once a month at about the time of full moon. Although the patient's sexual awakening occurred at five or six with infantile fancies about female members of the household and active masturbation began at the age of ten, periodicity in his sexual excitement, coincident with lunar changes, was not observed until he reached puberty. As a boy of thirteen he experienced nosebleed during one of his excited periods, but there has been no periodical epistaxis.
>
> While he has observed that though once a month, at the time of full moon his erotic cravings are strong, it is curious that unless he is in his period, his sexual desires are very mild indeed. His citation of many examples of relative absence at one time of his desires and extreme augmentation at others with the same or different women (the patient has lived in common-law relations with a woman in London for two years) substantiates his assertion. Because he appreciates that during these periods his sexual cravings are almost uncontrollable, he has made it a practice for some years to avoid women at such times for fear that he will commit some serious indiscretion. At the time of the period he usually also feels a marked increase in energy, physical power, and ability to play on his violin, but at others experiences restlessness, depression, and anxiety. During one of his periods at the age of sixteen he was so excited as to require commitment to the Leeds (England) Insane Hospital. Judging from a retrospective account this appears to have been a maniacal attack.[27]

Oberndorf's second case study was of another young man, this one twenty-six years old, whose family arrived in America aboard the *Mayflower,* or some ship arriving soon after (Oberndorf is vague for the sake of his patient's privacy). The doctor described this man as a homosexual employed as a clerk, with a thin build and hairy chest, legs, arms, and back, whose "voice, gait, and many mannerisms are distinctly feminine." After infrequent attempts at intercourse with a particular woman and several traumatic homosexual encounters, the young man withdrew, psychologically and socially. His only sexual release was masturbation, of varying frequency but always at full moon. Oberndorf's account:

> Patient began masturbation at the age of five and has continued it practically up to the present time. At first, masturbation was practised alone, but later he became passive agent in pederasty with his two brothers, who were respectively fourteen and eight years older than the patient. Sexual relations with his brothers ceased after a bitter fist fight with his younger brother at the age of fifteen. Heterosexual intercourse only on three occasions at the age of twelve with a girl of the same age.
>
> Since the age of fifteen the patient has abstained from any form of physical sexual relations with persons of either sex. His psychical homosexual component is very pronounced, as there are at least five instances of marked attraction toward men of the definite masculine type. He has roomed with most of these men, and while, as before stated, he has never had relations with them, he made many sacrifices to retain their friendship, such as cooking, washing, and keeping house for them and lending them money. With women he has always been more of a companion than a suitor, a receiver of intimate confidences, and a friend whom they met on a basis of equality. In his tastes he is an esthete, with strong likings for the artistic in music and painting and an aversion for the gross and vulgar.
>
> Periodicity.—When he returned to masturbation after the quarrel with his brother at fifteen, the patient gratified himself too frequently to observe any periodicity in his desires. At nineteen, however, when he began to attempt to suppress his habit, he noticed a regular variation in the intensity of his desires, therein that at the time of full moon no amount of effort succeeded in controlling them.
>
> This lunar increment in his sexual cravings has continued without fail up to the present time. He believes that the psychical effect of moonlight is a negligible influence in his case, for, as he points out, the moon remains bright for several days after full moon, but his sexual longings disappear completely after reaching a climax at or about full moon, only to recur after another [29.5] days. Moreover, the same excitability exists at [the full moon] when the moon is not visible. Of recent years, since the patient has almost conquered his masturbation, nocturnal pollutions occur regularly at such times.[28]

Oberndorf's third case study concerned a near-hermaphrodite, a male with some female sexual characteristics. The man was a twenty-eight-year-old native of Illinois who made his living as a machinist. His health was normal, even if his physiognomy was not. Dr. Oberndorf observed that his patient became overwhelmingly lustful once a month, usually several days, often even a week or more, after the full moon. His left breast would swell and become more firm, and the nipple would spontaneously secrete an "oily" substance. Merely rubbing his breast with a towel after a bath, let alone affectionate fondling, was all it took to prompt his penis erect.

> From the age of 15 to 18 the patient indulged in masturbation about three times a week, but then abandoned this practice for normal sexual intercourse. It was then that he became aware that his sexual desires were active only once a month . . . at which time they became extremely strong. At the same time of the month he would also notice that the left breast would become firmer and more erect, and would also be subjectively sensitive and tender for about four days. For the past two years an oily secretion has appeared about the nipple at such times.
>
> Seven years ago while rubbing the left breast with a coarse towel after bathing he observed that the friction caused an erection of the penis. The same reaction occurred subsequently when a physician whom he consulted for his neurasthnenic symptoms, in administering electricity, happened to place an electrode over the left breast, and subsequently manipulation of the breast has produced erections.
>
> [A]t the time of his periods . . . [h]e becomes restless, easily frightened, irritable, and is subject to an annoying vertigo and flushes of blood to the head. For the past two years he has avoided sexual intercourse because of waning sexual desires, but at the time of his periods he is troubled by frequent involuntary nocturnal emissions. While actual failure in coitus has never occurred, his pollutions have led him to fear impotency. Homosexual traits or even masks of homosexuality, which often accompany such secondary sex traits, have not been revealed.[29]

Of course, sexual desire is no more the only expression of

monthly periods for men than it is for women. The laborers and managers studied by Dr. Hersey of the University of Pennsylvania experienced a wide range of emotional changes which affected all other aspects of their lives from hobbies, to job performances, nightly sleep, and family relationships.[30,31,32] Men are upset and distracted during their periods just as surely as women are. This was something the Omi Railway Company of Japan had to find out the hard way. The company operates an armada of 700 buses and taxis in the dense traffic areas of Kyoto and Osaka, and during the 1960s the firm's directors became worried about large losses resulting from accidents. In 1969 the company's efficiency experts set out to discover the reason for this big drain on the company's resources. What they found was nothing short of incredible. The drivers were men, and Dr. Estelle Ramey writes that when they adjusted their drivers' "routes and schedules to coincide with the appropriate time of the month" according to "each man and his lunar cycles," Omi's accident rate plunged an astounding one-third. And that happened despite the fact that during the same period traffic increased. The benefit to the company—and to the men—has apparently been substantial.[33] So much for men's jokes about women drivers.

Still, stereotypes die hard. Many men simply refuse to consider women seriously for sensitive jobs in business, the military, and politics because of the emotional carnage they believe women suffer each month. Dr. Edgar Berman, a friend of Hubert Humphrey and a member of the Priorities Commission of the Democratic National Committee (DNC) in 1970, said at a policy planning session of the DNC in April 1970 that women are not as capable as men for positions of public leadership because of their "raging hormonal imbalances."[34,35] Janet Delaney, a feminist author, has suggested that Dr. Berman and like-minded men (and women, for that matter) consider the fact that that criterion would have excluded from the presidency Thomas Jefferson, because he had periodic migraines, Abraham Lincoln, with his periodic depression, and John F. Kennedy, who presided over the Cuban missile crisis despite his affliction with Addison's disease, "a serious hormonal disorder" (adrenal insufficiency).[36]

The truth is that male sexual cycles (and their effects, physical and emotional) are no more unaffected by the moon than all women are totally incapacitated by theirs. Both sexes' sexuality is influenced, if not equally obviously. Moreover, in upcoming chapters we'll examine a psychiatric ward's worth of nonsexual emotional disturbances and violent criminal activities that equally afflict men and women. All have unmistakable lunar rhythms and many follow the full moon as faithfully as a cobra follows its snake-charmer.

21

Murder and Mayhem

The full moon made Herman Heppel steal. In a county courtroom in Brooklyn, New York, in 1938, the New Jersey man reportedly was charged with the theft of an automobile and accused of running it into a bus while trying to avoid arrest for traffic violations.[1] Judge William O'Dwyer, however, allowed Heppel to plead guilty to a reduced charge, petty larceny, after Heppel's father and pastor swore that the defendant suffered "periodic 'mental explosions,' especially when the moon is full."[2] A court board had already ruled Heppel otherwise quite sane.[3]

* * *

Similarly, the moon drove Alan Dennis Witcomb to murder. A British court found the Birmingham, England, baker's assistant guilty of murder in 1963, according to one science publication.[4] But the court tempered its own judgment by declaring Witcomb insane on the basis of his sister's testimony that he had often told her, "The moon does strange things to me."[5]

* * *

The moon was early in its full phase the day Sarah Jane Moore tried to assassinate President Gerald Ford in September 1975.[6,7,8] It was 3:30 on the afternoon of the twenty-second. When Ford walked out of San Francisco's St. Francis Hotel, Moore was waiting forty feet away across Post Street on the edge of a large crowd. She was ready. She had her chrome-plated .38-caliber Smith & Wesson revolver loaded with six rounds. Her mind, however, was momentarily wrestling with something mundane: would she have time to pick up her eight-year-old son at school? It took the sudden sight of the President, exposed, to bring her back to the task at hand. She stared. She had a clear view. She was astounded, in fact, that she had so much time.

She almost capitalized on it.

As Ford made his way slowly toward a waiting limousine, Moore pulled the .38 from her purse and aimed. It was so easy. She held the gun with her right arm out straight and her left hand under her right wrist. Then she squeezed off one round. But before she could fire again, Oliver Sipple, a disabled Vietnam veteran standing next to her, knocked her arm down. A swarm of police officers converged on her like linebackers on an enemy halfback. One grabbed her hair and tumbled over a rope cordon with her. Another handcuffed her. In the scuffle, her nose began to bleed.

Police took care of her other worry. Cops in an unmarked car picked up her son.

* * *

The full moon's reputation for inciting violence is unassailable. The familiar cadre of professional and amateur social scientists swears to it. Harvey Schlossberg, director of the New York Police Department's psychological services unit in 1978, told *The New York Times,* "There's really no way to explain it scientifically, but there is an increase in the number of assaults and crimes between people at a full moon."[9] Detective Captain Michael Wilson, of the Providence, Rhode Island, police department, has said, "I know we joke about it. But in a way, it does seem like we get all the unusual calls during a full moon."[10] And he is backed up by Lieutenant Frank Smith of the department's criminal records division, a man whose opinion is based on more than a personal impression.[11] Dominick Longo, Police Chief in the seashore resort of

Ocean City, New Jersey, has said that the full moon always brings a rise in crime, nuisance complaints, and assaults on police officers.[12]

Boston may call itself the Hub of the Universe, but its citizens are nonetheless plagued by earth's humble satellite. The day of one recent full moon Boston police officer John Shea warned a reporter that from past experience he knew that that night the police emergency telephone number would ring incessantly and the department would be "busy as hell—with all the kooks coming out."[13] It was that way every full moon, he said. Jack Gifford, a district patrol supervisor, assured a reporter in 1977, "Sure. It never surprises an officer who's seen someone act irrational or a little whacked out to realize there's a full moon."[14]

The full moon is like an alarm to firefighters, too. Andrew Casper, Chief of San Francisco's Fire Department, once said there are more arson fires at full moons, as well as false alarms, climbers stranded on cliffs, cats in trees, and frightened people calling to report they smell smoke when there is none.[15] Across the continent, New York's chief fire marshal in 1938, Thomas P. Brody, said that pyromaniacs were especially active at full moons. In fact, "Certain districts where pyromaniacs are suspected of setting fires are always placed under special surveillance," Brody said.[16] (A few years before that, authorities in a township not far from New York City had sought a firebug "whose madness apparently came from the moon," because each time the moon reached the first quarter, some major structure in the town was burned, according to a study in the *American Journal of Psychiatry.*)[17]

Bartenders get to see their fill of the full moon's intoxication. Ronald Ross, for example, at The Last Hurrah, a swanky saloon in Boston's posh Parker House hotel, has said, "You see it every time. Just one drink brings it out. Everybody's louder, more aggressive, and, as they drink, progressively crazier."[18]

Hospital workers can also be counted on to add their voices to the lunacy litany. An emergency medical technician who rides an ambulance in Boston told one reporter that at full moons he prepares for "the physically and emotionally traumatized victims of shootings and knifings . . . not just for the usual cuts and bruises. . . ."[19] A hospital emergency room attendant in Portland, Oregon, said she anticipates a sudden increase in bloodshed from domestic quarrels and what she described as "weird admissions."[20]

The collective impression of these urban gladiators and saviors is only reinforced by the list of full-moon victims compiled by journalist Collie Small:

"Jesus Christ was crucified under a full moon. Julius Caesar was stabbed to death in the same phase of the moon. President Abraham Lincoln was assassinated three days before the full moon had peaked.

"Alexander II of Russia was assassinated while the moon was full, as were Russian war minister Leon Trotsky, UN Palestine mediator Count Folke Bernadotte, King Abdul ibn Hussein of Jordan, Mexican President Francisco Madero, Austrian Chancellor Engelbert Dollfuss and Dominican dictator Rafael Trujillo Molina. . . ."[21]

Small also wrote, "Japanese atrocities in the Mindanao concentration camps in World War II were said by survivors to increase both in savagery and fiendish ingenuity at the time of a full moon.

"The My Lai massacre of twenty-two South Vietnamese men, women and children in the Vietnam War occurred during a full moon."[22]

Her most graphically horrifying example, however, involved tragedy inflicted by the victims themselves. The scene was a soccer stadium in Lima, Peru, where rioting erupted on May 24, 1964, "the world's worst sports-oriented disaster." Small described it:

"Peru was playing Argentina with Argentina leading 1–0. There were about five minutes left to play when an Argentine player inadvertently kicked the ball into his own goal. Presumably that tied the score, but the referee disallowed the point, ruling that Peru had been guilty of excessive roughness. Suddenly hell broke loose.

"Tens of thousands of furious fans streamed onto the field, screaming epithets. One policeman was killed and his dog dismembered by flying knives. A second policeman was thrown from high in the stands and killed. Scores of people were trampled to death or smothered.

"When the melee was finally stilled, bodies were found piled 10 feet high in front of the locked gates. All told 328 persons died in the riot while a full moon looked down impassively."[23]

The full moon may have illuminated a path for the most infamous murderer in recent days, New York's Son of Sam. The killer struck on eight nights between July 29, 1976, and July 31, 1978, and five of those evenings were during (or, in one case, right before) the full or new moon phases.[24]

The full moon's murderous notoriety was already well established when it was accused of having had a bloodstained hand in one of the most sensational murders of the Roaring Twenties. Psychiatrist Douglas Kelley, in the *Psychoanalytic Review,* said, "In New York's Snyder-Gray murder case, it was alleged that the full moon caused Ruth Snyder to lose part of her senses."[25] Although Ruth Snyder's attorneys apparently did not base her defense on that, they might as well have, because nothing else seemed capable of saving her. Snyder and her lover, Henry Judd Gray, a corset designer and salesman, were convicted of murdering Mrs. Snyder's husband, Albert, the art editor of *Motor Boating* magazine, on March 20, 1927,[26] early in the full moon phase.

Blonde, blue-eyed Ruth Snyder and her dapper, poised playmate said they had plotted editing Albert out of their lives for six months before their opportunity finally came in the wee hours of Sunday that March morning.[27,28] The Snyders had spent the previous evening partying with friends, and Ruth Snyder saw to it that Albert drank much more than usual. When they got home shortly before 2 A.M., the forty-five-year-old editor went right to bed. His thirty-two-year-old wife waltzed downstairs to rendezvous with Gray.

When they returned upstairs together, Ruth tested the door of her nine-year-old daughter's bedroom to make sure it was locked, then the two conspirators tiptoed into the master bedroom. The end was quick. Gray stuffed a piece of fabric soaked with chloroform over the sleeping man's nose and mouth, then clubbed his head with a heavy iron window sash.

Albert Snyder, with two gashes in his skull, was next garrotted with heavy picture hanging wire so he would appear to be the victim of burglars. The wire necktie was certainly tight enough; it tore two patches of skin from his neck. Police would find his bedsheets piled in a heap and stained with blood.

The police became suspicious, though, as soon as they began their investigation. An autopsy revealed traces of the chloroform, and detectives said the phony signs of forced entry and theft were pathetically amateurish, totally unconvincing. Jewels, for example, that Ruth Snyder would claim were stolen were hidden under a mattress, where police quickly found them.

Ruth Snyder was the first to confess. She and her beau went to the electric chair at Sing Sing on January 12, 1928.[29]

Now the question is, Is all of this coincidence? Or do all of these murders, riots, robberies, and torch jobs happen at the full moon because the full moon causes them? Are all those cops, fire fighters, bartenders, and hospital workers wrong? Or *should* Ruth Snyder have based an insanity defense on the full moon, in similar fashion to what Herman Heppel, Alan Witcomb, and—way back in our first chapter—Charles Hyde did?

A growing body of evidence suggests she should have. One after another, serious, valid, scientific studies are showing an astounding correlation between lunar phases and human mayhem. If the moon is not actually making harmless men and women into vicious monsters, it certainly seems to be triggering people who are ready to go—turning the Dr. Jekylls of this world into Mr. Hydes.

The most important and probably best known of these studies demonstrated a correlation between full moons and the murder rates in two metropolitan areas, Greater Miami and Greater Cleveland. This is the inquiry performed by Dr. Arnold L. Lieber, a psychiatrist, and clinical psychologist Carolyn Sherin, both of Miami.[30] They found that murders over a fifteen-year period (1956 to 1970) in Dade County, Florida, clustered dramatically around full moons. In fact, when they subjected their data to mathematical analysis, they found that the correlation was, in scientific jargon, "statistically significant"; that is, a correlation much stronger than chance alone should allow, a correlation that presumably indicates exactly what it seems to, that full moons somehow cause murders. And there was more. They also found a statistically significant cluster right after the new moon. Just as the moon creates the highest ocean tides of each lunar month at full and new moons, Lieber and Sherin had found an ominous surge in murder at syzygy as well. They also recorded smaller peaks at the first and third quarters. It was as though killers were setting their schedules by the moon.

When Lieber and Sherin turned their attention to Ohio's Cuyahoga County, they obtained similar results. Again, they found four peaks each lunar month in the murder rate, this time over a thirteen-year span (1958 to 1970), although none as tall as Miami's. And again the tallest peak was after the full moon. One thing, however, puzzled them. The peaks were shifted so they each occurred after the quarters, rather than right at them.

Lieber and Sherin had to wonder whether this deviation knocked the apparent full-moon rhythm right out of orbit. A trip to the research library, though, suggested just the opposite. What they found, in a study of the metabolic activity of hamsters by scientists at Northwestern University,[31,32] was a lunar pattern strikingly similar to the Cuyahoga murder pattern. Significantly, they noticed that Cleveland and Evanston, Illinois (Northwestern's location), are on nearly the same geographic latitude. Here was evidence that the delay between a full moon and its effect varies according to the distance from the Equator. The delay appeared to be consistent and predictable, two crucial criteria for scientific verification.

In addition to these monthly rhythms, Lieber has pointed out another cycle, one following the lunar day. In a 1973 paper published under his name alone, Lieber reported that a review of the murders in Greater Miami during 1969 and 1970 revealed that statistically significant clusters occurred at *lunar* noon and midnight (that is, when the moon is highest in the sky and lowest beneath the horizon, respectively, in its daily circuit), the "times of maximum daily gravitational attraction."[33] By the same token, the fewest homicides occurred at moonrise and moonset.[34] Lieber interpreted this as added evidence in support of a "biological tides" theory explaining the moon's influence.[35]

Lieber mentioned another piece of evidence in his earlier work with Sherin. Murders committed when the moon is full or new and at perigee were "often of a particularly bizarre or ruthless nature."[36] An article in *Science Digest* elaborated on this observation by Lieber:

> In September and October of 1970 the number of homicides in Dade County was double the usual monthly average. The following examples typify many of the crimes which occurred during this period:
>
> On September 22 police were notified that several parts of a dismembered body had been found along a major highway. From fingerprints the victim was identified but neither his head nor the murderer were found.
>
> On September 23, Socrates 'Shorty' Johns, a 69-year-old retired racing driver, was held up by three men while working in his son's tire store. Johns resisted, was shot and wounded. He then ran from behind the counter and chased the three out of the store and down the street whereupon one of the assailants turned and fired again, killing Johns.
>
> That same evening Gyorgy Virag was leaving a restaurant with three companions when they were confronted by two men with a shotgun. One shouted, 'This is a holdup,' Virag then yelled, 'I'll get our gun,' and ran toward his car. He was attacked and clubbed by one of the assailants, then shot in the head.
>
> The next day, September 24, Debby Oldham, 23, was working as a barmaid at the Casino Bar when two men entered and ordered sandwiches. Then one drew a pistol. Miss Oldham began to run about hysterically, waving her arms and screaming. She was shot four times by the panicky gunmen before the pair fled the scene.[37]

Lieber and Sherin's work was a breakthrough, but it is no longer unique. A 1974 study of crime patterns in New York City confirmed the Miami and Cleveland results. Doris Ann Stahl, a graduate student at John Jay College of Criminal Justice, found a significant increase in crime at full moons in two "representative" police precincts, the 110th and the 32nd.[38] In fact, Stahl's investigation covered a wider range of violent behavior than Lieber and Sherin's had. Stahl found that robberies, assaults, and motor vehicle thefts all peaked at full moons over the 24 months studied.[39] The single exception was in the first year surveyed, 1971, when robberies were ever so slightly higher at new moon than full moon in the 110th precinct.[40] Arson also followed a monthly lunar pattern. In 1971 it peaked at full moon and last quarter; the next year it rose dramatically before and after full moon until it again peaked at last quarter.[41]

Stahl took the shrewd precaution of isolating other possible influences. She compared the patterns of crime in each category to weather, and found no correlation whatsoever.[42] She did the same thing with the days of the week, and again found no correlation.[43] The only variable crimes were following was the moon's motion.

Two years after Stahl's study appeared, more concurring research emerged. Jodi Tasso and Elizabeth Miller, of the Department of Psychology at Edgecliff College in Cincinnati, Ohio, found that "eight categories of rape, robbery and assault, burglary, larceny and theft, auto theft, offenses against family and children, drunkenness, and disorderly conduct occurred significantly more frequently during the full moon phase than at other times" in metropolitan Cincinnati.[44]

Tasso and Miller found this pattern by screening police data for 34,318 criminal offenses in Hamilton County during 1969. They also found a fascinating underlying periodicity. Crimes of personal violence against family members and children showed the largest clusters around full moons, whereas offenses against material objects—like auto theft—formed smaller clusters, although they still clearly corresponded to full moons with statistical significance.[45]

There was also a study done by the Philadelphia police department in 1961, which confirmed the impression of some seventy officers working the department switchboards that there is an increase in such violent crimes as pyromania, homicide while drunk, destructive driving, and kleptomania when the moon is full.[46]

Frightening as these lunar patterns of violent crime in large metropolitan areas are, a much smaller group has displayed the most chilling cycle of full-moon violence. And those who witnessed it not only tolerated it but often applauded!

It seems that penalty minutes in the now-defunct World Hockey Association (which was partially absorbed by the National Hockey League in 1979) soared like the cow jumping over the moon on nights of the full moon. The number of minutes that players spent in the penalty box during the 1976–77 season skyrocketed by 33.6 percent at the full moon, compared to the night before.[47,48]

This pattern was discovered by Frank Polnaszek, chief statistician of the league. "I was listening to a radio show and they were talking about the effect of the full moon on people's behavior," Polnaszek told Allen Abel, of the *Toronto Globe and Mail.* "It got me to thinking about how the full moon might affect hockey players. I figured that it wouldn't show up in the scores of games and number of goals, because both teams would be affected equally, but that it might show up in the number of penalty minutes."[49]

Indeed it did. Polnaszek found that there was an average of 26.1 minutes in penalties in each game. On nights when the moon was as full and round as a hockey puck, though, there were 34.8 minutes on average, and twenty-four hours later penalty minutes subsided to 28.6 minutes. Such tidal waves of violence were impossible to ignore. The *Courant* of Hartford, Connecticut, whose Whalers had played the Houston Aeros on the full-moon night before, began its report of the February 4, 1977, game this way: "It was a long, drawn-out World Hockey Association game, thanks to referee Steve Dowling, lasting nearly three hours."[50] The beleagured Mr. Dowling was forced to interrupt the game with his whistle for no less than twenty-seven so-called "minor" penalties and one five-minute "major." Players served almost as many minutes in the penalty box, fifty-nine, as there are minutes in a game.

Although Polnaszek studied only the WHA, there is no reason to doubt that full moons affect the National Hockey League (NHL) as well. Take the NHL Boston Bruins, who were doing battle with the Atlanta Flames the same night the Whalers warred with Houston. That game featured a wild bench-clearing brawl, which is hockey's version of gang warfare, assorted skirmishes, and a total of 119 minutes in penalties—only 60 seconds shy of being twice as many minutes of penalties as playing time.[51,52]

Like the War in Vietnam, hostilities between the two ice clubs escalated inexorably. In the first period the Bruins were penalized when their goalie conked an opponent on the head with his stick, an indiscretion formally designated as "highsticking." Another Bruin was soon sent to the penalty box for tripping and beefing to the ref. In the second period, a Boston player was assessed for tripping and for unsportsmanlike conduct. Minutes later yet another Bruin was whistled for "spearing"—using his stick like a cattle prod upon the tender ribs of an opponent. Then came the slugfest that Boston reporter D. Leo Monahan described as "a wild donnybrook."[53] Bruins goalie Gerry Cheevers skated behind his net to clear a loose puck idling along the boards. Players usually refrain from mauling a goaltender who meanders from his goal, but on this night Flames rookie Willi Plett rammed Cheevers against the boards. In an instant players were off their respective benches, battling on the ice. Boston's ace defenseman, Brad Park, was the first Bruin to Cheever's rescue, then brawlers Stan Jonathan and Terry O'Reilly both tore into the big Atlantan. John Wensink and lanky Ed Kea of the Flames got into one of those fights in which each man tries to hamstring the other by pulling his jersey over his head, then batter the blind man senseless; even second-string Bruins goalie Gilles Gilbert exchanged punches with an Atlantan, bearded Daniel Bouchard. No one was declared winner of the fight, but Atlanta won the hockey game, 6 to 3.[54,55,56]

In his Hartford, Connecticut, office after the season, Polnaszek learned more about lunar rhythms.

"All summer," Abel wrote, "as the WHA tottered on the brink of extinction, Polnaszek was stretched out on the floor with game statistics on one side of him and the Farmer's Almanac, Dr. Zolar's Pocket Guide to the Stars and the latest predictions of Bernice Bede Osol on the other. The merger negotiations [between the WHA and NHL] were a distant distraction as Polnaszek made another startling discovery."[57]

What he discovered was that "on the night of the new

moon, with just that big, black thing going across the sky, penalties were *down* 30.4 per cent from the night before, and the next night, they increased by 17.5 per cent."[58]

Writing facetiously, Abel suggested a simple way to reduce this banditry on blades. Players should either wear a clove of garlic around their necks, "the traditional method of repelling werewolves," or the league should "appoint an Official Augurer to slaughter chickens and read their entrails before each game. If the fowl predicts fouls, the game shall be cancelled."[59]

Fine, for fun and games. But where does that leave the police in Miami, Cleveland, New York, Philadelphia, and Cincinnati? And your town?

22

Madness

Mr. L. was cracking up. Shortly before his graduation from high school, the world began to look as remote and two-dimensional to him as the images on a television screen. Then he became afraid he was nothing more than a character in one of his father's dreams who would disappear should his father awake. An imaginary friend, "Eddie," began to keep Mr. L. company in his increasingly isolated world.

Somehow, Mr. L. also managed to elope with his fiancée from that world out there, and he entered college, where he excelled at mathematics but avoided classmates. It was just Mr. L., his wife, and "Eddie." A most private *ménage à trois.*

Mr. L., whose psychiatrist does not reveal his full name, found it harder to concentrate. He became depressed. He gained weight. He began to perform compulsive rituals. He was hospitalized twice and subjected to shock treatments both times. Although his depression cleared temporarily, he dropped out of college. Then things got bad.

Mr. L. spent one afternoon alone in his apartment, singing, dancing, and writing notes to himself on a blackboard there. "[H]e would get certain words in his mind and repeat them over and over, rhyming them with other words in his mind," his psychiatrist wrote in a study published in the journal, *Psychiatric Annals.* "He also became enveloped by a feeling of being watched from somewhere in the living room, and while in the shower he imagined people calling his name."[1]

He was given medication so he could sleep at night. He was "grossly overweight." His mood swung in dizzying arcs from one extreme to another. "[S]ome days he would be cheerful and talkative, while on others he was severely depressed and suicidal. He reported self-destructive and violent acts around his apartment, continued feelings of unreality, auditory hallucinations, and violent nightmares. On his 'good days' he was able to pursue his course of home study with excellent discipline and managed to tutor some college students in advanced calculus; except for therapy sessions, however, he did not leave the apartment, with or without his wife."[2]

That is a condition diagnosed on the streets, if not in psychiatric circles, as *the pits.* It was also at this time, however, that his psychiatrist (a prominent New York practitioner and Assistant Professor of Clinical Psychiatry at Columbia University's school of medicine) made the discovery that eventually led to successful treatment. Mr. L. had been on several types of daily medication. After making certain changes, his psychiatrist began to chart the response on a graph. Sure enough, there it was. For four or five days Mr. L.'s depression would subside enough for him to be able to study. Then it would return, like a heavy, dark curtain shutting out the world. The deepest gloom and anguish, though, lasted only a day or so, twenty-four to thirty-six hours, arriving but once a month. And when was that?

Within twenty-four hours of the full moon.[3]

* * *

Mr. L. had no control over the fluctuations of his emotional disturbance. Apparently on its own it followed a lunar timetable, surging at full moons. Moreover, more and more health professionals recognize this lunar influence on human emotions, ranging from Mr. L.'s relatively withdrawn and private turmoil to the violence we saw in the previous chapter.

"[T]hose employed in hospital wards, particularly in mental institutions and those employed on police forces, to a large extent accept the proposition that the levels of activity in their respective and overlapping realms are indeed affected by lunar cycles," wrote biologist Harry D. Rounds, in his 1975 study (See chapter 25) of why human, cockroach, and mouse hearts beat faster at full moons.[4]

Concurring voices can be heard throughout the realm of medicine. Health workers in Boston, the medical mecca of America, are certainly no exception. Eleven members of the emergency room staff at Boston City Hospital (BCH) recently told the *Boston Globe* that "full moon nights are busier and crazier than normal nights."[5] No one else on the staff said full moon nights were the same as any other, and few of the eleven had believed in such a full-moon influence before joining the emergency room staff.

"There was a time when I didn't believe it because all my conditioning and education had told me that anything that can't be substantiated should be disregarded," an ambulance driver told the reporter.

"But since my emergency room service (which began three years ago), my experience tells me that on the night of the full moon, I have to be prepared for more trauma by violence and more psychiatric disorders.

"On the night of a full moon, what I see are not the accidents between a person and a fixed object, but the results of person-to-person problems. At one time, I was not a believer. Now I am."[6]

A veteran nurse at the BCH emergency room said it seems drunks stagger in "drunker than usual," and other workers said that a whole maternity ward's worth of mothers would all come in to deliver at once.[7]

At Project Place, a crisis center catering mostly to youths in Boston, a staff member doing graduate work in psychology at Boston University said that a review of the records of more than 100,000 telephone hotline calls received during an eighteen-month period revealed an increase in the "intensity" of calls at the full moon, including more suicide threats "and situations where there was more emotion than usual coming out."[8]

Dr. Thomas Stair reported something similar in the *New England Journal of Medicine.* After analyzing admissions for traumatic injuries and psychiatric problems over twelve lunar months in 1975 at Symmes Hospital in the Boston suburb of Arlington, he wrote that no significant full-moon pattern emerged; night admissions showed only a slight increase at full moons. Nevertheless, he agreed with one emergency room colleague who insisted that patients who come at the full moon seem "loonier than usual."[9]

A twelve-year veteran of nursing home work has noticed that "the elderly patients [who are already] confused and senile are definitely affected by the full moon. They become very restless and difficult to handle starting from three days before the full moon to about three days after." This woman felt confident that other nursing home workers have observed the same thing: "This is not only my opinion. I'm sure if you questioned others who work with this type of patient they would agree with me. . . . Also, a friend of mine is a Special Education teacher and she also believes that it affects her children that she teaches."[10]

Nor is Greater Boston unique. Dr. Arnold Lieber (who studied the lunar patterns to murder rates in metropolitan Miami and Cleveland) has said that in his own psychiatric practice in Miami many of his manic-depressive patients would call around the same time, at full moons, with similar feelings of restlessness and depression despite ongoing lithium medication which stabilized them on other days.[11]

A Manhattan psychiatrist wrote that a colleague studying sexual cycles in men found that two of his patients suffered episodes of abnormal behavior or emotions at full moons.[12] A Washington, D.C., physician thought enough of his own similar experience to report it in the *Psychoanalytic Review.*[13] And a Tallahassee surgeon suggested the full moon's influence may be restricted to those people already on the psychiatric brink. He cited an observation by one Dr. Bolton, whom he identified as head of the Psychiatric Department at Temple University's school of medicine: "It has long been accepted by psychiatrists that the moon is known to have a serious effect on the minds of persons afflicted with nervous disorders."[14]

The conventional wisdom is quick to blame such impressionistic reports on the power of suggestion: knowing it is the day of a full moon, a doctor, nurse, or counselor becomes more conscious of normal amounts of aberrant behavior or emotional disturbance. And that is precisely the reception that unsubstantiated reports would deserve. But what makes these informal observations all the more fascinating is that a mass of solid research has now accumulated, mostly in the last three decades, that says these isolated examples are samples of reality; they are the truth rather than fragments of a modern mythological mosaic.

Roger Osborn, for example, reported in the *Journal of Psychiatric Nursing and Mental Health Services* (*JPN*) in 1968 that he had found a statistically significant plurality of patients admitted to two psychiatric hospital facilities in Ohio during the full moon phases of 1965.[15] Osborn, a Clinical Instructor in Psychiatry at Ohio State University College of Medicine, first examined the dates that 1,043 patients had been admitted to Upham Hall, a 125-bed facility run by the medical school. Then he made a shrewd analytic maneuver. "If the moon phase does influence psychiatric hospital admissions," he wrote, "any moon-influenced disturbance might not be recognized as serious enough to warrant hospitalization until it had existed for a few days. If so, the higher admission rate would trail the actual moon phase."[16] Thus, Osborn decided to measure the full moon's influence by giving hospital admissions time to reflect that influence. He defined the full-moon "phase" as the latter half of the actual phase and the first half of the next phase, and so on for each phase.

Osborn's insight was accurate. He found 315 admissions during the full-moon "phase," fully 35.6 percent more than the first "quarter," 32.3 percent in front of the new moon "phase," and 27.5 percent beyond the last "quarter." The differences were clearly significant. The probability of such differences happening by chance alone were less than one in a thousand.[17] Moreover, Osborn noted that the socioeconomic segment of society served by the hospital was in no way different from society at large, and that most of the increased full-moon admissions were for psychotic disorders and transient situational personality disorders, as opposed to, say, disorders brought on by physiological changes (i.e., a brain tumor).[18]

That wasn't all that Osborn discovered, though. He next

turned to the medical school's Special Care Units, which are "used for particularly disturbed patients or those patients who are overly disturbing to other patients. Some typical symptoms are extreme suicidal tendencies, gross psychotic behavior, embarrassing regression, hyperactivity, aberrant psychotic sexual behavior, overaggressiveness and hostility, acting out behavior, and extreme anxiety. Assignment to Special Care is typically used only as a last resort."[19] The only complete records then available were for female admissions during the first nine lunar months of 1965. Reviewing them, Osborn found that admissions were highest in the last quarter, but that this was "consistent with the previous findings" because patients were not admitted to Special Care until they had already been admitted to Upham Hall. In other words, the symptoms entitling them to enter Special Care had been observed before the last quarter, in the full moon phase.[20,21]

Sheldon Blackman and Don Catalina found a similar trend in patient contacts at the North Richmond Community Mental Health Center on Staten Island, New York, in the early '70s. They analyzed the number of patients served in the clinic's emergency room from August 1971 to July 1972 and found a clear full-moon pattern. One aspect of this pattern was that far more patients "were seen on the day of the full moon at this Emergency Service than in the ten-day period before that day."[22] And, reminiscent of the Osborn study, Blackman and Catalina found a similar number of patient contacts after as well as during the full moon, which they suggested "may be the result of a residual full-moon effect, that gradually dissipates."[23]

Alex D. Pokorny (Chief of the Psychiatry and Neurology Service of the Veterans Administration Hospital in Houston, Texas, and Professor of Psychiatry at Baylor University medical school) conducted a survey which disclosed several apparent lunar patterns to admissions to the psychiatric unit of a large Veterans Administration hospital over the three years 1959 to 1961. (Presumably for reasons of patient privacy, Pokorny identified the hospital only as a 400-bed facility, without specifying whether it was the Houston VA Hospital.) There was a total of 4,937 admissions, which Pokorny first analyzed according to actual lunar phases, then by Osborn's method of delayed phases.

For 1961 alone, he found a statistically significant correlation between admissions and both the actual and "lagged" phases.[24] For 1959 and 1961 there was a strong correlation falling just below statistical significance for lagged phases.[25]

Admissions for all three years during lagged full moon phases were above what should have occurred merely by chance.[26]

A study reported to the Virginia Medical Society in 1951 showed related admission patterns for men and women, both following a lunar route. Dr. Eleanor Beamer-Maxwell, of Eastern State Hospital in Williamsburg, Virginia, and Mrs. Hannah F. M. Hendrick, a retired mathematical astronomer of the U.S. Naval Observatory, analyzed a decade's worth of admissions to a psychiatric hospital and found that female patients entered most frequently on the day of the full moon; most men were admitted just after new moon, but the second largest number of men went in after the full moon.[27,28]

Nor are our neighbors north of the border immune from the full moon's influence. A Canadian study published in *JPN* documented the lunar cycle of admissions to Lakeshore Psychiatric Hospital in Toronto. Upon examining the hospital's telephone inquiry and admission records, "It was found," wrote Sheldon H. Geller and Herbert W. Shannon, "that both the number of new patients presenting themselves for assessment and the number of new patients desirous of continuing with out-patient treatment after the initial assessment, increased the closer the moon was to its full phase."[29]

Geller and Shannon were as clear as possible about what their work demonstrated. "[T]he notion that deviant and violent human behavior occurs most frequently when the moon is full . . . can be defined as . . . the Transylvanian hypothesis" because of its association with folklore, they wrote.[30] Thus, given the trend of hospital admissions: "The results of the present study are consistent with the Transylvanian hypothesis that abnormal behavior is more likely to occur during the full moon."[31]

Researchers along North America's southern border found

practically the same exact pattern. Gerald N. Weiskott and George B. Tipton studied admissions to all Texas state hospitals during the nine months of 1974, January to September. Twelve thousand ninety-three patients were counted, and Weiskott and Tipton found a statistically significant majority had been admitted during the fortnight around full moons.[32]

Of course, such statistical surveys are not unique to the latter half of the twentieth century, as an 1843 study published in *The Lancet* illustrates.[33] T. Laycock referred to a survey in Massachusetts (a state often in the vanguard of social welfare innovation in the United States) which had demonstrated a lunar rhythm to psychiatric hospital admissions. Records showed that admissions to the State Lunatic Asylum in Worcester, Massachusetts, ebbed and flowed with the moon like ocean tides, surging most at the new moon, the full moon's alter ego.

* * *

Suddenly, the casual observations about full-moon frenzy that we are so used to hearing, but equally accustomed to treating with skepticism, take on new authority. Considered in view of this growing wave of documentation of moon's might, they have a louder ring of truth to them.

Doris Ann Stahl's comment, in her study of police administration in New York, that many police patrolmen, state police officials, psychologists, and a teacher of neurologically disturbed children agree there is "an increase of deviant behavior on the days of the full moon as well as on the contiguous days"[34] makes more sense than ever.

The observation by a small claims court clerk in Boston that complaints against dating services seem to run in batches at each full moon[35] no longer sounds like some line overheard at a singles bar.

It is easier to understand how more than 500 readers could provide first-hand accounts of the moon's effect on them or their relatives when a science reporter for the London *Daily Express* solicited information in the mid-1960s.[36]

Suddenly, we just *know* that a certain FBI agent in San Francisco has company at a lot of FBI offices around the country. He's the agent who takes routine telephone calls for the office, and every full moon he gets them from people who believe they are being "watched." That Bay City agent gets them all, too. Everyone from street winos to briefcase-toting business types who complain they are being staked out by "the Communists, the neighbors, or even creatures from outer space who are sending rays up through their pillows, keeping them from sleeping at night."[37]

A cautious little voice in the back of your head stops whispering, "That's jive!" when you read that Al "Jazzbeaux" Collins, the host of a weekend all-night talk show on KGO radio in San Francisco, once told a reporter that he gets weird calls on the full moon.[38] Collins recalled the night in the midst of one of the West Coast's droughts several years ago that a female caller assured him on the air that frogs attract water. Next thing he knew, calls were coming in from places like Ketchum, Idaho; Pasco, Washington; and Williams, Oregon, from people wanting to know where they could get frogs.[39]

And that isn't just isolated California craziness, either. Darrell Martinie, Boston's radio astrologer known to thousands of New Englanders as the "Cosmic Muffin," says the number of calls he gets from anxious people triples at each full moon, and they come from as far away as California and Europe.[40]

We're certainly not as skeptical about what Sylvia C., who has taught grade-school in Syracuse, New York, in New Hampshire, and towns in Eastern Massachusetts, has to say about youngsters. "Third graders, whom I taught for about eight years, had more accidents and fights during full moons. Generally, kids who were more prone to violence or lots of activity seemed most active or violent at full moons. I'd go into the teachers' room and say my kids are crazy today, and the other teachers would say the same thing. I used to joke that there's a full moon causing it all, but I don't [joke] now. There's definitely something to it. I began to believe it after seeing this go on for about six years."[41]

Is there a tavern-keeper in the country who would not toast what Marvin Feiden, a longtime bartender at Charlie Brown's in Manhattan's Pan Am Building, told *The New York Times* in 1978? "Customers do the craziest things for no reason—

scream, sing at the top of their voices. Even couples who are lovey-dovey all the time, comes a full moon and one of them will haul off and smack the other and get into terrible fights."[42]

And why doubt the "veteran Veteran's Cab driver" in San Francisco who told that city's *Chronicle* that people are more likely to imagine a cab is late when they call one at the full moon. Also, like bartender Feiden, this Frisco cabbie said, "We have people who climb in the cab together, all friendly, and within three blocks they are fighting and hitting each other. Our no-go rate, the phony calls, shoots sky high. You better believe it. When that moon is full, I know it."[43]

C. Eugene Emery, Jr., of the Providence *Journal-Bulletin*, took his own look at aberrant behavior in 1977 in that Rhode Island community and found few clues pointing at the full moon, but plenty pointing at its ghost, the new moon.[44] The police blotter showed reports of all "incidents" clustering roughly four times, once at the start of each lunar phase, with the second largest group right after the new moon. Rape reports showed a minor peak at the new moon and a major one shortly before it. Emergency admissions to the Institute of Mental Health in Providence reached a minor peak exactly at the new moon and a major one afterwards; in fact, tandem clusters occurred around each phase. Similarly, cases of sexual assault on minors, which were reported to Women and Infants Hospital, bunched after the start of each phase. There were practically none on the day of the new moon, but a rash shortly after. Reports to the police department of "Assaults" reached a minor plateau at the new moon, but pinnacled before it.

All of a sudden, we're not so quick to dismiss as a lunatic the hospital guard encountered by medical historian George Sarton on a winter visit to St. Vincent in the British West Indies in 1936. Sarton had sailed from Boston aboard the Canadian ship *Lady Drake*, which reached the island on December 15. At the first good opportunity, Sarton set out to visit "Fort Charlotte upon Berkshire Hill, one of the many fortified places established during the eighteenth century in the West Indies when the peace of those heavenly islands was frequently troubled by wars. Some of the old military buildings are now used as hospices for the poor of the colony, one of them being devoted to the insane."[45] It was at that facility that Sarton was guided on a tour by a guard who said that the patients "were generally easy to handle, except about the time of the full Moon when special precautions had to be taken in order to restrain them."[46]

And what do we make of reports that up to the year 1808 psychiatric patients at England's Bethlehem Hospital "were bound, chained, and even flogged at particular phases of the Moon, to prevent the accession of violence"?[47,48] Obviously, the treatment was cruel and an act of ignorance. The staff's timing, however, was not foolish at all.

Just ask "Mr. L."

23

Suicide

Mecca may be the religious center of the Islamic world, but Tehran is the mecca for suicide. In the midst of a heat wave several years ago, more than a hundred people tried to take their own lives during a single 24-hour period. Many succeeded. Reports of that black day described the victims as mostly young people who had failed either in love or in school. Most reports failed to mention that the moon was full.[1]

America has its own realm of fanaticism. It's called California. Between April 1976 and April of the next year, nine people committed suicide by leaping off the Golden Gate Bridge at a full moon. Twenty-three people altogether that year had taken their lives by jumping from the famed span.[2] Simple arithmetic tells you that that is lots more leapers at the full moon than chance alone would push over the edge. For example, if you compute a year as thirteen lunar months (actually, it is about twelve-and-three-quarters synodic months), any given day stands about a one-in-twelve chance of hosting a Golden Gate suicide. That means the ghoulish odds favor only one full-moon suicide each year, let alone the nine that in fact occurred.

Tehran and San Fran. East and West. Two cities a world apart, culturally as well as geographically. Yet both illustrate the same grim reality that pays no heed to political borders.

Suicide, like other expressions of mental illness and distress we've examined, shows a lunar inspiration. Take what investigators in Erie County, New York, found. When David Lester, Gene Brockopp, and Kitty Priebe, of Buffalo's Suicide and Crisis Service, took a look at the 399 suicides in their area during the five years from 1964 through 1968, they found that more people took their own lives around full moons in four of the five years than chance should have accounted for.[3]

Then there was the research by Paul and Susan Jones. Poring through records in the Cuyahoga County, Ohio, coroner's office, they found 928 suicides during the four years from 1972 through 1975. They defined the full and new moons as the calendar days of the full or new moon plus the day before and after; that is, each was defined as a three-day "window," a common and valid statistical device. The picture that emerged was striking. For 1972 and 1974 the number of full-moon suicides was more than should have happened by chance, but the figure did not reach statistical significance.[4] New-moon suicides, though, were way above what bad luck alone would explain for the entire four-year period. One hundred twenty-nine people killed themselves at new moons, 43 percent more than "should" have, a figure which is both dismal and statistically significant.[5]

The Joneses double-checked their results to be sure their figures were not reflecting some underlying influence. (Researchers have found that illness and suicide occasionally follow weekly, holiday, and certain weather patterns.) They compared suicide dates against the holidays of New Year's, Memorial Day, Independence Day, Labor Day, Thanksgiving, and Christmas as well as individual days of the week, months, and even years. None revealed a suicide rhythm working its way in disguise into their lunar data.[6]

A University of Nevada at Reno study in 1977 reminds us that wine, women, and gambling do nothing to mitigate the full moon's traumatic effect. Researchers Susan De Voge and James K. Mikawa decided to see whether they could find a relationship between suicide *threats* and lunar phases. (As they pointed out, research published in 1965 had explained that there are important differences between people who commit suicide and those who merely attempt it, perhaps without hoping to succeed.)

With that in mind, they examined records for the 7,844 calls made to the Suicide Prevention and Crisis Call Center, a 24-hour telephone hotline service in Reno, serving northern Nevada. The calls spanned a two-year period. They found the number of calls involving suicide threats was statistically significant at the new moon and first quarter.[7] They also found that calls prompted by nonsuicide crises like family problems, marital fights, and acute depression were most common at the new moon, although not with statistical significance.[8]

Over and over, new and full moons crop up as the favorite times for suicide. When suicide patterns among women only are examined, what emerges is a pattern which seems to be different but actually confirms that new- and full-moon tendency.

First, two researchers found that human emotions turn topsy-turvy Down Under at the first quarter.[9] That was the time of lunar month when a significant plurality of women in metropolitan Melbourne, Australia, tried to commit suicide during 1970 and 1971. Next, two University of Manitoba psychologists tried to see whether they could find the same results in Canada—and succeeded. Records at Winnipeg General Hospital in Winnipeg, Canada, covering the first seven lunar months of 1971, showed unquestionably that the Canadian ladies also preferred the first quarter for suicide attempts (almost all of which, incidentally, involved swallowing poison).[10] Unlike their Aussie sisters, however, many patients of Winnipeg General had taken a stab at suicide right after full moons, though not quite in statistically significant numbers.[11]

At any rate, it was these Canadian researchers, Margitta and K.P. Ossenkopp, who brought these first-quarter tendencies into line with other studies showing a new- and full-moon pattern. They pointed out that the actual attempt at suicide may be merely the tragic climax to psychological events taking place earlier; say, about one week earlier at the new moon! For support, they cited the work of Malek, Gleich, and Maly (see chapter 19) on menstruation, which argued that the onset of menstruation depends on earlier biological events:

> Malek et al. (1962) found a certain relationship between menstruation onset and the lunar cycle. The frequency of menstruations was lowest at new moon, in the first and third quarters menstruation was more frequent, and at full moon the expected frequency was confirmed. These findings are consistent with those of the present study [i.e., Winnipeg suicides] since the mid-luteal phase and consequent increases in attempted suicide correspond to the distribution of menstruation onset. For example, the lowest frequency of self-inflicted injuries occurred just prior to new moon, which corresponds to the midluteal phase for menstruations starting at new moon. The relationship found by Malek et al. (1962) between menstruation onset and the phases of the moon, may also involve a disturbance in tryptophan metabolism which might facilitate menstruation onset.[12]

The Ossenkopps' survey also disclosed one lunar pattern the Australian study did not consider. Both men and women attempted suicide (successfully or not) with statistically significant regularity at lunar perigee and apogee. Two clusters of attempts by females took place just after perigee, one right before perigee, and one occurred during apogee.[13] There were two male clusters right after apogee, two right after perigee, two more during apogee, and one during perigee.[14] Interestingly, Alex Pokorny, in a study published by the *American Journal of Psychiatry* in 1964, cited German research in the 1940s and '50s which indicated "there may be a positive relationship between suicide and the day before the perigee of the moon."[15]

Finally, as with the studies of psychiatric hospital admissions and counseling, there is a study of suicide which demonstrates this subject's ancestry is of an old and proven pedigree. Dr. P. Foissac, president of the Medical Society of Paris, in an 1855 volume of the *St. Louis Medical and Surgical Journal,* discussed "the prize essay" on suicides at Provence and Alençon between 1842 and 1846 by a fellow French physician, Chereau. "The greatest number," wrote Foissac, "were found at the full moon."[16]

24

Biological Rhythms

Hippocrates had a hunch.

Some 2,400 years ago the Greek physician was advising colleagues that "regularity" was a sign of health in people and "irregularity" a warning of illness.[1]

But it was another 100 years before anyone actually measured and defined such a "regular" biological function. With the aid of a water clock, Herophilus of Alexandria counted a patient's pulse.[2] This came shortly after an amateur naturalist made the first study of a plant related to peas that folded its leaves each night and raised them like a sun-worshiper to Sol every morning.[3]

Now we know that people are veritable factories whose assortment of biological machinery chugs, huffs, wheezes, whirrs, and flows to a variety of yearly, monthly, daily, and near-daily rhythms, and that similar things can be said about other animals and plants. Of course, people are used to thinking of the sun as the basic clock for all this activity. After all, the 24-hour cadence of night after day is so obvious. Yet, as we've seen, both the lunar day and month play important roles in biological rhythms. Most that we've examined involve sexual or emotional cycles of one sort or another. In this chapter, we'll consider a number of human cycles better classified under "biological rhythms" in general. That includes everything from cycles of body temperature and sleep, to the cyclical course of disorders like epilepsy, alcoholism, and sleep-walking, to death.

* * *

Man's body responds to a multitude of daily lunar and solar rhythms simultaneously. Often the lunar rhythms become apparent only when the usual course of things is disrupted. One of the most vivid examples of this was brought to light in 1977. A trio of scientists at Stanford University and the Veterans Administration Hospital in Palo Alto, California, reported in *Science* the remarkable case of a blind man, who was otherwise healthy and living normally in society, with circadian (i.e., approximately 24-hour) rhythms matching the lunar day of 24.84 hours.[4] The man, identified only as "J. X.," was twenty-eight years old and a "healthy and active postgraduate student in biostatistics at a major university." Unfortunately, for years he had been plagued by insomnia and excessive daytime sleepiness for two to three weeks at a time, which severely interfered with his work and leisure activities. He had even resorted unsucessfully to hypnotic and stimulant drugs, hoping for a cure. J.X. finally entered a hospital for treatment by the Palo Alto team and it was there that his lunar rhythms were discovered.

He was allowed normal contact with people and provided with whatever he needed to work, eat, sleep, and interact with others. As biological and psychological measurements of him were made at regular intervals, it became apparent that his temperature, alertness, secretion of certain vital hormones, urinary electrolyte excretion, and ability to perform particular tasks all had a 24.9-hour circadian cycle, imitating the length of the lunar, rather than solar, day. Most welcome from his own perspective was the fact that his insomnia disappeared when he was allowed to regulate his days according to 24.9 hours, instead of being forced to conform to the typical 24-hour day. Now, his daily fatigue could correspond to bedtime, while before it was moved away from bedtime by about 50 minutes every day so that sometimes his body wanted to sleep when it was the middle of everyone else's day. As if his lunar synchronization were not clear enough, the researchers treating him noticed that "there was a remarkable coincidence between his sleep onset and a local low tide."[5] Moreover, when he returned home and tried to entrain himself to a socially normal 24-hour day, his body clung to its lunar-day cycle. That, despite the fact that he was given a strict schedule for sleep, meals, and other activity. He was in bed at 11 P.M. with orders to sleep, and his watch, radio, and books were removed. He was prohibited from getting out of bed until 7 A.M. except to urinate, and at seven he *had* to be out of bed; he was forbidden to sleep the rest of the day. All to no avail.[6]

In their *Science* report the Palo Alto investigators cited research by others who had found similar patterns in their own subjects—in one case, a blind person, and in another, a person suffering from manic-depression.[7] The Palo Alto group also double-checked themselves by examining fifty additional blind people, and they found thirty-eight afflicted with a sleep-wake disorder resembling J.X.'s.[8] And while blindness had brought most of the study's subjects to the attention of investigators, the Palo Alto trio emphasized that J.X.'s lunar syndrome is very probably not unique to blind people.[9]

The results of experiments by other scientists concur with that. Jurgen Aschoff, a German researcher, reported in 1965 that he had kept a man in a soundproof underground bunker for twenty-four days. Aschoff's human mole had no way to know what time it was. There were neither clocks nor windows, only light bulbs which were illuminated constantly. All of this subterranean subject's bodily functions remained in synch with each other, but unknown to the man himself he was going to sleep later each "night." He soon was living a "day" with 25.04 hours, roughly the length of a lunar day.[10]

Aschoff also cited similar experiments by J.N. Mills and the French researcher Siffre and his colleagues. Mills kept a man secluded in a cave for three months. For the first three weeks, this cave man's sleep and body functions followed a day 24.1 hours long, but after that he shifted into a 24.7-hour "day."[11] Siffre observed a woman living in one cave for 88 days and a man in another for 125 days. Almost all of the woman's circadian rhythms followed a 24.6-hour cycle; the man's were 24.8, even closer to the lunar lap. Heartbeat for both of them peaked every 24.7 hours.[12]

A physicist living in similarly isolated circumstances was

kept under observation by two other scientists, Jay Shurley, of the University of Oklahoma Medical School, and Chester Pierce, of Harvard Medical School.[13,14] The physicist spent nearly a year "in a high polar desert remote from social activity and alterations in light and darkness." And, like subjects isolated completely in caves and bunkers, his circadian rhythms drifted away from synchronization with the solar day. He began to retire 15 to 30 minutes later each night, awakening that much later each morning. He was soon sleeping during the "day" and active at "night," terms which lose some meaning in the land of alternating perpetual sunlight and night. This drifting continued for 28 days, almost precisely the length of the sidereal month, the time it takes the moon to revolve once around earth. Then, the physicist's sleep schedule suddenly shifted backwards to his original bedtime hour, and his drifting cycle began again.

* * *

There is an even wider array of biological rhythms marching to the beat of the lunar month. One of the most extensively documented rhythms concerns one of man's most dogged and dreaded adversaries, the migraine headache. The Swedish chemist Jons Jacob Berzelius (1779–1848), one of the founders of modern chemistry and a man not inclined toward superstition, was tormented by periodic migraines, which he believed were induced by the full and new moons.[15] In his autobiography, not published until 1901, he wrote that the migraines had been a problem since age 23. They would begin at 8 A.M. on the day of a full or new moon and last until 8 that night. This went on for fourteen years, but his friends simply could not believe it had anything to do with the moon. When he visited Paris in the winter of 1818–19, his friend, the famed mathematician and astronomer Pierre LaPlace, assured him no such connection could exist and even conspired to persuade poor Berzelius of this. The chemist wrote:

> The next time I was seized with the migraine and had prepared myself to remain at complete rest in a dark room, I was disagreeably disturbed by an invitation to dinner with LaPlace,

> which naturally I could not accept. When we met several days afterward he reported that it had been a snare laid for me; that is to say, he desired, with the calendar in hand, to convince me that such a regularity did not exist, at a time when I myself certainly would not have such exact knowledge of the days of the changes of the Moon as at home. I answered him that in this he predicted correctly, but nevertheless, I was unfortunately not left in ignorance of when they occurred.[16]

Periodic asthma is another disease whose attacks have occasionally been described as lunar-monthly. One well-documented case comes from early in the nineteenth century. It was reported by a Dr. Franzieri, physician to what was then the royal court of Spain. For twenty-one years his regal patient's attacks arrived promptly at the full moon and day before the new moon, with relief during the rest of each lunar month. The same pattern applied to a second patient, whose medical history covered several years.[17]

Around the same time, reports in American and British medical journals argued that diseases in tropical climates seem especially susceptible to lunar influence, and for evidence they cited reports from English and native physicians at Minocra (in the Mediterranean), Jamaica, India, and parts of the East Indies.[18,19] They also referred to medical reports about an unidentified "pestilence" which in 1636 ravaged Noyon, a town north of Paris, doing its worst damage around the full and new moons.[20,21] The epidemics of 1692, 1693, and 1694 in the northern Italian community of Modena were also described by physicians on hand as striking hardest around full moons.[22,23]

The same journals also considered case studies of ulcers and an odd urological affliction.[24,25] The subject of one was a "young man of high character" who developed an ulcer high up in his intestine, and a whopping ulcer it was. It burned a passage right through to the outside of this upstanding young man's belly, through which partially digested foods in a mucous soup seeped. He had to put up with this most often "during the waxing moon, but when the moon began to decrease, the excretions almost insensibly diminished." This happened so consistently that physicians could predict the affliction's course by the phase of the moon. The urological ailment concerned a clergyman "who was affected with suppression of urine, accompanied by severe pain in the back, at each period of the full moon." Much to the minister's relief, the pain and symptoms gradually disappeared after each full moon.[26]

Miscellaneous disorders with some sort of lunar-monthly periodism seem as common as germs from a sick man's cough. Clark Timmins cited a report indicating that rheumatism is more painful at the full moon.[27] A sixteenth-century French medical text attributed the successive outbreaks of bubonic plague in the fourteenth century to phases of the moon.[28] And more than one researcher has suggested there is a connection between periodic alcoholism and the moon's phases. "Dipsomania, or periodic alcoholism, was investigated first by Cramer, who almost a hundred years ago cited his famous case in which violent paroxysms of intemperance occurred regularly every four weeks at the new moon," John Oliven wrote in the *American Journal of Psychiatry* in 1943. "Most, a psychiatrist of the same period, reported similar cases. Other instances can be found scattered in the literature. Laycock's case (1843) of intolerance to alcohol at every full moon in a patient otherwise well accustomed to alcohol, deserves special mention."[29,30] Furthermore, we've already come close to belaboring the fact that there isn't a bartender alive who would not swear that the moon and moonshine don't mix well.

Epilepsy is another disability frequently associated with the moon. Edson Andrews, in his study of post-surgical bleeding at full moons (see chapter 25), said he had found numerous references to a correlation between full moons and epileptic attacks in medical literature. "In fact, the word epilepsy comes from the Greek meaning 'to seize upon from the moon.' "[31] One early but authoritative study of epilepsy's cosmic connection was written by Richard Mead, the renowned eighteenth-century British physician. The work, "Concerning the Action of the Sun and the Moon on Animal Bodies," overflowed with such case histories as this one:

"The girl, who was of lusty full habit of body, continued well for a few days, but was at Full Moon again seized with a most violent fit, after which, the disease kept its periods constant and regular with the tides: She lay always speechless during the whole time of flood, and recovered upon the Ebb. . . ."[32]

Dr. T. Laycock, of York, England, wrote that at least one medical authority "recommends the remedies for epilepsy to be given a day or two before the new and full moon, as the disease returns at the periods of the moon, especially the new and full. He mentions another convulsive disease in which the accessions of the fits keep exact pace with the phases of the moon."[33]

Modern practitioners are also aware of the moon's possible influence on this disease. In a 1942 article in *The Psychoanalytic Review,* Douglas Kelley, although skeptical, ticked off a list of patients and symptoms described in the medical literature:

> Kerchringuis tells of a French woman whose face was round and pretty at the full moon but was so disfigured because of changes in her eyes, nose and mouth as to be unable to appear in public during its last quarter; and Bartholin reported a case of a young epileptic female who showed upon her face certain dark spots which changed as regards size and color according to the phases of the moon.
>
> Mead recalls in discussing epilepsy that, "The power of the moon was so greatly felt that it was not difficult to predict the occurrence of the attacks at the approach of the new or full moon." Pison reports a case of hysteria recurring each spring at the full moon and another case of chorea, the paroxysms of which coincided with the changes in the moon and tides. Boyle observed that the most violent cephalalgias; Lepois, cerebral conjestions [*sic*]; and Wepfer, severe apoplexias occurred during the full moon; and Hoffman, Sauvages, Bauce and Pitcain cite many cases of epileptic attacks occurring at this time. . . . [S]imilar findings are given by Rutters in a case of hysteralgia which showed great increase of pain at the new and full moon.
>
> . . . Olbers, an astronomer, writes that he has not "remarked any influence of the moon's phases on accidental injuries in dropsies, in paralysis, in epilepsy, or in any of the neuroses." However, he goes on to say that he cannot deny all human influence in the face of so many supporting authorities and that

> . . . the action of the moon may be more apparent in cases of epilepsy.[34]

In a 1977 magazine interview, Dr. John Gambill, an assistant professor of psychiatry at Boston University School of Medicine, said that a colleague's pet Siberian husky had suffered epileptic fits "only during full moons" ever since being hit by a car a couple of years earlier, and was being treated with conventional anticonvulsant medication.[35] Then there are those notorious agents of the full moon, werewolves. In their case study of a married woman suffering from lycanthropy (see chapter 7), Doctors Rosenstock and Vincent theorize that many werewolves are actually people suffering from psychomotor epilepsy.[36] Werewolf or epileptic, either diagnosis may make full moons the villain.

Sleepwalking has been blamed on the moon so often that it is often referred to as moonwalking, and it is the full moon in particular that attracts these periodic perambulators the way a lighted bulb attracts moths. The first clinical study reported in the modern medical literature was by one Dr. Ebers, of Breslau, Germany (now a part of Poland), in 1838, who described an eleven-year-old boy whose "paroxysms of moon walking" occurred every full moon.[37,38] Much more recently, Edson Andrews cited the work of Ebers and a fellow European, J. Sadger, for support in his study of lunar hemorrhaging.[39] Oliven noted that the anatomist and physiologist K.F. Burdach periodically moonwalked from ages ten to thirteen.[40] And Clark Timmins quoted the psychiatrist, Carleton Simon, who said that moonwalking is more prevalent at full moons, as are several other things we happen to have discussed in earlier chapters: as Simon put it, arousal of sexual organs and mating impulses, and molting by hardshell crabs.[41] He also said that menstruation is "influenced" by the lunar phases.[42]

Sadger's study, "Sleep Walking and Moon Walking," is a comprehensive and impressive work. He places the phenomenon in a conventional medical context, and what it boils down to is that full moons are the catalyst. His case studies are dramatic, to say the least. The sad subject of one was a thirteen-year-old boy living in a lodging house run by an older woman.[43] One morning the youngster awoke, immediately feeling guilty but not knowing why. All he had was "the dark suspicion that I had done something in the night. What, I did not remember. I merely felt stupefied," he recalled during a psychoanalysis session. "Suddenly the boys who slept with me began to laugh, for from under my bed ran a stream of urine. In the night the full moon had shone upon my bed," and the boy had relieved himself in a box of neckties and hats kept under there. After the next full moon, one of his roommates wasn't laughing anymore, because the shoe, so to speak, was on the other foot. The boy had again urinated while moonwalking, but this time into one of his bunkmate's shoes. That made the thirteen-year-old move his bed so the full moon's light could not shine onto it. No matter, for at the third full moon he somnambulated into his landlady's bedroom and tried to rape her.

Another one of Sadger's subjects was a forty-year-old woman who had never consummated her marriage, "although her husband was thoroughly sympathetic to her and very potent," as Sadger put it.[44] The psychiatrist said she had a powerful ambivalence about sex, lusting for it and avoiding it with equal, offsetting energy, which he traced to a traumatic episode in her childhood. Hers was a rural family, and she had shared her parents' bedroom until she was thirteen years old. She had often seen her parents making love, and years later confessed to her psychiatrist that she had frequently fantasized about taking her mother's place. Now, when she was nine or ten years old, her brother became ill with typhoid fever. She and her sisters were sent away to stay with friends or relatives, which is when she met a boy with whom she played sexual games. Sadger doesn't elaborate, but the erotic recreation presumably consisted of some undressing, fondling, relatively innocent sexual show-and-tell. At night, she would dream about him and their games. She said she also began touching and stimulating herself. It was also at this time that she began to have insomnia, lying awake, obsessed with images of her fevered brother. What little sleep she did catch was violated by nightmares of a burglar who attacked her with a knife. Sadger felt she never resolved the conflicts of this experience.

Moonwalking was one way this conflict expressed itself. One moonlit night when she was about ten years old, she got out of bed and woke up to find herself standing between a chest and a desk, drumming the desk with her fingernails as if it were a piano.[45] Years later, after she was married, she woke up in bed, still confused by the lunar trance she had not quite dispelled. "I could not think consciously, I was quite incapable of thought. I knew neither where I was nor what was happening to me; I could remember nothing. I did not know whether I was Jew or Christian, man or woman, a human being or a beast, only stared straight ahead into the next room, at a point of light."[46]

A third patient was a twenty-eight-year-old single woman who first moonwalked at age six.[47] Once, when she was nine years old, she rose from bed and walked, fast asleep, over a chair and piano, heading for a nearby window. Her father interrupted this hike through the house by waking her with a sharp smack on the derriere. Her moonwalking continued periodically, however, until she was sixteen, which is when her menstrual periods began.

Yet another case history is of a twenty-two-year-old woman whose moonwalking Sadger attributes to a sexual fixation. It began at an early age. She slept with both parents until she was seven, and bedtime was frequently preceded by a playful ride on the knee of her father, who affectionately stroked her buttocks at the same time. Once in bed, she would wrap herself "like a serpent" around her mother. When she was only two, this contact actually often led to genital secretion that in a woman would be the lubricating prelude to sexual intercourse. At an age when she must have been oblivious to any pun, she herself described this secretion as "The good comes."[48]

When she was four years old, she was temporarily banished to a crib. She reacted by having nightmares, which made her moan and cry, and which prompted her mother to take her into her parents' bed, where she would wriggle and press herself against her parents until achieving what she later claimed was orgasm. Sadger said she would climax and secrete vigorously, her face would flush, and she would almost lose herself "in her great pleasure."[49]

Her sexual precocity was remarkable. To Sadger, she must have seemed like an infant version of the insatiable Catherine the Great. She recalled being terribly aroused even at age two when she was breast-fed. She connived any way she could for physical contact with her parents. "Even at two or three years old Mother at my entreaties must soothe me to sleep," she wrote in a personal journal. "As we lay together in bed I pretended often to be asleep and reached as if 'in my sleep' after my mother's breast in order to revel in sensation there. Also I often uncovered myself, again ostensibly in my sleep, and laid myself down quite contentedly. Then I awoke my mother by coughing, and when she awoke she stroked me and fondled me, and as was her custom kissed me also upon the genitals. Frequently I stood up in bed between my parents—a forerunner of my later sleep walking—and laid myself down at my mother's feet, asleep as she thought, but in reality awake only with eyes closed. Then I pulled the feather bed away from Mother and blinked at her in order to see her naked body, which I could do better from the foot than if I had lain near her.

"If she awoke she took me up to my place, kissed me repeatedly over my whole body and covered me up. I opened my eyes then as if just awakening, she kissed me on the eyes and said I should go quietly to sleep again, which I then did."[50]

This randiness hardly diminished as she grew older. Sadger wrote that "her greatly exaggerated vaginal eroticism . . . at menstruation was abnormally pleasurably excited."[51] As a young woman in school her attention frequently wandered away from the chalk-dry lessons to wild sexual fantasies.[52]

Sadger suggested that a lamp kept on her parents' night table became associated with these infantile sexual feasts, like a beacon marking the way to her erotic haven. He also suggested that the full moon eventually became a surrogate for this lamp, triggering her desire to return to those simple days of satisfaction. It was a desire she acted out by moonwalking, an unconscious pursuit of a route home. Once, she awoke after a night of somnambulism and realized she was wearing her mother's lingerie.[53] Another time she got out of bed, unbolted her bedroom door, and walked down the hallway to a window overlooking a courtyard. Wearing only a nightgown, she crawled onto the window ledge and sat there with her feet dangling, staring at the moon. She climbed back inside, started back to her bedroom but turned and went downstairs and outside, where she tried unsuccessfully to open the courtyard gate onto the street. She stood there a while before waking up. Then she was frightened and shaking with cold, and rushed back to bed.[54]

When she was eighteen she went for a vacation in the country. She rented a room in a house occupied by her landlady and the woman's twenty-six-year-old daughter. Sure enough, one night she began to moonwalk. She left the house, but here too she could not get past the locked front gate, so she returned to the house. Instead of going back to her own room, though, she walked into her landlady's bedroom, where the daughter also slept. When she pushed the room's door open, both of the other women woke up "and were, as they told me next day, frightened to death."

Word of this little escapade quickly made its way around the nearby village, earning Sadger's patient hostile stares from everyone she encountered. Although she had paid a month's rent in advance, she decided to leave two days later.[55]

Sadger wrote that his patient's moonwalking happened most frequently when she reached "sexual maturity and leads to the most complicated actions before the menses, that is at the time of the greatest sexual excitement. . . . The shining of every light stimulates her sexually, especially that of the moon. The wandering about in her nightgown or in the scantiest clothing is plainly erotically conditioned (exhibition), but [so is] the going about in the ghostly hours . . . finally the being awakened through the softest calling of her name by the mother, with whom alone she stands in a contact like that of a hypnotic somnambulism."[56]

Sadger records that his patient's moonwalking abruptly ceased when she began to date—and sleep with—men.[57]

Even death seems to swing its lethal scythe in tempo with the moon's phases. A Chicago physician, W.F. Petersen, found not long ago that deaths caused by tuberculosis peaked one week after the full moon and waned eleven days before the full moon each and every lunar month.[58] Dr. Michael Allen, of the York Lunatic Asylum in Britain, found that eleven York patients had died at a full moon, fifteen at a new moon, one at a first quarter, and three at a last quarter over the course of the year 1831.[59,60]

Another study of deaths over a forty-three-year period at the same institution also revealed that most mortalities were at new moons. Laycock alludes to a study (without providing details) that indicated that elderly people—specifically, those aged 113 to 169—died more often at the new and full moon than other times of the lunar month.

Laycock also reported that most lives lost in the cholera epidemic in the summer of 1832 in York expired at the full and new moons.[63] And the "pestilence" that ravaged the French town of Noyon in 1636 spread most rapidly at the full and new moons and also took lives most often then.[64]

In hearty contrast to this mortuary math is a survey begun in 1951 by the Frenchman Michel Gauquelin. After reviewing the date and hour of birth of thousands of Western Europeans prominent in the professions, sports, science, military, arts, humanities, politics and so on, Gauquelin concluded that "successful" men and women are usually born shortly after the daily rise over earth's horizon of the moon, Mars, Jupiter, or Saturn.[65] Gauquelin said the birth pattern for these achievers differed significantly from the pattern yielded by his control group.

In his original report of this work, *Les Hommes et les Astres,* Gauquelin even indicated which professions followed which planet's rising. Politicians and writers were born most frequently after moonrise, for example, whereas soldiers, athletes, scientists, physicians, and businessmen popped up most often after the ascension of Mars.[66] Gauquelin also claimed his study revealed a strong tendency for children to be born just after the rise or set of their accomplished parents' birth planets.[67] When the child is born on the day of a geomagnetic disturbance (such as a solar flare), that parental correlation doubles.[68]

Despite its aura of astrology, there may be something to Gauquelin's work. He categorized writers as moon people, and at least one prominent man of letters would have agreed wholeheartedly. That was Thomas Chatterton, the eighteenth-century English poet admired by such luminous literati as Wordsworth, Keats, Coleridge, and Shelley. It was, you see, Chatterton who once told his friends that his own celebrated intellect was more vigorous, not in the morning or after a spot of tea, but at the full moon.[69]

25

Bleeding

Plastic surgeons in ancient India would not operate during a full moon. Instead, they postponed all surgery until after full moons, when the moon would be waning. This was considered simply proper medical procedure, done to avoid unnecessary scarring.[1] Far from being a ridiculous notion confined to primitive practitioners, however, this idea that wounds bleed more at full moons is attracting believers among modern surgeons and biologists.

Bleeding from an injury *is* worse at the full and new moons than other times of the lunar month. The body's fluids, like earth's oceans, atmosphere, and terrestrial torso, seem to respond to the moon's tidal pull.

Dr. Edson J. Andrews, of Tallahasee, Florida, proved this in 1960 when he published the results of a four-year study of surgical patients at Tallahasee Memorial Hospital. First, Dr. Andrews considered over a thousand tonsillectomy patients, and defined bleeders "as those patients who had to be returned to the operating room, those who bled sufficiently post-operatively to require medical management, namely, Premarin, Koagamin, et cetera, and those who bled persistently on the operating table, requiring unusual means of control such as suture." Then each instance of bleeding was compared to the dates of lunar phases. What he found was an "amazing association of the full moon and the increased incidence of bleeding."[2]

Bleeding peaked dramatically at full moons. In fact, an overwhelming 82 percent of all such bleeding episodes occurred between the moon's first quarter and one day before the third quarter, a period which straddles the full moon.[3] What impressed Andrews all the more was the fact that the number of people admitted for surgery actually declined around each full moon, so the increase relative to the patient population was even higher than 82 percent.

Seeking confirmation for his findings, Andrews branched out. He enlisted the assistance of Dr. Carl S. McLemore of Orlando, who had kept records of the dates his tonsil and adenoid patients had bled during or after surgery from 1950 to 1956. When the two physicians compared those dates to the dates of the lunar phases, they had a chart almost identical to Andrews's.[4] Again, hemorrhaging clearly peaked at full moons.

Andrews took his investigation yet another step. This time he examined the dates that bleeding peptic ulcer patients had bled at Tallahasee Memorial and found a "definite trend of increase in the area of the full moon."[5]

Andrews's findings do not represent his own statistical quirks or some peculiarity of northern Florida, either. Just last year, the *Milwaukee Journal* reported, "Dr. Norman Shealy, a Wisconsin neurosurgeon and head of the highly respected Pain and Health Rehabilitation Center near La Crosse, surveyed his fellow surgeons and confirmed Dr. Andrews's conclusions.

"Dr. Shealy also checked with blood banks all over the country and found that 'the demand for blood transfusions is always highest at the time of the full moon and the two days following. Surgeons should definitely not perform any surgery except emergencies during the full moon.' "[6]

Another concurring medical opinion was conveyed in a brief report to the *Journal of the Medical Association of Georgia* not long ago. The physician, W.P. Rhyne, indicated that he encounters the most bloody noses ("probably the most common occurrence in the practice of medicine") when the moon is full and certain other celestial conditions are in effect.[7] And anyone seeking a second opinion about this nasal-hemorrhage diagnosis need turn only as far as the celebrated eighteenth-century doctor, Richard Mead. In a medical text published in London, Mead described the experience of a patient of one Dr. Pitcairne. The patient, nearly nine years old, had begun to have severe nosebleeds, "followed by pain in the arms and loss of consciousness. When consciousness returned his fingers were insensible and his arms agitated with violent convulsions; then he lost the power of speech." Every March and September these attacks came, for an unspecified number of years. Mead and Pitcairne did specify that the attacks struck only at the full moon.[8] And whether or not you'd trust any eighteenth-century doctor, celebrated or not, to perform any procedure or make any diagnosis on your twentieth-century body, you can be sure that Mead and Pitcairne were perfectly capable of recognizing nosebleeds and reading a calendar.

The new moon, too, has been accused of causing excessive bleeding just as it is responsible for one of each lunar month's two highest tides and for a higher than normal incidence of menstrual bleeding (see "Reproduction"). Ironically, one such report of excessive new-moon bleeding concerns the good Dr. Pitcairne himself, as well as several of his acquaintances. An 1843 issue of *The Lancet* reported, "Dr. Pitcairne was seized at a country seat near Edinburgh with a bleeding from the nose and faintness, at the exact hour of the new moon, namely nine o'clock, A.M. On returning to Edinburgh he was informed that Mr. Cockburn, professor of philosophy, had died suddenly at the same hour, from hemorrhage from the lungs, and also that five or six of his patients had been seized with hemorrhages."[9]

The *St. Louis Medical and Surgical Journal* published an article which discussed the plight of a young man who coughed blood from his lungs for six months, but only at each new moon, and the dilemma of another man who hemorrhaged from his left thumb every new and full moon. From infancy until age 16, he bled about 125 grams, which is about four and a third ounces. He bled twice as much when he was older. The hemorrhaging was eventually prevented by cauterizing the responsible artery.[10]

The tendency of new moons to aggravate bleeding from any wound was even taken into account by physicians who employed bleeding, that dimwitted practice whose use was intended to flush infectious spirits from diseased people. Attention to lunar phases may have been the only thing such foolish physicians were doing right. At least it decreased their chances of inadvertently bleeding a patient to death. British Bishop John of Beverly showed how important he considered lunar phases in this matter when he arrived at the nunnery in Wetton, Yorkshire, to examine an ailing sister, whose condition had deteriorated alarmingly after a bleeding.[11,12] When John learned that the sister had been bled shortly after a new moon, he chewed out the abbess who had invited his assistance. Had not Archbishop Theodore, he scowled, recently reminded everyone that bleeding should not be done around the time of a new moon? History records that John was eventually canonized. History, however, does not record whether the gentle sister survived.

Finally, there is Andrews again. In his study of hemorrhaging at Florida hospitals, he refers in passing to a hemophiliac whose blood had been under analysis by another researcher elsewhere. That analysis revealed that the subject's blood took more time to clot at some times of the lunar month than at others. In fact, its coagulation followed a monthly rhythm, with one maximum and one minimum in clotting time.[13] Andrews also cited studies showing there is a steady monthly increase and decrease in the number of red blood cells in a given amount of blood.[14]

What could cause all of this? Why should people bleed more from wounds at one time of the month than another? How does the blood's chemistry know what time of month it is? A remarkable answer was discovered recently by Harry D. Rounds, a biologist at Wichita State University in Kansas. What he uncovered was the reason a heart sometimes beats faster and pumps more blood through a wound. His experiments in the summer of 1973 involved dipping cockroaches in melted paraffin, jostling mice enough to make them edgy, and having humans run up and down a few flights of stairs.

Rounds's goal was to produce stress in his test subjects, which he believed would trigger the biological manufacture of whatever chemicals are pumped into the blood and carried to the heart to make it beat faster around the full and new moons. He made his mice nervous by moving their containers, and that's why he had human subjects run those stairs. After five minutes of this, he took blood samples from both.

To produce stress in his adult male cockroaches, he shook them in a small jar for twenty minutes, hard enough to prevent them from clinging to the sides or bottom. The bugs were then knocked out with carbon dioxide and dipped into melted paraffin, first one end, then the other, to seal their gut openings. Their antennae and legs were amputated, and the bodies were placed in a centrifuge tube, which whizzed around for one minute at 1,900 revolutions per minute. Cockroach "blood" was obtained that way, and mixed in a chemical cocktail before being given a steam bath. After a little more preparation, this concoction was placed, one drop at a time, onto the heart of a cockroach from which nearly all other organs and tissue had been removed. Rounds's question was, would the eviscerated cockroach's heart now beat? The answer was yes, but only around full and new moons.

In the end, Rounds had discovered that around full and new moons, the blood of men, mice, and male cockroaches does indeed contain more of certain substances that speed up heartbeat. Two days after full moons and three after new moons, to be exact, those chemicals peak.[15] Rounds became a believer.

He wrote, "The data . . . leave little alternative to the hypothesis that there is some sort of a direct or indirect relationship between lunar movements and the blood chemistry of cockroaches, mice and men. The event to which the organisms appear to be responding is a direct or indirect effect of gravitational maxima with a periodicity of between 14 and 15 days. This, of course, exceeds the time it takes the Moon simply to orbit the Earth and corresponds to the 14.8 day periodicity displayed by the 'phases' of the Moon and which are accompanied by gravitational maxima."[16]

As for the slight lag behind the precise day of the full and new moons, no problem. Rounds reminded his readers that some ocean tides exhibit the same delayed reaction, and so do the lunar-related actions of numerous marine animals.[17] Of far more importance was that Rounds (who had started out, incidentally, to investigate something that had nothing to do with the moon) had demonstrated, under steadfast scientific conditions, exactly what causes the fabled lunar bleeding, making it fable no more.

Part Three

A Search for the Mechanism

What if the moon's influence is psychological, not physical? If that is so then people act crazy at the full moon because they see the moon and act as they believe they're supposed to. Or, someone acts odd or violent because the sight of the full moon unconsciously triggers psychotic behavior. Psychiatrists say that might happen to someone who is already emotionally disturbed, someone who panics when he or she sees an object with the apparent size of an eye and an ominously cold, yellow color (in contrast to the warm orange sun). To such a person, the full moon may seem to be God's angry eye, a malevolent eye capable of seeing into his mind—or heart. Psychiatrists recognize the extreme behavior this might elicit.

The drawback to this psychological theory is that it does not seem to explain why something like post-surgical bleeding increases at the full moon or why cloudy weather, which obscures the moon, does not decrease the correlation between lunar phases and aberrant behavior. It certainly does not explain correlations between, say, stormy weather and the full moon or animal reproductive cycles and the full moon or other lunar phases.

All of which means the moon's effects cannot always, if ever, be merely psychological. Unless the effects themselves are merely statistical aberrations, the effects must result from a cause-and-effect connection between the moon and things on earth. The question is, what is that connection, that mechanism?

26

Moonlight

Among his many accomplishments, Pliny the Elder was the Frank Perdue of the Latin world: an expert on poultry. It was he who advised farmers to have hens sit on eggs after the new moon because the moon's increasing light would help hatch vigorous chicks.[1] The Egyptians of antiquity felt much the same way about melons and marrows; even the least skilled farmer knew they grow quickest on moonlit nights.[2] And a little over a century ago, the French physician E. Esquirol rhetorically asked his colleagues, "[I]s it not the bright of the moon that excites" the insane so much at each and every full moon?[3]

You don't have to be Lou Harris or George Gallup, Jr., to know that moonlight more than anything through the ages has been blamed for the effects of full moons. In our own time, much serious study has been devoted to proving the matter once and for all. Edmond M. Dewan believed he showed that women's menstrual cycles could even be regulated and tamed by manipulating moonlight. Dewan, a physicist, reasoned that light might trigger the release of enzymes and hormones crucial to the start of ovulation. That could be the role played by the full moon in regulating women's menstrual cycles. And if that's the case, then an artificial full moon just might re-synchronize an irregular menstrual cycle. Dewan set out to demonstrate his hypothesis.[4,5]

One of his subjects was a twenty-six-year-old woman whose

menstrual cycle had lurched unpredictably between 33 and 48 days for sixteen uncomfortable years. Dewan placed a common table lamp at the foot of her bed, with the shade arranged so light from the 100-watt bulb shined on the walls and ceiling rather than directly on the woman, for the sake of her comfort. The lamp was kept illuminated throughout the fourteenth, fifteenth, sixteenth, and seventeenth nights of her menstrual cycle. Quickly as a moth returning to its favorite flame, her cycle returned to a normal 29 days. Was this merely a demonstration of the power of suggestion? Impossible, because Dewan's subject had not been told what sort of experiment she was participating in. A second subject who had suffered severe menstrual cramps began to experience even worse ones after being subjected to similar photic stimulation.

Dewan and a colleague, John Rock (a father of the birth-control pill), later performed similar experiments at the Rock Reproductive Clinic in Boston with another seventeen women suffering irregular menstrual cycles. Bedroom lighting was used on the fourteenth through sixteenth nights of each woman's cycle, and again the result was success. Fifteen of the seventeen women reverted to cycles of about 29 days.[6,7,8]

One woman not from that group, a newspaper reporter in Washington, D.C., who had suffered from an irregular cycle ranging up to 45 days long, used that three-night light system on herself for three years, and was soon able to report that it helped her achieve a regular, 29-day cycle. When she neglected her artificial moon for two months, though, her cycle slipped out of phase again.[9]

Another woman, Louise Lacey, resorted to simulated moonlight for the sake of birth control. She had been relying on the pill for contraception, but abandoned it after her physician advised her it was responsible for the lumps he had discovered in her breast.[10] Contraception by abstinence was an appealing alternative.[11] All she needed to know with certainty was when she would ovulate, and she decided to do that by using photic stimulation to make her ovulation as predictible and regular as possible.[12] She described this experience in her book, *Lunaception.*[13,14]

Then there was Josy Laures, a young midwife who volunteered to isolate herself from all moonlight for three months, and suffered the menstrual consequences. Laures moved herself into a deep, subterranean cave where her physiological functions and behavior could be monitored by Dr. Alain Reinberg and his colleagues in Paris. She could communicate with the surface world only by telephone. Moreover, the only illumination in her dark new world was a miner's lamp she wore, which did not provide much light. Before going underground, Laures had lived a normal 24-hour day schedule and had had a regular 29-day menstrual cycle. In her cave, however, she drifted into a 24.6-hour day (almost exactly the length of a lunar day) and a 25.7-day menstrual cycle. Once she returned to the world of sun and moonlight above ground, she also returned to days of 24 hours and a menstrual cycle with 29 days.[15]

Animals show the same apparent susceptibility to moonlight. Lemurs whose orgies in Yale's zoological tower happened every other full moon (see chapter 17), for example, also happened to be living in a room with windows facing all parts of the sky. A control group of lemurs which exhibited no lunar lust dwelt in an area with much less view of the sky. This prompted the experimenters to observe that "the data appear to suggest a *prima facie* case for a correlation between peaks of sexual activity and the lunar cycle . . . when the animals are exposed to appreciable illumination, due to changes in the amount of moonlight."[16]

Worms also recognize the romantic value of moonlight. A German biologist showed that it seems to be moonlight, rather than anything else, which turns on certain worms. He imitated the full-moon phase by shining dim light on his slimy charges for six nights out of every thirty, and right on cue the worms ripened sexually.[17,18]

H. Munro Fox described experiments performed by other scientists that demonstrated that it was moonlight and not tides which trigger sexual swarming among certain worms. In one of those experiments, eleven mature Atlantic Palolo worms were placed in water tubs thirty days before they were due to swarm. When the time arrived, though, only four did;

all of their kin in nature responded normally. "Mayer also put 22 worms in floating boxes protected from moonlight," Fox wrote. "None of those animals swarmed. The light seems therefore to be a necessary contributory cause of swarming."[19]

A bird commonly known as the nightjar starts its normal evening activity during the breeding season twenty minutes later than usual at the time of the full moon. Actually, the disruption occurs several days before and after full moon when, according to J.L. Cloudsley-Thompson, the moon is high enough in the sky at the time of sunset and sunrise to have an effect on twilight.[20] A similar influence may be responsible for the disruption of a particular large European grouse's breeding cycle. When the bird's mating season falls near the new moon, its females seem to get "headaches" until the next full moon when their normal nightly activity resumes.[21]

Cloudsley-Thompson cites certain East African winged insects as still another example of animals affected by the light of the moon. In this case, it is "the flight activity . . . [which] may be greater on moonlit nights resulting from a positive response to light of low intensity."[22]

Erwin Bunning wrote in *The Physiological Clock* that the beetle *Calandra granaria* responds more or less actively to light depending on which phase the moon is in.[23] And the number of *Heliothis zea* moths zapped by light-traps varies according to the moon's phase.[24]

Plants also seem sensitive to moonlight. Fox cited demonstrations of response to moonlight among certain flowering plants and the fact that the stomata, or respiration holes, on leaves of some plants open in moonlight. Even photosynthesis, he wrote, may be caused by moonlight. He conceded that it would be slight, but he insisted it is conceivable. After all, he wrote, the propagation of plankton and algae according to lunar rhythms had already been proven, and the scientist demonstrating that cycle for plankton had attributed "the algal maximum occurring about full moon to a photosynthetic effect of moonlight." In addition, one researcher had found that *Euglena* (plants which resemble animals in certain ways) breathe more oxygen into their surrounding water during moonlit nights than nights with no moon at all. Granted, lunar photosynthesis is hard to believe, wrote Fox. But it is possible.[25]

Other scientists agree. In the summer of 1921, the Englishwoman Elizabeth Semmens reported that the "plane-polarised" light of the moon "at certain periods" increases the speed with which mustard seeds germinate. Crushed seeds had been placed in petri dishes with water. Some were exposed only to moonlight, some to non-polarized daylight, and some to no light at all. The moonlit seeds churned out 15 percent more sugar than either of the others, and Semmens got similar results when she repeated her experiment with oats, wheat, and cornflour.[26]

A Kansas Agricultural College researcher found a related reaction for the leaves of certain trees in the Philippines. Frank Gates showed that after dusk the leaves of all the trees he was observing would fold up or down into their natural nighttime positions, but on moonlit nights that were warm and dry the respiration holes of leaves would reopen and the leaves themselves would resume their daytime posture, spread out.[27] Spread out, that is, like hands held open in prayerful supplication to a lunar god.

The simplest explanation for these effects would be that the amount of moonlight is what makes a difference; at full moons, there is more than at any other time. A number of researchers have placed this theory under the scientific spotlight. For example, Ursula Cowgill and her colleagues at Yale made it clear that they believed "changes in the amount of moonlight" were responsible for their lemurs' full moon randiness.[28] When Margaret Klinowska verified Frank A. Brown, Jr.'s study of the full moon's effect on hamsters in 1972 (see chapter 17), it was the moon's light that appeared significant. Exposing his hamsters to artificial light—12 hours on, 12 off—Brown had found a monthly peak in their daily activity around full moons. Using varying natural light, Klinowska later found that the peak was actually on whatever day after the full moon that the moon happened to rise after solar twilight.[29] The day of longest uninterrupted light was thus the critical one, and the moon was shown to be the crucial variable.

An American biologist reported in 1941 that simulated moonlight could trick Atlantic Palolo worms into turning "tricks" in the laboratory. What the biologist did was simulate the light of the waxing moon by increasing the duration of artificial light to which the worms were exposed each day. One result was that the worms mated sooner each month than they would have naturally.[30] The worms also responded to these sexual traffic lights in another way. Once the biologist had increased the daily duration of light, the change between successive day's amount of light also made a difference in sexual behavior, with the worms mating most often during days of least change.[31]

Much more recently, a professor of dairy physiology at Michigan State University in East Lansing demonstrated that dairy cows exposed to sixteen hours of light a day give three and a half more quarts of milk than cows exposed to either more or less light.[32] That comes out to a 7 to 10 percent gain in milk. Those cows also gained weight 10 to 15 percent faster than other cows.[33]

Boyce Rensberger, describing this six-year experiment in *The New York Times* in 1978, wrote, "Sensitivity to photoperiod, a phenomenon well known in plants for centuries, is now increasingly being recognized in animals. The shortening length of day in autumn, for example, is believed to play a role in triggering bird migrations.

"Egg production in poultry has been known for some years to peak with a photoperiod of 14 to 16 hours. Just three years ago, it was reported that lambs subjected to 16-hour days grew 21 to 66 percent faster than those kept under 8-hour illumination."[34]

The way that changes in the amount or timing of moon (or sun) light may affect an animal is through the two important hormonal regulators, the pituitary gland and the hypothalamus. One way this was demonstrated was with sexually maturing birds.[35] A scientist who had captured juncos migrating south in Saskatchewan, Canada, held them in outdoor aviaries, where he turned on light bulbs longer each day in imitation of spring's lengthening days. Sure enough, by mid-December the birds were singing their mating songs and their testes had developed fully. Another scientist showed how light had played a role in this. He removed the eyes of sexually immature drakes. None of the ducks matured until light was shined directly into its hypothalamus.

Gay G. Luce, editor of the U.S. Public Health Service's *Biological Rhythms in Psychiatry and Medicine,* describes the normal hormonal chain reaction in human females this way: The ovulatory cycle starts when light makes the hypothalamus produce more "follicle stimulating hormone releasing factor" (FSHRF). FSHRF then prompts the pituitary gland, which is the size of a pea in humans and located beneath the brain, to secrete more "follicle stimulating hormone," or FSH. FSH induces development of the small follicles of the ovary, in which eggs develop, and secretion of estrogen by the ovaries. "FSH is followed by another pituitary hormone, known as luteinizing hormone, LH, which makes possible the final maturation of the ovum and its release through the rupture of the follicle. The ruptured follicle then becomes transformed into the yellow body—corpus luteum—that secretes progesterone to complete preparation of the uterus for the coming ovum, and to develop the environment for the implantation of the fertilized egg."[36]

The reason that the moon, which reflects so much less light than the sun casts, may be important to this cycle is that the time of day seems to be as important as the light itself. The critical time is before dawn, when the moon may indeed be the biggest show in the sky.

When two Duke University researchers performed a series of experiments on his hormonal network in rats during the late 1940s, they found that injecting the rats with particular barbiturates would interrupt this light chain reaction—but only if done at a certain time of day "related to the beginning of illumination."[37] By the same token, rats kept in constant darkness in the laboratory went into continuous heat.[38] "More recently," Luce wrote, "it has been shown that rats in darkness will not ovulate if given two hours of light during the critical period before ovulation. By turning light on and off, people are now able to turn on and off the hormonal mechanisms controlling reproduction in the rodent just as they can control flowering in the soybean plant."[39]

Which also brings us full circle to what Edmond Dewan, John Rock, Louise Lacey, and that Washington, D.C., reporter had discovered about the effect of artificial moonlight on women's ovulation. Nor should we overlook the *daily* relationship between births and the absence of light (as well as their *monthly* relationship to full moons). Jiri Malek and colleagues in Prague (see chapter 19) showed that most births by far take place at night.[40] Irwin H. Kaiser and Franz Halberg reported in *Annals of the New York Academy of Sciences* in 1962 that the bulk of more than 600,000 spontaneous births in Western Europe and North America from 1848 to 1960 for which they could obtain records occurred between 3 and 4 A.M. The slowest hour was between 5 and 6 P.M.[41] In contrast, most stillbirths and newborns with fatal complications occurred in the later afternoon.[42]

One British study of some 16,000 births during 1951 and 1952 found a clear plurality starting between 2 and 3 A.M.; the fewest began between 1 and 2 P.M. Most actual deliveries were at 3 A.M.[43] Another British study of a different location confirmed that a majority of 4,031 births recorded over a two-year period happened between 11 P.M. and 11 A.M.[44] Likewise, most births among 4,154 women at Sloane Hospital for Women in New York during parts of 1958 and 1959 were between 2 and 4 A.M.[45]

Why are most births at the full moon but in the dark of night? Perhaps evolution has merely perpetuated some simple facts of life: it was safer for prehistoric women to give birth at night because fewer of her natural enemies were on the hunt at that time, and it is less traumatic for an infant to be born into a dark world which more closely resembles the comfortable womb from which he or she just arrived.

Whatever. In addition to the pituitary gland and hypothalamus, the pineal gland may play a part in moonlight's effect. "The gland is shaped like a tiny pine-cone situated deep in the middle of the brain between the two hemispheres," Gay

Luce wrote. "Many people think of the pineal body as a vestigial third eye, mentioned by Indian mystics and Yogic [*sic*] practitioners. This curious gland, which protrudes on the skulls of lizards like a skin-covered eye, indeed, responds to light."[46]

Luce went on to explain that recent studies suggest that the pineal may act as a brake upon the pituitary production of a hormone involved in sexual ripening. In fact, many "children with pineal tumors have been known to reach sexual maturity grotesquely fast, arriving at puberty while still in kindergarten while overactive pineals have been known to delay puberty.[47] . . . Infant rats deprived of their pineals also have been observed to show precocious sexual mounting and copulating."[48] And when two University of Wisconsin researchers "implanted melatonin [which is secreted by the pineal] in weasels [they] saw an arrest in gonadal development."[49]

The effect of moonlight, however, apparently is to retard the pineal's action, in effect releasing the brake on sex. Luce cited several experiments which showed that animals exposed to constant light had smaller pineal glands than animals exposed to natural amounts of light.[50] A research chemist in Tokyo, Japan, reported just last year that exposure to light at night most certainly does inhibit the pineal.[51] He found that in healthy, ten-day-old chickens the production of a sexually restraining hormone skyrockets eight- to elevenfold after dark. But when the chickens were exposed to light during the night, hormone productions only doubled. Pineal glands removed from chickens killed in the laboratory and kept in a culture in continuous darkness reacted the same way to light and dark. Thus through the pineal gland the full moon may be the equivalent of a red light in a brothel.

In addition to this, the pineal plays some part in regulating other biological rhythms. Sparrows kept in constant light in a laboratory, for example, show a regular circadian rhythm of activity alternating with restful perching. When the pineals are removed from sparrows, though, their alternating rhythm disappears.[52] Moreover, recent studies suggest that the pineal gland plays a key villainous role in manic-depression, a disease whose mysterious lunar rhythms we've discussed in other chapters.[53] Beyond this, however, the pineal's precise role in life is not completely understood.

The varying amounts of light reflected by the moon during successive phases may be the most obvious thing about moonlight, but it's not the only way moonlight might affect living organisms on earth. When Elizabeth Semmens found that moonlight increased the speed with which mustard seeds germinated, she said, "A possible explanation for these results is to be found in the fact that at certain periods moonlight is plane-polarised, and in order to test this suggestion the experiments with crushed mustard seed were repeated with daylight after polarisation [*sic*: British spelling], either by reflection or by a Nicol prism."[54] Polarization has to do with the direction of wavelength of individual particles of light. In the case of moonlight, it means that the moon has reflected toward earth mostly only those particles moving the same way. Electromagnetic properties aside, the result was impressive. Seeds showed a "remarkable increase" in growth processes.[55] In a similar vein, Princeton University scientists revealed in 1979 that honeybees use polarized light in the sky to tell their humming colleagues the location of food when the sun cannot be used for orientation because it is obscured by clouds.[56]

Another theory confines itself to the problem of moonwalking: somehow moonlight stimulates muscle action. In American experiments, a sensitive electromyographic instrument was connected to the flexor muscles of the arms of sleeping patients. When light was cast on each patient, the device detected tiny electrical impulses in the patient's arms. Furthermore, 30 out of 33 times patients who had been exposed to light during their sleep later reported dreaming, whereas in 62 instances when no light was shone patients reported dreams only nine times.[57]

The moon's influence may also have something to do with the fact that each color of light has different effects on living things. Three University of California biomedical researchers found that mice in lab cubicles are more active the longer the wavelength of light they are exposed to.[58] (Wavelengths in the visible spectrum range from the shortest—violet—progressively through blue, green, yellow, orange, and red, which has the longest wavelength.) Red light and darkness elicit the most activity in mice, which are nocturnal animals.

A jungle's worth of responses among many plants and animals to different colors came to light in a film and paper presented by John Nash Ott to the New York Academy of Sciences in 1964. Ott, in the course of making a film involving time-lapse photography for the Walt Disney studios, found that apples would not mature and turn from green to red when they were covered with ordinary window glass that had been used to construct a photography greenhouse. Instead, the apples used all their energy to grow to twice normal size. It seems the glass had filtered out ultraviolet light from sunlight, and the ultraviolet wavelengths (which are shorter than visible light) are essential to the sexual maturity of apples.[59] Ott also worked with guppies. He placed fifty in each of two aquarium tanks. A "daylight white" fluorescent tube hung 12 inches above one tank was illuminated for 14 hours a day, and a "cool white" over the other. The daylight white tube actually cast a slightly bluish light, the other a slightly pink light, and the daily durations of illumination were gradually reduced to nine hours over the course of several weeks. Each tank's guppies reacted differently. The blue-tube guppies would not reproduce. The pink-tube guppies produced 80 percent females and 20 percent males instead of the usual 50-50 breakdown, and the male guppies did not develop normal sexual characteristics.[60]

Mammals, which is what men and women are, of course, also react to color changes. Ott told of determining the sex of chincilla offspring by exposing them to particular colors of light. Under natural sunlight, for example, they produce equal numbers of male and female young. Under bluish incandescent lights, though, they produce practically no males. Under ordinary incandescent, which is rich in red and infrared, no females.[61] In additional research that Ott published four years later, he described how hens and roosters exposed to pink fluorescent light for 12 hours a day produced nearly all infertile eggs.[62]

One man who fancied himself as the ruling cock of his own Fascist roost also paid quite a bit of attention to the light of the moon. This was Benito Mussolini, dictator of Italy from 1925 to 1943, whose early schooling had included exposure to lots of superstitious lore at the hands of an elderly woman, "la vecchia Giovanna," whom many local people feared as a witch.[63] As a result, even as an adult Mussolini subscribed to a wide assortment of lunar saws, including a belief in the debilitating effect of the moon's light. This was an imposing threat to a strutting, fists-on-hips man like Mussolini, who wrapped himself in so much macho imagery. The jut-jawed bully was simply deathly afraid of having moonlight fall on him while he slept.[64]

Now it seems that this fear of moonlight, though foolishly exaggerated, may have been one of the few things Mussolini was even half right about. Mussolini was probably totally ignorant, however, of the fact that this folklore was first recorded for posterity by another Italian, whose renown will be perpetuated much more favorably by history: Pliny the Elder.[65]

27

Biological Tides

Darrell Martinie, perhaps the best-known astrologer in New England, puts it this way. "Each cell in your body is, what, ninety-seven percent water, right? Well, if the moon can move something as big as an ocean, it stands to reason it can also move something as small as a body. Pressures build up, and a full moon triggers their release. It doesn't create *different* pressures. It just works on existing emotions, work strain, hassles in your love life, whatever. And each full moon represents the culmination of that pressure cycle."[1]

That's the theory that tides of the human body's own liquids are responsible for the moon's effect on people. Next to moonlight, these biological tides are the most often nominated explanation for the moon's influence. But astrologers like Martinie aren't the only people who blame biological tides. Numerous hard-nosed scientists also think the theory holds water.

"As our bodies are about two-thirds 'sea' and one-third 'land,' we must sustain 'tidal' effects," wrote Walter and Abraham Menaker (whose detailed studies of birth rates we reviewed earlier) in the *American Journal of Obstetrics and Gynecology.*[2] And Albert Feingold, an emergency room psychiatrist at Boston City Hospital, observed in 1978, "I think the full moon does have something to do with behavior.

After all, we are mostly water and the moon does move tides."[3]

Most body water is found in three places. There is water in individual cells, called "intracellular." There is water outside individual cells within the body's tissues, called "extracellular." And there is water in the blood, with about the same chemical composition as sea water, called "intravascular." When too much water accumulates, the result can be a sensation of bloating, tension, and depression. The premenstrual disturbance experienced by so many women is merely one example of this, and the alarming tendency of women to attempt suicide more often during the onset of menstruation is a sad confirmation.

The way these tidal variations are translated into emotional disturbances for men and women is by the disruption of normal neurological functions. Paul and Susan Jones described this in "Lunar Association with Suicide": People are "comprised of essentially the same elements, in similar proportions, [as the earth is]: approximately 80% water and 20% organic and inorganic minerals. [Therefore, it's easy to assume] that gravitational forces of the moon exert a similar influence on the water mass of the human microcosm [as on the water mass of earth]. Just as a tide is produced in large bodies of water, 'biological' tides are produced in a human body. The tides are comprised of cyclic changes in water flow among the fluid compartments of the body such as the intracellular, extracellular, and intravascular. These changes, together with associated electrolytic [i.e., body fluids and chemicals involved with the electrical firings of nerves and muscles] and hormonal shifts, may set the stage for neural triggering or altered levels of neuromuscular irritability."[4]

But this sort of interference with the body's electrical wiring doesn't always lead to blown fuses or abnormal behavior. It does only when the person is already at some sort of biological high tide about to flood over whatever dams there are that normally protect people. The person is ready to go.

As the Joneses put it, "The overall result [of neurological interference] is 'normal' variations in emotional tone of 'normal' individuals. The overall result in constitutionally predisposed individuals, on the other hand, is severe emotional disturbance."[5]

One batch of precisely those "predisposed individuals" appears to be people suffering from the disturbance known formally as manic-depression. Clinical studies back this up. They've shown that manic-depressives suffer from disruptions in their reservoirs of body water, and that one key to medication for the psychosis also happens to stabilize levels of body water and the firing of nerve synapses, which may be roughly thought of as the nervous system's spark plugs.

One medical study in 1970 said this: Manic-depressives have "gross change of mood . . . [and] more variability of mood than do normal subjects. It has been shown . . . that this variability is associated with a greater variability of total body water. In recent years it has been suggested that the permanent administration of lithium carbonate in this illness prevents further mood changes . . . Three cases studied over five years suggest that daily doses of lithium carbonate may prevent both large mood and TBW [total body water] changes in at least some manic-depressive subjects."[6]

Another study, this one published in 1976, said virtually the same thing about the association between premenstrual emotional symptoms and water imbalance, and the effectiveness of lithium treatment. That, it said, just might explain the "increased vulnerability of women to manic-depressive disorders . . ."[7]

In either case, menstruation or manic-depression, New York psychiatrist Michael Stone argues that it is the moon that could push such "predisposed individuals" over the edge by disrupting their body water, hormonal, and electrolyte balances. "Should a number of patients exist with emotional disturbances that coincide with phases of the moon, it would not be surprising if they were concentrated in the manic-depressive spectrum. Here, cyclical, including seasonal, disturbances have been recorded for a long time."[8]

Ever since the first cave man, in fact, accused his neighbor of being a lunatic.

28

"P.I." in the Sky

It was like the opening scene in a horror movie. The village animals somehow knew disaster was about to strike while the human inhabitants remained oblivious. In fact, the animals knew enough to panic.

In the hours before an earthquake ripped apart the Italian hamlet of Friuli in May 1976, deer in the nearby mountains formed flocks and fled from the heights, cowering in a group outside the village as if they knew the high ground would soon be unsafe. No villager had ever seen anything like it. Mice and rats began to swarm from their hidden burrows, seeking open ground. People were quite peeved by this because every last pet cat had fled the village. Fowl refused to roost. Twenty minutes before the ground began to heave, cattle became visibly nervous, bellowing, tearing at their chains, and pawing their boxes. Dogs began to bark for no apparent reason. It was night, and a cuckoo normally active only during the day began to repeat its strange call.[1]

A similar scene evolved at Marine World–Africa USA, the aquarium and zoological park just south of San Francisco, shortly before that city's 1979 quake, its worst in decades.[2] "[A]nimal handlers and trainers reported erratic behavior among the animals in the hours preceding the quake.

"Mary O'Herron of Marine World said that a cougar had been very restless and had paced most of the night Sunday and that a baby tiger 'normally very nice'—had remained curled up in a corner all day, refusing to respond to friendly gestures."[3]

This sort of peculiar behavior before earthquakes has been observed and reported for hundreds of years.[4] It's the same sort of thing that animals seem to do before the eruption of an electrical storm,[5,6] but now scientists think they understand why. Animals can sense the colossal accumulation of something known as "positive ions" in the air,[7] and this overload of positive ions is a by-product of stormy weather and earthquakes (both of which we've seen are under lunar influence), as well as of the moon itself. Since we'll take up the moon's influence over geophysical phenomena in more detail in chapter 30, suffice it to say here that one explanation for how the moon could directly increase ionization of earth's atmosphere is that the moon reflects ultraviolet radiation and x-rays from the sun back to earth,[8] where they cause ionization.[9] The second explanation (both could operate) suggests that the moon periodically becomes electrostatically charged, like a statically electric wool blanket, and deflects clouds of ions from the sun towards earth.[10] Both these effects would peak around the full moon.

What's more important, such accumulations of positive or negative ions can affect the physical and emotional health of man and beast and the physical well-being of plants.

These ions are molecules of the gases that make up the atmosphere, but molecules which have been altered. Molecules normally consist of a certain number of atoms, which in turn have a particular number of electrons and protons. In contrast, an ion molecule has either lost or gained a stray electron, which are the negatively charged particles surrounding the nucleus of each atom; the nucleus consists of protons having positive electrical charges.[11] A positive ion is a molecule that has lost one of its negatively charged electrons. A negative ion is one that has gained an electron.[12]

Alone, an ion molecule is of little consequence. As everyone's grade-school science teacher tried to make eminently clear, a single atom is infinitesimal. There are millions, we were assured, in the period at the end of this sentence. The only reason ions do affect us is because they attack or assist us in such huge armies. We are actually surrounded by staggering numbers of these mutilated molecules. A single cubic inch of air contains anywhere from 16,387 to 32,774 of them,[13] and we not only bathe in them, we also breathe 2;500 gallons of air full of them every day.[14]

Their relationship to the weather and to earthquakes is simple. Positive ions are produced by several types of friction associated with changing weather: the friction between conflicting masses of air, layers of wind, air and ground, and the air and particles of dirt blown through it. The friction simply shears away electrons.[15] Recent German investigations suggest that earthquakes, with their colossal shoving matches between vast stretches of earth and rock, create ions in much the same way.[16] Negative ions, meanwhile, seem to require complicated atmospheric cauldrons. The sun's rays cooking clean air can create them. So can naturally radioactive rock and soil, or a frothing waterfall with its halo of electron-absorbing mist, or waves crashing against rocks at the seachore.[17] Those processes, plus the fact that the naturally negatively charged Earth repels like-charged negative ions, account for the usual five-to-four ratio of positive to negative ions in the air near earth's surface.[18]

What makes all of this interesting to people other than physicists is that radical variations from either the normal amount of atmospheric ions or the five-to-four ratio can have drastic effects on living organisms. A laboratory environment free of all ions, for example, will kill test plants and animals, plain and simple, a fact not lost on NASA scientists responsible for creating manned vehicles that will bring 'em back alive.[19] A more benign result is that the proper abundance of negative ions creates a pleasant freshness in the air, while an accumulation of positive ions may be tiring, depressing, or annoying.[20] Scientists now think this may account for some of the pleasure people feel at the beach or after a shower, and the relief many people have after an electrical storm has passed.[21] Negative ion generators for home or office use have been vigorously marketed for years, but subject to certain government restrictions.

Experiments with ionization have yielded results that Ripley would have cherished for his "Believe It Or Not." California researchers found that barley, oats, lettuce, and peas grown in chambers containing only sixty positive and negative ions were quickly stunted and became diseased. The same plants in air with twice that number of ions grew much more rapidly. The U.S. Department of Agriculture has been able to grow cucumbers 18 inches longer than normal by nurturing them in ion-enriched air. In the Soviet Union, mice, rats, guinea pigs, and rabbits placed into enclosed pens without any ions at all died within days.[22] And late in 1978, *Science News* reported that University of California scientists had been able to manipulate the health of plants by altering the ionization and certain other conditions of their test chambers.[23]

Research with humans has proven just as startling, as Fred Soyka showed with a series of examples in his book, *The Ion Effect.* In 1927, an Italian scientist, L.M. Spolverini, reported that ionization caused a "remarkable" increase in the amount of milk new mothers were able to secrete.[24] Soviet scientists have recently reported that mothers exposed to loads of negative ions recovered more quickly from the debilitating effects of giving birth, and it made suckling easier for mothers who had been having trouble breast-feeding their infants.[25]

Soviet scientists also staged a sort of domestic ion Olympics shortly after World War II to measure the effect of ions in athletes. What they found was that ions make jocks iron-strong. Weightlifters nurtured with large doses of negative ions performed better and recovered faster from fatigue than those kept on a diet of normal air or large doses of negative and positive ions.[26] The endurance of athletes simply running in place improved an impressive 240 percent over a ten-day period in which they breathed negative-ion-enriched air. In contrast, stationary joggers breathing normal air improved only 7 to 24 percent.[27] Other athletes were affected in similar ways.

Since the mid-1950s, researchers in California, Israel, and France have shown that ions work their apparent magic through subtle effects on certain hormonal and glandular activities.[28] The causal role in this of certain weather patterns is so well accepted in some parts of the world that the most common of those weather culprits have acquired ominous nicknames connoting the trouble they make. These are usually a steady, warm, dry wind, laden with positive ions. In central Europe such a wind is known as the "foehn," which commonly blows from the southeast. To Israelis it is the "sharav." Elsewhere in the Middle East it is the "hamsin."[29] In southern France it is the "mistral."[30] Southern Californians may call it a "Santa Ana," and in the Pacific Northwest and Canada it is the "chinook."[31] In parts of Germany the presence of the wind is reportedly admissible in courts of law as a mitigating circumstance in crimes of passion.[32] Soyka says hospitals in parts of southern Germany will actually cancel surgery a day or so before a foehn blows into town, and when it does, the rate of traffic accidents rises more than 50 percent and suicide attempts (successful or not) reach epidemic proportions.[33] Israelis, too, blame everything from spates of murder and suicide attempts to asthma attacks and aching joints on the sharav. One Jerusalem shoe salesman claims his sales swell by 300 percent when the sharav arrives because people's feet swell, as well.[34]

There is also an Israeli medical researcher who blames the sharav for the 1969 death of Bishop James Pike, who was the controversial Episcopalian Bishop of San Francisco until his resignation in 1968.[35] Pike died of hunger, thirst, and exhaustion when he lost his way during a drive into the desert near the Dead Sea, and the physician says that descriptions of Pike's behavior before this ill-fated journey suggest Pike was a likely candidate for the hormonal ravages resulting from a positive ion overdose. That hormonal insurrection could have triggered the emotional disorientation that allowed Pike to embark on his fatal foray into the sandy wasteland.

In a lighter vein, it is Soyka again who recounts the frustration of a Swiss woman whose sex life was wiped out by headaches brought on with each arrival of the foehn, and the joy discovered by a rather quiet and shy man who made his living installing negative ion generators in people's homes. Eventually he installed one in his own home, and Soyka asked about the results. The salesman replied instantly.

"Well, the biggest effect has been on my sex life; my wife loves it."[36]

29

Weather Effects

Who doesn't have an elderly aunt who predicts rain for the next day when her arthritis acts up, or who hasn't heard of the proverbial farmer who knows it will snow when his big toe hurts?

The belief that weather affects health is widespread, though often consigned to the category of claptrap, always by those people whose big toes don't hurt or who don't have arthritis. Recent research, however (much of it as current as the 1970s), has shown that this meteorological mythology is often a crude reflection of reality. The weather *does* affect our health, and not just in the manner of cold weather leading to the sniffles.

This is all the more interesting because, as we saw in chapter 15, the moon affects the weather. The full moon in particular is prominent in patterns of heavy rainfall, hurricanes, typhoons, tropical storms, and coastal floods. So weather is one more way that the moon manipulates us.

There is a veritable deluge of studies documenting the relationship between weather and health. Sheldon Geller and Herbert Shannon, whose study of the correlation between full moons and admissions to psychiatric hospitals we discussed earlier, pointed out in 1976 that a drop in barometric pressure often precedes stormy weather, and they found that such barometric plunges are significantly correlated to telephone calls to the outpatient department at a psychiatric hospital in Toronto, Canada, and to the number of new patients seeking outpatient services there.[1]

Suicide rates also peak when barometric pressure is low and air temperature high, according to a five-year study published in 1934 by C.A. Mills in the *American Journal of Psychiatry*.[2,3] Julian Fast, a biometeorologist and author of *Weather Language*, writes that as much as a third of our population succumbs to back pains, headaches, depression, dizziness, sleeplessness, loss of appetite, mental confusion, nervousness, and a half dozen other ailments due to the meteorological conditions that constitute the familiar calm before a rainstorm.[4]

Yugoslavian researchers have found a significant correlation between the number of strokes and changes up or down in atmospheric pressure, with a larger increase in the number of strokes occuring when the change happens to be a decline.[5] In their 1968 report to the *Journal of Neurological Sciences*, these researchers noted that another European study published in 1960 had reported the same thing.[6] A University of Pennsylvania study in 1973 confirmed that more people who were intoxicated sought help from the University's medical school facilities during periods of low barometric pressure.[7]

Several studies have documented the connection between a variety of serious health problems and changes in weather, with or without falling barometric pressure. A sixteen-year Dutch study found that suicide attempts (successful and otherwise) increased an astounding 300 to 750 percent on days "with strong atmospheric turbulence, accompanied by drastic changes in thermal balance (either cold or warm) and heavy precipitation (rain, snow or hail), causing serious thermoregulatory disturbances."[8] That Yugoslavian study also found an increase in strokes during the passage of certain types of weather fronts, and they noted similar reports by other investigators.[9]

An American study reported in 1935 confirmed that stormy weather apparently causes "acute psychotic reactions" among certain people.[10] Another investigation in 1967 found a correlation between "uncomfortable" weather and admissions to a psychiatric hospital in the South. The focus fell on hot weather, making summer months the major culprits.[11,12] Edson Andrews, that Florida surgeon who studied the correlation between full moons and post-surgical bleeding, cited research showing a correlation between nosebleeds and times of changing weather, as well as between the passage of cold fronts and an increase in the number of stomach ulcers, intestinal ulcers, post-surgical hemorrhages, fatal coronaries, migraine headaches, asthma attacks, and eclampsia, an illness involving convulsions and coma connected with pregnancy.[13] Those University of Pennsylvania researchers found an increase in the number of people seeking professional assistance for depression when barometric pressure was high.[14]

More and more research suggests that the way bad weather precipitates illness is through the hormonal system.[15] The prime suspect is the hypothalamus, which seems to crop up in any discussion of biological disturbances, and it's no wonder. That section of the brain is involved with everything from body temperature to sleep and fluid retention.[16,17] Whatever the precise biochemical mechanisms involved, medical concensus seems to be that people with faulty systems are the most likely to be affected by rude or changing weather, and that's certainly the thinking in the case of mental disorders.[18] One American physician has even said that the biochemical changes induced by disturbed weather might make a disturbed person "shift to normal or a phase of quiescence . . . "[19]

More and more members of the health and meteorology sciences are coming to appreciate the usefulness of biometeorology. The American Meteorological Society, for example, devoted a three-day national conference in the spring of 1979 to the subject.[20] And in ever-efficient Germany, physicians today may dial a particular phone number and hear a forecast of the weather and its likely effects on their patients.[21]

30

Magnetism and Electricity

In A.D. 160, the Greek satirist Lucian wrote about a sailor whose boat is sucked into the sky by a waterspout, is swallowed by a whale, and ends up floating to the moon.[1,2,3] Lucian called this flight of fancy *True History,*[4] and the flight he described takes all of seven days and seven nights.[5] It was the first work of science fiction to describe a journey through space, an idea not achieved in reality until 1,800 years later, when the Soviet Union launched Yuri Gagarin into orbit.

The Soviets' success with Gagarin was an early lap in what would soon be called "the space race." The landing of Apollo 11 was the victorious climax to that contest, of course, but man climbed closer to the moon in other ways, for in the first half of those eight years between Gagarin and *Eagle* some of the most important discoveries about how the moon affects earth and its inhabitants were made.

These advances, however, are still as obscure as military secrets. None was especially dramatic. None was the sort of stuff that could compete with the heroics of the astronauts. Separately, each was a rather anonymous, esoteric accomplishment in the science of geophysics. Taking place one at a time as they did, it was easy to overlook their significance. Taken together, though, along with other more recent breakthroughs, they are the reason that more scientists are seriously considering whether the moon does indeed affect man. Ironically, the general public probably regards the notion of lunar influence more skeptically than an increasing number of scientists does.

What the space program did was provide scientists with significantly superior research tools. Satellites, rockets, radar, radio, high-altitude balloons—all of these suddenly offered scientists a much closer look at space. It was as if biologists had just invented the microscope. Incredibly more detailed information was available to researchers, which enabled them to see previously unknown astronomical events as well as new relationships among familiar fixtures in the sky. Effects of the moon, which had been too subtle to measure, suddenly came into scientific sight. Most of all, it gradually became apparent that the moon has a regular, rhythmic effect on two things whose influence on man and other living things has also become clearer only recently: earth's magnetic field and the electric field created by every living thing.

In one four-year period, 1961 through 1964, researchers reported that all of the following adhere to monthly lunar patterns: the number of meteors attacking the earth,[6] the number of hail-like ice nodules which form in the cold air of high-altitude rain clouds,[7] the amount of ozone in the atmosphere,[8] and the dates of heavy rainfall in the United States and New Zealand, which we discussed in chapter fifteen. In that same period, scientists also reported that disturbances of the earth's magnetic field follow lunar cycles.

The Australian radiophysicist E.K. Bigg found that certain critical types of magnetic storms on earth (which do things like interrupt radio broadcasts with static) over an 81-year period had peaked significantly just after full moons.[9,10] Two Harvard College Observatory investigators reported virtually the same thing for the 30-year span they examined,[11] and so did a pair of NASA scientists working in New York.[12] All three reports said that the fewest magnetic disturbances were at the new moon. In addition, a University of Michigan study found that the smallest numbers of certain atomic particles in the so-called "solar wind" reach the earth just after the full moon.[13] A European study found much the same thing for other particles in the solar wind.[14]

These reports added enormous weight to studies done before World War II that had indicated the earth's magnetic field fluctuates according to daily and monthly lunar rhythms.[15] In fact, as far back as 1852[16] scientists had noticed what they believed to be lunar tides in earth's magnetic field, but those fluctuations turned out to be ones caused by the sun's rotation on its axis (the solar "day"), which takes about twenty-seven days, almost exactly the same length as the sidereal lunar month.[17] Also, changes in the electrostatic strength (amount of electricity) of the atmosphere, partially caused by lunar-induced fluctuations in ionization, had been known about since before the war.[18,19]

Now, for those effects to have extra importance, they must in turn affect living things; and that's what scientists have found. Turning their attention from the heavens back to earth, researchers have discovered that plants, animals, and people can sense those forces, especially magnetism, which are juggled by the moon just as they can sense heat or light, or, in the case of animals and people, hear sounds and taste flavors. This has astounded scientists because they have always believed that the effects of magnetism were well beyond the range of our five senses. But the proof is there. Experiments in the 1960s and '70s have proven that living organisms can sense earth's magnetic field and other related geophysical phenomena, and they can sense ever-so-slight changes in them.

One of the earliest and most impressive of these demonstrations was by Frank Brown, Jr., and Young H. Park in a series of experiments first reported in 1965. Their work was with the common planarian worm, which has an aversion to light and crawls away from it. Brown and Park first showed that the angle at which these flatworms crawl away from light changes systematically over the course of a lunar month. The closer it is to a new moon, the more sharply they turn away from light (see chapter 17). In subsequent experiments, they placed a bar magnet beneath the planaria's playpen, with its north pole facing north, then with its north pole facing south. The bar's magnetic field was twenty times stronger than earth's own natural field. When the pole was turned south during a full moon, the worms turned as much as if it were the new moon; and when it was south at a new moon, the worms "thought" it was a full moon.[20] Furthermore, the worms could remember what phase of the moon it seemed to be for five to ten minutes, a long time to a planarian.[21]

German and American scientists have done similar experiments with birds. The husband-and-wife team of Wolfgang and Roswitha Wiltschko put European robins in a cage at migration time. The birds could not see the sun or stars from the cage, and the Wiltschkos surrounded the cage with Helmholtz coils, which create a magnetic field when electricity runs through them. When the Wiltschkos oriented this artificial field so that magnetic north pointed geographical east, the birds began flying in the wrong direction when released from the cage.[22,23]

William Keeton of Cornell took this idea further. Keeton put small bar magnets on the backs of some pigeons, and nonmagnetic brass bars on the backs of others. Keeton's theory was that the birds with magnets would have trouble orienting themselves by earth's magnetic field. He was right. When the pigeons were released in sunny weather, all of them could find their way home without any trouble. But when they were released in overcast weather, the birds with bar magnets became confused and lost.[24,25] Obviously, when the birds could not see the sun they tried to rely on earth's magnetic field.

Keeton and a colleague have reported one other remarkable thing about how pigeons orient themselves. The scientists took precisely detailed notes about where pigeons flew upon being released, and after several years they noticed a lunar pattern. Each day the pigeons took off at a slightly different angle relative to north. What Keeton and company noticed was that the exact direction varied over the course of a lunar month, returning to the original departure direction about every thirty days.[26] This change in initial orientation was not dependent upon any other variable.

Another Empire State scientist, Charles Walcott, went one up on both Keeton and the Wiltschkos. Walcott, of the State University of New York (SUNY) at Stony Brook, placed Helmholtz coils on the head and neck of pigeons, and by remote control changed the direction of this artificial magnetic field while the birds were in flight. Immediately, the birds would change course.[27] In cloudy weather, Walcott could also make the homing pigeons fly away from home.[28]

Other investigators have found that birds are confused by radar and sunspot activity, both of which affect earth's magnetic field, and when flying over mineral deposits that disrupt the local magnetic field.[29]

About the same time Frank Brown of Northwestern University was testing planaria with magnetic fields, an Illinois neighbor was performing similar experiments on green algae. J.D. Palmer, of the University of Illinois, placed the green algae, *Volvox aureus,* into corrals mounted on petri dishes and kept track of which way the aquatic plants turned when they left the corrals. These algae each have a slender, whiplike tail called a flagellum that they use to swim in whatever direction they want, which—in contrast to Brown's worms—happens to be toward light. Like Brown, however, Palmer found that the local magnetic field affected the exact direction his test subjects moved in. Palmer placed bar magnets in a variety of positions relative to earth's magnetic field beneath the algae's petri dishes, and after putting nearly 7,000 of the flagellates through their paces he could see that each change in the magnetic bar caused the algae to change their departure direction.[30]

Moreover, Palmer wrote that because the algae are so evolutionarily primitive and "a direct descendant of one of the earliest forms of life," their responsiveness to magnetism must be equally primitive and therefore "quite widespread in Nature" today as a result of heredity.[31]

Another of Brown's observations was that the metabolic rates of rats, potatoes, salamanders, quahogs, oysters, fiddler crabs, and several other plants and animals were the mirror images of fluctuations in the intensity of primary cosmic radiation reaching earth. The more radiation that came near earth, the slower the metabolic rates of those plants and animals, and vice versa. But Brown realized that it could not be the radiation itself causing the changes in metabolism since primary cosmic radiation does not reach earth's surface. It is deflected by earth's magnetic field high above our planet's surface. Brown saw that regular daily fluctuations in the strength of earth's magnetic field affected the amount of radiation reaching as low as the outer atmosphere—still not anywhere near the earth's surface. The stronger the field, the less radiation making its way in. And those daily geomagnetic fluctuations correspond exactly, Brown wrote, to the lunar day. Just like ocean tides, the earth's magnetic field is "highest," or strongest, twice a day: when the moon is directly above and directly below.

So, since the plants and animals could not be reacting to the radiation, it had to be earth's magnetic field that affected their metabolism.[32]

In 1971, Michael Persinger, a Canadian scientist working at the University of Tennessee in Knoxville, reported that a local magnetic field could affect the natural gusto of newborn rats. Mentally and physically healthy lab rats will show more curiosity about their environment than unhealthy rats, and one way to demonstrate this is by counting the number of squares on a checkerboard surface that each rat covers when it is released from a pen.

Persinger kept pregnant rats in pens on top of continuously rotating magnets. When their litters were able to walk, they covered less ground in open-field tests than rats not exposed to a rotating magnetic field during gestation. Persinger also found that not all "exposed" rats performed the same. The closer exposed rats were born to lunar perigee, the fewer squares they covered. Those born at lunar apogee were least restrained.[33]

Frank Brown, Jr., and Kate Scow coaxed hamsters into following a 26-hour "daily" activity schedule by exposing them to artificial magnetic fields in 26-hour cycles.[34] The rodents were kept in cages balanced on a pivot point. Any motion by the hamster would rock its cage, and any movement of the cage was electronically recorded. Each cage was surrounded by an artificial magnetic field which would be made strong for 12 hours, then weak for 14 hours. The hamsters were soon pulled away from their normal, 24-hour day to this 26-hour magnetic day like so many cuddly pieces of iron.

A Hungarian scientist who eventually moved his research to Brown's Northwestern University found that mice exposed to an artificial magnetic field gained less weight and grew more slowly than unexposed mice.[35] And in 1960, the British journal *Nature* reported that the roots of certain plants grew away from small magnets hung near them in glass jars filled with liquid nutrients.[36] But leave it to Soviet scientists to come up with the most bizarre example of magnetic influence. One researcher recently wrote in *Izvestia* that the moon can disturb the earth's magnetic field even beneath the surface of oceans. Those disturbances can wreak havoc with an airplane's gyroscope, causing even the best navigator to lose his way long enough for his plane to run out of fuel.

And that, he seemed sure, explains the mystery of the Bermuda Triangle, where, he said, most disappearances occur while the moon is full, new, or at perigee.[37]

* * *

In just the last few years, lots of fruitful research has emerged shedding light on how living things perceive magnetic fields—and the answer appears to be simpler than you might expect. In the case of several creatures, each of which uses earth's magnetic field for navigation, it is because they have built-in magnets!

Two Princeton scientists and Charles Walcott of SUNY (whose work with pigeons is discussed above) have found tiny crystals of magnetite, a powerfully magnetic mineral commonly known as "lodestone," between the brain and skull bone of pigeons.[38] This was reported late in 1979. About a year earlier, one of those Princeton researchers, James Gould, and two of his colleagues reported that they had found magnetite in the abdomen of honeybees.[39] Early in '79, a trio of scientists from M.I.T., the University of New Hampshire, and the University of Illinois published their discovery of magnetite in several species of aquatic bacteria; the first one they found it in lives in fresh water on Cape Cod.[40,41,42] The M.I.T. man, Richard Frankel, said there is no doubt the bacteria use the magnetite like "an internal compass and [use it to] orient in the geomagnetic field just like a mariner's compass needle."[43] He also said their tests proved the bacteria biologically manufacture the magnetite; it is not something they ingest, which is already made.[44] Then, with an expedition to New Zealand and Australia in January 1980, the Frankel team demonstrated that magnetite-toting bacteria in the Southern Hemisphere use their built-in lodestone to home in on the South Pole just as particular Northern Hemisphere bacteria use it to find north.

Furthermore, monarch butterflies have magnetite in their wings,[45] and both the Gould and Walcott teams noted that the teeth of chitons (sea creatures related to clams that resemble the shell of an armadillo) contain the magnetic substance as well.[46,47]

Animals without magnetite can detect earth's magnetic field by using the same principle used by hydroelectric dams to generate electricity. (Picture a horseshoe magnet. One end of the magnet is its north pole, the other end is south. A magnetic field fills the gap between those poles at the open side of the horseshoe. Now, take a piece of wire made of something like copper that will conduct electricity, and bend it into a loop. Water cascading through tunnels in a dam turns a waterwheel whose axle is the stem of that copper loop. That makes the loop rotate, and since the loop is in the middle of the horseshoe magnet's field it is churning through the field the way the loops of an egg-beater churn batter; the loops are crossing and breaking the lines of the magnetic field. That creates an electric current in the copper loop because, in terms of physics, magnetism and electricity are related. In fact, they're simply different forms of the same force, which physicists call "electromagnetic force.")

How do animals use this principle to sense earth's magnetic field? It appears to work like this: An animal that can generate an electric current (as an eel can) can conduct electricity like that copper wire. And when that animal swims east to west or west to east, it is swimming across the lines of earth's magnetic field. Then, just like a rotating copper loop that breaks the lines of a magnetic field, an electric current is generated through the animal, which the animal is perfectly capable of sensing.[48] If the animal swims north-south no magnetic lines are broken and no current is generated. If the animal knows it is swimming fast and only a weak current is being generated, it understands that it could not be crossing as many lines of the magnetic field as it does when moving east-west; it must be swimming diagonally (e.g., southwest toward northeast) across the lines of magnetism. A change in swimming direction can even change the direction of the induced current.[49]

Several experiments have shown that eels can navigate this way.[50,51] Sharks are certainly equipped to. They have sensory organs that can pick up an electric field as low as a hundred-millionth of one volt per centimeter.[52] Since all living things generate an electric field, sharks can detect the electric field of prey that might be hiding beneath sand.[53,54] Stingrays can detect a magnetic field the same way.[55] Gould says salamanders, too, might use electromagnetic induction to navigate; at any rate, they do use earth's magnetic field.[56]

This sensitivity of living things to magnetic fields is demonstrated in one more way: the vulnerability of plants and animals to electromagnetic radiation.[57] This is what the controversy over microwave radiation is all about, but *Science 80*, the new publication of the American Association for the Advancement of Science, recently explained that microwaves are hardly the only radio-wave frequency which can endanger man. Potentially dangerous radio-frequency electromagnetic radiation is also produced by everything from television to citizens band radio to walkie-talkies.[58]

That threat, however, is just from radio-frequency waves, which occupy only part of the entire electromagnetic spectrum. Research has shown that plants and animals are sensitive to radiation from all over the electromagnetic spectrum, and at strengths far below that of any radiation which might leak out of a microwave oven or flood out from a military radar installation. (Something illustrated in part by our chapter, "Moonlight," because visible light is a narrow portion of the electromagnetic spectrum, lying between infrared and ultraviolet radiation.) Frank Brown, Jr., and two colleagues, for example, have shown that exposure even to exceedingly weak gamma radiation will change a mouse's rate of metabolism.[59]

In another experiment, Brown and Carol Chow found that

bean seeds can even detect the electromagnetic fields generated by groups of bean seeds nearby.[60]

A Missouri researcher exposed test subjects to something whose influence is usually considered psychological rather than physical—television. A pair of three-month-old rats were placed in a cage directly in front of a color TV set. Half the tube's screen was shielded by a sheet of lead about a third of a centimeter thick, the other half shielded only by black photographic paper; then the set was turned on without sound for about six hours a day. Both rats began to act as if they had swallowed barbiturates, the paper-shielded rat becoming lethargic before his partner.[61]

When an entire breeding colony of rats was placed in front of the set, the effect on their sex lives was disastrous. The rats, which had been producing eight to twelve babies each, immediately were reduced to litters of one and two, many of which quickly died. It was fully six months after the rats were removed from in front of the TV before they began reproducing normally again.[62] Which just vindicates what Johnny Carson has been joking about all these years. If it's a romantic light you're after, don't watch the lit tube. Watch the full moon.

* * *

Of course, humans are also sensitive to magnetic fields and electromagnetic radiation. A Czechoslovakian study showed that fewer women than usual menstruate during disturbances of earth's magnetic field, and during periods of geomagnetic calm more women than usual begin menstruation.[63] Scientists in India found a clear and ominous correlation between heart attacks and magnetic disturbances. They analyzed admissions to two major Indian hospitals over a six-year period and found that heart attacks followed magnetic activity as faithfully as a puppy follows its master.[64] Ironically, the investigators remarked that an earlier study in the United States had not found such a correlation, but they were confident they knew why: there is so much artificial magnetic "smog" in America that it obscures subtle changes in the natural magnetic environment.[65]

Canadian researchers overcame that problem and documented a significant relationship between outbursts of hostile, violent, and excited behavior by psychiatric patients at a Montreal hospital and disturbances in earth's magnetic field.[66]

Investigators in neighboring New York State discovered the same pattern. They found a clear correlation between some 29,000 psychiatric admissions in eight central New York hospitals and aberrations in earth's magnetic field over 4 1/3 years.[67] Their study had been prompted by earlier inquiries, one showing this type of correlation for psychiatric admissions at two Syracuse hospitals, and another charting the same sort of relationship for suicide and other emotional disturbances among 40,000 patients in Germany.[68]

These same New York investigators later refined their study by using an indirect but more precise measurement of changes in earth's magnetic field: the amount of cosmic rays reaching the earth. Again, they found a clear relationship between geomagnetic fluctuations and grossly abnormal, clinically detailed human behavior.[69]

In yet another study, the New Yorkers showed that the reaction time of human test subjects deteriorated sadly as they were subjected to increasingly strong, but modulated (that is, "warbling" like a police siren), magnetic fields.[70]

The Soviets have demonstrated the flip side of the same thing: subtle changes in earth's own magnetic field produce headaches, fatigue, memory loss, irritability, insomnia, and emotional instability in human guinea pigs.[71] Scientists in West Germany studied people being housed in underground bunkers, one of which was heavily shielded against ordinary electromagnetic fields, one of which was not. Volunteers in the unshielded bunker had shorter circadian rhythms than their shielded counterparts,[72] whose cycles were shortened when artificial electric fields were beamed into their subterranean habitat.[73]

Finally, there was the study by two Canadians, who pointed out the medical research suggesting extremely low frequency (ELF) electromagnetic waves are especially likely to disrupt hormonal activities involved with menstruation.[74] Several studies have in fact documented identical lunar patterns to suicide and menstruation among women (see chapter 23). Moreover, research has shown that suicides rise on days when long electromagnetic wavelengths are being powerfully disturbed.[75] The Canadian team cited German research showing that weather disturbances create ELF electromagnetic waves and pulses. Thus, the moon may manipulate suicide, particularly among women, through electromagnetic disturbances it induces by way of its influence on weather, earth's magnetic field, or some means scientists have yet to pinpoint.

* * *

Most high school chemistry and biology students are familiar with Luigi Galvani's eighteenth-century experiments with twitching frog legs. When Galvani accidentally attached two copper wires to a source of electricity and touched one to an exposed leg nerve and the other to a muscle, the frog's leg muscle contracted. Galvani had demonstrated that nerves and muscles conduct electricity.

In fact, electricity can move among many types of cells in living plants and animals. Before there is electric current, though, atoms of substances like sodium and potassium with opposite electric charges must accumulate on opposite sides of a cell's membrane. Since opposite charges attract, the charged atoms will move towards each other when permitted through the cell wall. That motion is the electric current.[76] (Nerve cells, for example, only permit that when stimulated.) The push behind that current is caused by those charged atoms building up like water behind a dam. This potential push is what is known as "electric potential" or the "potential difference," and it is measured in terms of "volts."[77] One more bit of science: anything that has an electric charge is surrounded by an electric field. It is that electric field that lets a comb charged with static electricity tug at your hair (which has the opposite charge) without ever touching it.[78]

Two Yale scientists demonstrated that living things are surrounded by an electric field, and thus possess electrical activity and are subject to the rules of electricity, by placing a salamander in a dish of salt water with electrodes attached to the dish's edge, very close to the salamander's head. The electrodes were attached to a galvanometer, which measures changes in the flow of electricity through it. Since salt water can conduct electricity, every time the salamander's head passed near an electrode there should have been a burst of current detected by the galvanometer—and that is precisely what happened. It could happen only because an electric field does exist in the salamander,[79] and the basic ingredient—electric potential—exists in every living organism from single-cell bacteria to jellyfish, plants, and man.[80]

More fascinating still is the fact that electric potential does not remain steady. Certain biological activity causes it to fluctuate, and vice versa: a change in electrical activity imposed by man or nature will visibly affect biological activity. Experiments done by placing electrodes at and near the vagina have shown that the electric potential of women and rabbits changes at ovulation.[81] Measurements across the chest of mice change when the mice are developing cancer.[82] And physicians in New York have accomplished the medically impossible by manipulating body electricity. Although natural regeneration of lost limbs has been the exclusive skill of such lower animals as starfish, these doctors have elicited regeneration of bone, muscle, nerves—even fingertips, in humans by enhancing the electric current and field of injured limbs.[83]

But, for our purposes here, the most fascinating thing of all is that the moon, too, is capable of influencing electric potential. A Yale researcher found that the electric potential of trees peaked right around new and full moons.[84] The pattern was utterly unaffected by other variables like barometric pressure changes, humidity, weather. The only variable it kept step with was the moon's changing phases. This same investigator later found the same cycle in mice.[85]

Another medical detective, Leonard Ravitz of the medical schools at Yale and Duke University, has documented lunar swings of electric potential in humans. Ravitz subjected seventeen men and women to close daily scrutiny during 1949 and 1950. During their daily physicals, such things as temperature, blood pressure, and pulse were recorded. At the study's start, each was classified in one of three psychiatric categories: "severely maladjusted," "moderately maladjusted," or "reasonably well adjusted." A psychiatric profile was sketched during each day's physical exam. And the difference in electrical potential between several points on the body was measured. At the end, Ravitz had some electrifying results: all the people had two peaks of "potential difference," at full and new moons.[86] Sometimes, two lesser peaks showed up—just before or after the first and third lunar quarters.[87] Whenever the peaks occurred, the more emotionally disturbed a test subject was, the higher his or her potential differences (or voltage measurements) were.[88] A year later, Ravitz said he had found the same thing in a new study involving 100 human subjects.[89]

One of Ravitz's subjects illustrated his findings with shocking clarity. The subject was a man, one of two schizophrenic twins whose psychosis progressed and regressed as predictably as the moon's phases.[90] Ravitz does not reveal the man's full identity. He only indicates that the man was raised in a rural, poverty-stricken setting somewhere on the southern Atlantic coast of the United States in a moderately religious Baptist family. His father was alcoholic and a blacksmith by trade; his mother, "an eccentric domineering" woman. He dropped out of school at age 16 after completing fewer than eight grades.

That same year his father died in bed, something the boy was an intimate witness to since he regularly shared his father's bed. Despite that, he showed no reaction to the death.

One year later, 1941, he joined the Navy. Not surprisingly, he never became anyone's close friend, although he proposed marriage to two women he had just met on blind dates. In 1945, back in the States, the Navy charged him with homosexuality while drunk. A general court-martial followed and he was clapped into the brig for a year and then discharged dishonorably in 1946. Home, he complained of pressure in his head and began to wander about the country working at various jobs, including one brief stint as a cowboy in California. Once, after seeing a child preacher, he decided to become a preacher himself. It was shortly after that that he was committed to a hospital for psychiatric treatment. He aggressively took to preaching to other patients. He did not have visual or auditory hallucinations, but he said God came to him as a "thinking wave." He claimed invulnerability to death or insanity. He claimed the power to produce earthquakes, hurricanes, tornadoes, and floods. And he told his psychiatrist that he could will himself not to have wet dreams. That seemed important. He suffered from periodic paranoia, irritability, restlessness, and tension.

He and his brother soon found themselves in the same veterans' hospital in Roanoke, Virginia. Ravitz made detailed daily physical and psychiatric observations of both men. When the would-be preacher's voltage readings were highest —which was at full and new moons—he felt the least healthy. Those were the times when he passionately tried to talk his brother out of his "sinful" goals, one of which was to become a baseball player. Those were the times when he talked about "slaying the wicked." And those were the times when he was "increasingly grandiose, paranoid, tense and irritable," according to Ravitz.

His highest bi-monthly voltage readings were during the winter of 1951. His voltage gradually declined during the following months, however, although each month still had two peaks at the full and new moons. A chart of his daily voltage readings would resemble a jagged but steadily declining graph.

This voltage reduction had its effect. Just as Ravitz's studies had indicated that mentally healthier patients have lower voltage readings, so this ex-sailor's mental health improved as his voltage readings declined. The young man began to relax. Some of his speech difficulties disappeared. His appetite improved and he gained weight—44 pounds, in fact. He admitted feeling better. And he became less possessed by visions of fire and brimstone. He stopped trying to talk his brother into becoming a fellow preacher. When his brother fantasized aloud about becoming a ballplayer, he merely shrugged his shoulders.

One of the most intriguing things about Ravitz's work is that it may forecast how the moon can be used for medical and psychiatric diagnosis. A former county medical examiner in Massachusetts, Edmund A. Jannino, speculated about that possibility during an international symposium on forensic immunology, medicine, pathology, and toxicology at London University in 1963.[91] In his lecture to the conclave, Jannino suggested that Ravitz's analysis of moon madness might be the key to unraveling two of the most baffling murder sprees of the last century. One of them remains unsolved to this day, and much uncertainty still surrounds the other, although a man was sent to prison for it in 1967.

The problem, Jannino pointed out, is that a motive is hard to detect. The cases have remarkable similarities. Women were the victims in both instances, and sex was an unmistakable ingredient. All seven of the first killer's victims in 1888 were prostitutes attacked outdoors in one of London's seedier neighborhoods, their bodies left grotesquely mutilated, cut open as if attacked by some deranged butcher. The man who claimed to be the second killer confessed to the murder of thirteen elderly Boston women. All were perfectly respectable, but most were strangled with such sexually associated pieces of clothing as brassieres and nylon stockings. Several were found lying "in suggestive sexual positions with variable minor genital trauma."[92]

The hunt for a logical explanation for the illogical acts of a homicidal mind can be frustrating, Jannino said. Perhaps the tides of bodily electricity are the only predictable, logical action involved. Jannino was making no premature jump onto any theory's bandwagon, mind you; merely thinking out loud in a structured way.

Oh, and the subjects of this suburban Bostonian's talk in London? Who else but Jack the Ripper and the Boston Strangler.

Reference Notes

INTRODUCTION: THE SILVER WATCH

1. Cottrell, John, "Moon Madness: Does It Really Exist?" *Science Digest,* October, 1969, 24.
2. *Ibid.*
3. *Ibid.*
4. Slaughter, J.W., "The Moon in Childhood and Folklore," *American Journal of Psychology,* 1902, *13* (2) 311.
5. Rosten, Leo. *The Joys of Yiddish* (New York: Pocket Books, 1970), p. 522.
6. Slaughter, *op. cit.,* p. 311.
7. White, William, "Moon Myth in Medicine," *Psychoanalytic Review,* 1914, *1* (3) 243.
8. Stahl, William H., "Moon Madness," *Annals of Medical History,* 1937, *9,* 260.
9. Kelley, Douglas, "Mania and the Moon," *Psychoanalytic Review,* 1942, *29,* 416.
10. White, *op. cit.,* pp. 251–252.
11. Scott, James G. *The Mythology of All Races,* vol. 12, ed. Louis H. Gray (New York: Cooper Square Publishers, 1964), p. 266.
12. Frazer, James George. *The Golden Bough,* vol. 1, part 1, 3rd ed. (New York: Macmillan, 1935), pp. 125–126.
13. *Ibid.*
14. *Ibid.,* pp. 121–122.
15. Kelley, *op. cit.,* p. 407.
16. *Ibid.,* p. 418.
17. *Ibid.,* pp. 421–422.
18. Laycock, T., "On Lunar Influence; Being a Fourth Contribution to Proleptics," *The Lancet,* 1843, *2,* 438.
19. Delaney, Janet; Lupton, Mary Jane; and Toth, Emily. *The Curse* (New York: Mentor, 1977), p. 219.
20. Frazer, *op. cit.,* p. 319.
21. Chartrand, Mark R. III, "Happy New Year," *Omni,* January 1979, 22.
22. Stahl, Doris Ann, "The Relevance of Hard but Unusual Data upon

Commanding Officers in Their Utilization of Manpower," Thesis for M.P.A., #396, John Jay College of Criminal Justice, 1974, p. 24.
23. Balmforth, Ed E., "Teng's New Year Plan," *New York Times,* January 12, 1979, A22.
24. Chartrand, *op. cit.,* p. 22.
25. Rosten, *op. cit.,* pp. 466–467.
26. Skilling, William, and Richardson, Robert. *Astronomy* (New York: Henry Holt, 1954), pp. 70–71.
27. *Ibid.,* p. 71.
28. Adderley, E.E., and Bowen, E.G., "Lunar Component in Precipitation Data," *Science,* 1962, *137,* 750.
29. Palmer, John D., "The Many Clocks of Man," *Cycles,* 1971, *22* (2), 40.
30. Brown, Frank A., Jr., letter to author, November 25, 1979.
31. Brown, Frank A., Jr.; Hastings, J. Woodland; and Palmer, John D. *The Biological Clock: Two Views* (New York: Academic Press, 1970), p. 15.
32. Menaker, Walter, and Menaker, Abraham, "Lunar Periodicity in Human Reproduction: A Likely Unit of Biological Time," *American Journal of Obstetrics and Gynecology,* 1959, *77* (4), 905–914.

CHAPTER 1: GREEN CHEESE

1. Hartley, Timothy. *Moon Lore* (Rutland, Vt.: Charles E. Tuttle, 1970), pp. 1–2.
2. Gill, David; Eddington, Arthur S.; and Jones, Harold S., "Telescope," *Encyclopaedia Britannica,* vol. 21 (Chicago: Encyclopaedia Britannica, 1951), p. 908.
3. Slaughter, J.W., "The Moon in Childhood and Folklore," *American Journal of Psychology,* 1902, *13* (2), 311.
4. Frazer, James George, *The Golden Bough,* vol. 2, part 4, 3rd ed. (New York: Macmillan, 1935), p. 130.
5. *Ibid.*
6. Rush, Anne Kent. *Moon, Moon* (Berkeley, Calif.: Moon Books, 1976)
7. Slaughter, *op. cit.,* p. 311.
8. White, William, "Moon Myth in Medicine," *Psychoanalytic Review,* 1914, *1* (3), 251.
9. Slaughter, *op. cit.,* p. 310.
10. Hartley, *op. cit.,* pp. 56–59.
11. Rush, *op. cit.,* p. 164.
12. Frazer, *op. cit.,* p. 130.
13. Langdon, Stephen H. *The Mythology of All Races,* vol. 5, ed. Canon John A. MacCullough (New York: Cooper Square Publishers, 1964), p. 287.
14. Slaughter, *op. cit.,* p. 302.
15. White, *op. cit.,* p. 242.
16. Slaughter, *op. cit.,* p. 303.

17. Hartley, *op. cit.*, p. 20.
18. *Ibid.*, pp. 35, 69.
19. White, *op. cit.*, p. 254.
20. *Ibid.*
21. Rush, *op. cit.*, p. 164.
22. Slaughter, *op. cit.*, p. 310.
23. White, *op. cit.*, p. 251.
24. Frazer, *op.cit.*, vol. 2, part 3, pp. 73–74.
25. *Ibid.*, p. 73.
26. Slaughter, *op. cit.*, p. 300.
27. Frazer, *op. cit.*, p. 72.
28. Morris, William and Mary. *Morris Dictionary of Word and Phrase Origins* (New York: Harper & Row, 1977), pp. 384–385.
29. *Ibid.*

CHAPTER 2: LUNACY

1. Oliven, John F., "Moonlight and Nervous Disorders," *American Journal of Psychiatry*, 1943, *99*, 579.
2. *Ibid.*, p. 581.
3. Stahl, Doris Ann, "The Relevance of Hard but Unusual Data upon Commanding Officers in Their Utilization of Manpower," Thesis for M.P.A., #396, John Jay College of Criminal Justice, 1974, p. 23.
4. White, William, "Moon Myth in Medicine," *The Psychoanalytic Review*, 1914, *1* (3), 246.
5. Hartley, William and Ellen, "Moon Madness," *Science Digest*, September 1972, 28.
6. Oliven, *op. cit.*, p. 580.
7. Stahl, William H., "Moon Madness," *Annals of Medical History*, 1937, *9*, 257.
8. "The Moon and Medicine," *Clinical Excerpts*, 1940, *14* (8), 7.
9. *Ibid.*
10. Kelley, Douglas, "Mania and the Moon," *Psychoanalytic Review*, 1942, *29*, 420.
11. Foissac, P., "The Influence of the Lunar Phases on the Physical and Moral Man," *St. Louis Medical and Surgical Journal*, 1855, *13*, 510.
12. "The Moon and Medicine," *op. cit.*, p. 8.
13. Oliven, *op. cit.*, p. 580.
14. *Ibid.*
15. Stahl, William H., *op. cit.*, p. 257.
16. *Ibid.*
17. Oliven, *op. cit.*, p. 580.
18. Timmins, Clark, *Planting by the Moon* (Chicago: Aries Press, 1939), p. 27.

19. Trapp, Carl E., "Lunacy and the Moon," *American Journal of Psychiatry,* 1937, *94,* 341–342.
20. Oliven, *op. cit.,* p. 581.
21. Kelley, *op. cit.,* pp. 412–413.
22. Oliven, *op. cit.,* p. 581.
23. Kelley, *op. cit.,* p. 413.
24. Timmins, *op. cit.,* p. 27.
25. Oliven, *op. cit.,* p. 581.
26. Ravitz, Leonard J., "Electrocyclic Phenomena and Emotional States," *Journal of Clinical and Experimental Psychopathology,* 1952, *13* (2), 94.

CHAPTER 3: LUNAR SYMPATHY

1. McDaniel, Walton Brooks, "The Moon, Werewolves, and Medicine," *Transactions & Studies of the College of Physicians of Philadelphia,* 1950, *18,* 115.
2. *Ibid.*
3. *Ibid.*
4. Laycock, T., "On Lunar Influence; Being A Fourth Contribution to Proleptics," *The Lancet,* 1843, *2,* 439.
5. Timmins, Clark. *Planting by the Moon* (Chicago: Aries Press, 1939), p. 15.
6. McDaniel, *op. cit.,* p. 114.
7. Stahl, William H., "Moon Madness," *Annals of Medical History,* 1937, *9,* 250.
8. Timmins, *op. cit.,* p. 14.
9. White, William, "Moon Myth in Medicine," *Psychoanalytic Review,* 1914, *1* (3), 248.
10. King, Howard, "Medicine and the Moon: Beliefs of Other Days," *Medical Record,* 1917, *92,* 1031.
11. *Ibid.*
12. *Ibid.*
13. White, *op. cit.,* p. 243.
14. Timmins, *op. cit.,* p. 14.
15. *Ibid.,* p. 13.
16. *Ibid.,* pp. 13–14.
17. King, *op. cit.,* p. 1031.
18. *Ibid.*
19. Stahl, *op. cit.,* p. 261.
20. Frazer, James George. *The Golden Bough,* vol. 2, part 7, 3rd ed. (New York: Macmillan, 1935), pp. 77–78, 301.
21. *Ibid.,* pp. 301–303.
22. "Mistletoe Kiss of Death for Some Trees," *Boston Evening Globe,* December 11, 1978, 5.

23. Stahl, *op. cit.*, p. 253.
24. McDaniel, *op. cit.*, p. 114.
25. Foissac, P., "The Influence of the Lunar Phases on the Physical and Moral Man," *St. Louis Medical and Surgical Journal,* 1855, *13,* 502.
26. Timmins, *op. cit.*, p. 30.
27. Trapp, Carl E., "Lunacy and the Moon," *American Journal of Psychiatry,* 1937, 94, 340.
28. Timmins, *op. cit.*, p. 30.
29. Stahl, *op. cit.*, p. 262.
30. *Ibid.*
31. *Ibid.*
32. Foissac, *op. cit.*, pp. 506–507.
33. Laycock, *op. cit.*, p. 439.
34. King, *op. cit.*, p. 1031.
35. McDaniel, *op. cit.*, p. 114.
36. Laycock, *op. cit.*, p. 439.
37. *Ibid.*
38. King, *op. cit.*, p. 1031.
39. Laycock, *op. cit.*, p. 438.
40. Foissac, *op. cit.*, p. 515.
41. Timmins, *op. cit.*, pp. 14–15.
42. Kelley, Douglas, "Mania and the Moon," *Psychoanalytic Review,* 1942, *29,* 420.
43. Stahl, *op. cit.*, p. 252.
44. *Ibid.*
45. Cottrell, John, "Moon Madness: Does It Really Exist?" *Science Digest,* October 1969, 25.
46. Frazer, *op. cit.*, vol. 2, part 4, p. 149.
47. *Ibid.*, p. 144.
48. White, *op. cit.*, p. 248.
49. *Ibid.*, p. 210.
50. Kelley, *op. cit.*, p. 407.
51. Trapp, *op. cit.*, p. 339.
52. Stahl, *op. cit.*, p. 254.
53. Frazer, *op. cit.*, pp. 144–145.
54. *Ibid.*, p. 144.
55. "The Moon and Medicine," *Clinical Excerpts,* 1940, *14* (8), 11.
56. Laycock, *op. cit.*, p. 441.
57. Hale, Jud, ed., *The Old Farmer's Almanac* 1979 (Berlin, N.H.: Yankee, 1978), pp. 76, 168–171.
58. Timmins, *op. cit.*, p. 16.
59. Stahl, *op. cit.*, p. 253.
60. Frye, Richard Nelson, "Darius," *World Book,* vol. 5 (Chicago: Field Enterprises, 1977), p. 30.
61. Kagan, Donald, "Greece, Ancient," *World Book,* vol. 8 (Chicago: Field Enterprises, 1977), p. 366.

62. "Marathon," *Encyclopaedia Britannica,* vol. 14 (Chicago: Encyclopaedia Britannica, 1951), p. 857.
63. Kagan, *op. cit.,* p. 366.
64. "Memorable Dates," *The World Almanac & Book of Facts 1977* (New York: Newspaper Enterprise Association, 1976), p. 709.
65. "Marathon," *op. cit.,* p. 857.
66. *Ibid.,* p. 858.
67. Hammond, Nicholas Goeffrey, "Marathon, Battle of," *Encyclopaedia Britannica,* vol. 14 (Chicago: Encyclopaedia Britannica, 1965), p. 845.
68. "Marathon," *op. cit.,* p. 857.
69. Frye, Richard Nelson, "Marathon," *World Book,* vol. 13 (Chicago: Field Enterprises, 1977), p. 150.
70. *Ibid.*
71. Hammond, *op. cit.,* p. 845.
72. Webster, Frederick, "Marathon Race," *Encyclopaedia Britannica,* vol. 14 (Chicago: Encyclopaedia Britannica, 1951), p. 858.
73. Hammond, *op. cit.,* p. 845.
74. Foissac, *op. cit.,* p. 515.
75. King, *op. cit.,* p. 1031.
76. Laycock, *op. cit.,* p. 439.
77. "Marathon," *op. cit.,* p. 858.
78. Hammond, *op. cit.,* p. 846.
79. *Ibid.*
80. "Marathon," *op. cit.,* p. 858.
81. Hammond, *op. cit.,* p. 846.
82. *Ibid.*
83. King, *op. cit.,* p. 1031.

CHAPTER 4: "THE MOON IS GOD"

1. "Preaching Pan, Isis and 'Om,' " *Time,* August 6, 1979, 84.
2. Fox, Selena, and Alan, Jim, interview with author, August 2, 1979.
3. "Preaching Pan, Isis and 'Om,' " *op. cit.,* p. 84.
4. Fox, Selena, and Alan, Jim, *op. cit.*
5. "Preaching Pan, Isis and 'Om,'" *op. cit.,* p. 84.
6. Passmore, Nancy, interview with author, September 1, 1979.
7. Rush, Anne Kent. *Moon, Moon* (Berkeley, Calif.: Moon Books, 1976), pp. 16–21.
8. Passmore, *op. cit.*
9. Rush, *op. cit.,* pp. 16–21.
10. Marshak, Alexander, "Lunar Notation on Upper Paleolithic Remains," *Science,* 1964, *146,* 744.
11. *Ibid.,* p. 743.
12. *Ibid.*

13. Kelsy, Rachel, "Stonehenge," *The 1977 Lunar Calendar,* ed. Nancy Passmore (Boston: Luna Press, 1976), p. 27.
14. Hawkins, Gerald S., "Stonehenge: A Neolithic Computer," *Nature,* 1964, *202* (4939), 1258–1261.
15. Sofaer, Anna; Zinser, Volker; and Sinclair, Rolf M., "A Unique Solar Marking Construct," *Science,* 1979, *206* (4416), 283–291.
16. Langdon, Stephen H. *The Mythology of All Races,* vol. 5, ed. Canon John A. MacCullough (New York: Cooper Square Publishers, 1964), pp. 3, 6.
17. *Ibid.*, p. 5.
18. "Memorable Dates," *The World Almanac & Book of Facts 1977* (New York: Newspaper Enterprise Association, 1976), p. 709.
19. White, William, "Moon Myth in Medicine," *Psychoanalytic Review,* 1914, *1* (3), 242.
20. King, Howard, "Medicine and the Moon: Beliefs of Other Days," *Medical Record,* 1917, *92,* 1030.
21. Slaughter, J.W., "The Moon in Childhood and Folklore," *American Journal of Psychology,* 1902, *13* (2), 314.
22. Langdon, *op. cit.*, pp. 152–153.
23. White, *op. cit.*, p. 242.
24. Slaughter, *op. cit.*, p. 315.
25. *Ibid.*
26. Stahl, Doris Ann, "The Relevance of Hard but Unusual Data upon Commanding Officers in Their Utilization of Manpower," Thesis for M.P.A., #396, John Jay College of Criminal Justice, 1974, p. 22.
27. Sheppard, Lancelot Capel, "Devil," *Encyclopaedia Britannica,* vol. 7 (Chicago: Encyclopaedia Britannica, 1965), p. 329.
28. Kelley, Douglas, "Mania and the Moon," *Psychoanalytic Review,* 1942, *29,* 409.
29. *Ibid.*, p. 410.
30. *Ibid.*
31. Slaughter, *op. cit.*, p. 315.
32. Ellis, Havelock. *Studies in the Psychology of Sex,* vol. 1 (New York: Random House, 1942), p. 130.
33. Slaughter, *op. cit.*, p. 315.
34. Frazer, James George, *The Golden Bough,* vol. 2, part 1, 3rd ed. (New York: Macmillan, 1935), p. 146.
35. "The Moon in Medicine," *Clinical Excerpts,* 1940, *14* (8), 3.
36. Slaughter, *op. cit.*, p. 313.
37. Frazer, *op. cit.*, part 6, pp. 140–141.
38. *Ibid.*, pp. 141–143.
39. Slaughter, *op. cit.*, p. 313.
40. Muller, W. Max. *The Mythology of All Races,* vol. 12, ed. Louis H. Gray (New York: Cooper Square Publishers, 1964), p. 38.
41. *Ibid.*

42. Trapp, Carl E., "Lunacy and the Moon," *American Journal of Psychiatry,* 1937, *94,* 339–340.
43. *Ibid.,* p. 340.
44. Stahl, William H., "Moon Madness," *Annals of Medical History,* 1937, *9,* 251.
45. Slaughter, *op. cit.,* pp. 313–314.
46. White, *op. cit.,* p. 241.
47. *Ibid.,* p. 242.
48. McDaniel, Walton Brooks, "The Moon, Werewolves, and Medicine," *Transactions & Studies of the College of Physicians of Philadelphia,* 1950, *18,* 113.
49. Slaughter, *op. cit.,* p. 314.
50. *Ibid.,* p. 304.
51. *Ibid.*
52. Frazer, *op. cit.,* pp. 281–283.
53. Frazer, *op. cit.,* vol. 1, part 4, pp. 72–74; vol. 1, part 6, p. 214.
54. *Ibid.,* pp. 218–221.
55. *Ibid.,* vol. 2, part 5, pp. 24–25.
56. *Ibid.,* vol. 1, part 6, pp. 53–54.
57. Geller, Sheldon H., and Shannon, Herbert W., "The Moon, Weather and Mental Hospital Contacts: Confirmation and Explanation of the Transylvania Effect," *Journal of Psychiatric Nursing and Mental Health Services,* 1976, *14,* 13.
58. Jones, Paul, and Jones, Susan, "Lunar Association with Suicide," *Suicide and Life-Threatening Behavior,* 1977, 7 (1), 32.
59. Slaughter, *op. cit.,* p. 307.
60. *Ibid.,* p. 305.
61. *Ibid.,* p. 307.

CHAPTER 5: FERTILITY

1. "The Moon and Medicine," *Clinical Excerpts,* 1940, *14* (8), 7.
2. Frazer, James George, *The Golden Bough,* vol. 1, part 1, 3rd ed. (New York: Macmillan, 1935), pp. 1–12.
3. *Ibid.*
4. *Ibid.*
5. Rush, Anne Kent. *Moon, Moon* (Berkeley, Calif.: Moon Books, 1976), p. 152.
6. Stahl, William H., "Moon Madness," *Annals of Medical History,* 1937, *9,* 251.
7. Luce, Gay G., ed. *Biological Rhythms in Psychiatry and Medicine* (Public Health Service Publication #2088; Washington, D.C.: U.S. Govt. Printing Office, 1970), p. 130.
8. *Ibid.*
9. Stahl, *op. cit.,* p. 252.

10. *Ibid.*
11. *Ibid.*
12. Kelley, Douglas, "Mania and the Moon," *Psychoanalytic Review,* 1942, *29,* 421.
13. Laycock, T., "On Lunar Influence; Being A Fourth Contribution to Proleptics," *The Lancet,* 1843, *2,* 438.
14. White, William, "Moon Myth in Medicine," *Psychoanalytic Review,* 1914, *1* (3), 250.
15. King, Howard, "Medicine and the Moon: Beliefs of Other Days," *Medical Record,* 1917, *92,* 1030.
16. Laycock, *op. cit.*, p. 438.
17. White, *op. cit.*, p. 250.
18. King, *op. cit.*, p. 1030.
19. Frazer, *op. cit.*, vol. 1, part 7, pp. 75–76.
20. "The Moon and Medicine," *op. cit.*, p. 5.
21. Stahl, *op. cit.*, pp. 254–255.
22. "The Moon and Medicine," *op. cit.*, pp. 6–7.
23. *Ibid.*
24. *Ibid.*
25. *Ibid.*
26. Kelley, *op. cit.*, p. 419.
27. King, *op. cit.*, p. 1030.
28. Stahl, *op. cit.*, p. 254.
29. "The Moon and Medicine," *op. cit.*, p. 6.
30. Frazer, *op. cit.*, vol. 2, part 1, p. 128.
31. Oliven, John F., "Moonlight and Nervous Disorders," *American Journal of Psychiatry,* 1943, *99,* 583.
32. White, *op. cit.*, pp. 250–251.
33. *Ibid.*
34. *Ibid.*, pp. 255–256.
35. Sadger, J. *Sleep Walking and Moon Walking,* trans. Louise Brink (Nervous and Mental Disease Monograph Series No. 31; Washington, D.C.: Nervous and Mental Disease Publishing Co., 1920), p. 19.
36. Oliven, *op. cit.*, p. 583.
37. Sadger, *op. cit.*, p. 34.
38. *Ibid.*, p. 35.

CHAPTER 6: MOISTURE

1. Kelley, Douglas, "Mania and the Moon," *Psychoanalytic Review,* 1942, *29,* 421–422.
2. Kelsy, Rachel, "Lost Civilizations of the Goddess," *The 1977 Lunar Calendar,* ed. Nancy Passmore (Boston: Luna Press, 1976), p. 5.
3. Stahl, William H., "Moon Madness," *Annals of Medical History,* 1937, *9,* 257.

4. Slaughter, J.W., "The Moon in Childhood and Folklore," *American Journal of Psychology,* 1902, *13* (2), 299.
5. *Ibid.*
6. *Ibid.*
7. *Ibid.*, p. 302.
8. Foissac, P., "The Influence of the Lunar Phases on the Physical and Moral Man," *St. Louis Medical and Surgical Journal,* 1855, *13,* 503.
9. Timmins, Clark. *Planting by the Moon* (Chicago: Aries Press, 1939), p. 10.
10. *Ibid.*
11. Harley, Timothy, *Moon Lore* (Rutland, Vt.: Charles E. Tuttle, 1970), pp. 195–197.
12. Charriere, Henri, *Papillon* (New York: Pocket Books, 1971), pp. 50–51.
13. Stahl, *op. cit.*, p. 255.
14. McDaniel, Walton Brooks, "The Moon, Werewolves, and Medicine," *Transactions & Studies of the College of Physicians of Philadelphia,* 1950, *18,* 115.

CHAPTER 7: LYCANTHROPY

1. Rosenstock, Harvey, and Vincent, Kenneth, "A Case of Lycanthropy," *American Journal of Psychiatry,* 1977, *134* (10), 1148.
2. *Ibid.*, p. 1149.
3. Baring-Gould, Sabine. *The Book of Were-Wolves: Being an Account of a Terrible Superstition* (New York: Causeway Books, 1973), p. 10.
4. Stahl, William H., "Moon Madness," *Annals of Medical History,* 1937, *9,* 259.
5. Frazer, James George, *The Golden Bough,* vol. 1, part 7, 3rd ed. (New York: Macmillan, 1935), pp. 314–315.
6. McDaniel, Walton Brooks, "The Moon, Werewolves, and Medicine," *Transactions & Studies of the College of Physicians of Philadelphia,* 1950, *18,* 119.
7. *Ibid.*
8. Eisler, Robert, *Man Into Wolf: An Anthropological Interpretation of Sadism, Masochism, and Lycanthropy* (New York: Greenwood Press, 1969), p. 148.
9. *Webster's Collegiate Dictionary,* 5th ed. (Springfield, Mass.: G. & C. Merriam, 1948), p. 664.
10. Rosenstock, *op. cit.*, pp. 1147–1148.
11. *Ibid.*
12. Surawicz, Frida, and Banta, Richard, "Lycanthropy Revisited," *Canadian Psychiatric Association Journal,* 1975, *20,* 537–538.
13. *Ibid.*
14. *Ibid.*
15. *Ibid.*

16. Rosenstock, *op. cit.*, pp. 1147–1148.
17. *Ibid.*
18. Copper, Basil. *The Werewolf in Legend, Fact & Art* (New York: St. Martin's Press, 1977), p. 27.
19. Baring-Gould, *op. cit.*, pp. 105–107.
20. Summers, Montague. *The Werewolf* (New Hyde Park, N.Y.: University Books, 1966), pp. 163–164.
21. *Ibid.*, p. 46.
22. Baring-Gould, *op. cit.*, pp. 112–113.
23. *Ibid.*, p. 113.
24. McDaniel, *op. cit.*, p. 116.
25. Summers, *op. cit.*, pp. 94–96.
26. *Ibid.*, pp. 73–74.
27. *Ibid.*, p. 118.
28. Copper, *op. cit.*, pp. 36–37.
29. Summers, *op. cit.*, p. 118.
30. *Ibid.*, pp. 123–124.
31. *Ibid.*
32. Copper, *op. cit.*, p. 44.
33. *Ibid.*, p. 74.
34. McDaniel, *op. cit.*, p. 121.
35. Copper, *op. cit.*, p. 28.
36. Summers, *op. cit.*, p. 15.
37. Hackler, Timothy, "That Ol' Devil Moon," *Milwaukee Journal,* March 18, 1979, Sunday magazine 52.
38. Copper, *op. cit.*, p. 27.
39. *Ibid.*, pp. 36–37.
40. *Ibid.*
41. *Ibid.*, p. 46.
42. Hackler, *op. cit.*, Sunday magazine 52.
43. Copper, *op. cit.*, p. 46.
44. Summers, *op. cit.*, p. 228.
45. *Ibid.*, p. 3.
46. Copper, *op. cit.*, pp. 46–47.
47. *Ibid.*, p. 44.
48. Summers, *op. cit.*, p. 228.
49. Copper, *op. cit.*, pp. 30–31.
50. Summers, *op. cit.*, p. 164.
51. *Ibid.*, pp. 164–165.
52. Copper, *op. cit.*, pp. 35–36.
53. Summers, *op. cit.*, pp. 116–117.
54. *Ibid.*
55. McDaniel, *op. cit.*, pp. 121–122.
56. Surawicz, *op. cit.*, pp. 540–541.
57. *Ibid.*, p. 541. (Surawicz and Banta submitted their patient to a full battery of psychiatric and physical tests, including a brain biopsy, re-

sults of which are discussed in the report text. They diagnosed his psychotic behavior as delusion; he was discharged from the hospital once successful medication was begun.)

58. *Ibid.*
59. Eisler, *op. cit.*, p. 166.
60. Fodor, Nandor, "Lycanthropy as a Psychic Mechanism," *Journal of American Folklore,* 1945, *58* (227), 310–316.
61. Summers, *op. cit.*, pp. 50–51.
62. Eisler, *op. cit.*, p. 165.
63. Rosenstock, *op. cit.*, p. 1149.
64. Summers, *op. cit.*, p. 51.
65. Surawicz, *op. cit.*, pp. 538–539.
66. Summers, *op. cit.*, p. 45.
67. Copper, *op. cit.*, pp. 32–34.
68. *Ibid.*, p. 81.
69. *Ibid.*, pp. 80, 108–109.

CHAPTER 8: HUNGRY DRAGONS

1. Moore, Patrick. *Suns, Myths and Men,* rev. ed. (New York: W.W. Norton, 1968), pp. 35–38.
2. Hopson, Janet, and Rogers, Michael, "The Last Eclipse," *Science News,* 1979, *115* (9), 139.
3. Moore, *op. cit.*, pp. 35–38.
4. Hopson, *op. cit.*, p. 139.
5. Scott, James G. *The Mythology of All Races,* vol. 12, ed. Louis H. Gray (New York: Cooper Square Publishers, 1964), p. 333.
6. Moore, *op. cit.*, p. 39.
7. *Ibid.*, p. 37.
8. *Ibid.*
9. Hopson, *op. cit.*, p. 138.
10. Browne, Malcolm, "Total Eclipse of Sun Races Across West," *The New York Times,* February 27, 1979, C4.
11. *Ibid.*
12. Moore, *op. cit.*, pp. 18–23.
13. *Ibid.*
14. *Ibid.*
15. *Ibid.*
16. *Ibid.*
17. *Ibid.*
18. Beazley, Sir Charles Raymond, *et al.*, "Columbus, Christopher," *Encyclopaedia Britannica,* vol. 6 (Chicago: Encyclopaedia Britannica, 1951), p. 83.
19. Moore, *op. cit.*, p. 43.
20. Foissac, P., "The Influence of the Lunar Phases on the Physical and

Moral Man," *St. Louis Medical and Surgical Journal,* 1855, *13,* 515.
21. Moore, *op. cit.*, p. 40.
22. Hopson, *op. cit.*, p. 139.
23. Foissac, *op. cit.*, p. 515.
24. Moore, *op. cit.*, pp. 40–41.
25. Foissac, *op. cit.*, p. 515.
26. Moore, *op. cit.*, pp. 40–41.
27. *Ibid.*
28. *Ibid.*, p. 42.
29. *Ibid.*
30. Foissac, *op. cit.*, p. 515.
31. *Ibid.*
32. *Ibid.*, pp. 514–515.
33. "Solar Eclipse—'Awesome,'" *Boston Herald American,* February 27, 1979, 29.
34. White, William, "Moon Myth in Medicine," *Psychoanalytic Review,* 1914, *1* (3), 251.
35. Cottrell, John, "Moon Madness: Does It Really Exist?" *Science Digest,* October 1969, 25.
36. Frazer, James George. *The Golden Bough,* vol. 1, part 1, 3rd ed. (New York: Macmillan, 1935), pp. 311–312.
37. Hopson, *op. cit.*, p. 139.
38. *Ibid.*

CHAPTER 9: EPILEPSY

1. McDaniel, Walton Brooks, "The Moon, Werewolves, and Medicine," *Transactions & Studies of the College of Physicians of Philadelphia,* 1950, *18,* 116.
2. Stahl, William H., "Moon Madness," *Annals of Medical History,* 1937, *9,* 256.
3. King, Howard, "Medicine and the Moon: Beliefs of Other Days," *Medical Record,* 1917, *92,* 1032.
4. McDaniel, *op. cit.*, p. 116.
5. Stahl, *op. cit.*, p. 256.
6. *Ibid.*
7. *Ibid.*
8. *Ibid.*
9. *Ibid.*
10. Trapp, Carl E., "Lunacy and the Moon," *American Journal of Psychiatry,* 1937, *94,* 340.
11. *Ibid.*
12. Kelley, Douglas, "Mania and the Moon," *Psychoanalytic Review,* 1942, *29,* 408–409.
13. "The Moon and Medicine," *Clinical Excerpts,* 1940, *14* (8), 8.

14. *Ibid.*
15. Foissac, P., "The Influence of the Lunar Phases on the Physical and Moral Man," *St. Louis Medical and Surgical Journal,* 1855, *13,* 508.
16. *Ibid.*
17. Kelley, *op. cit.*, pp. 411–412.
18. *Ibid.*, p. 407.

CHAPTER 10: SELENOLOGY

1. Shoemaker, Eugene, "Moon," *World Book,* vol. 13 (Chicago: Field Enterprises, 1977), p. 646a.
2. Burke, James, "Moon," *The Encyclopedia Americana,* vol. 19, intern'l rev. ed. (Danbury, Conn.: Americana Corp., 1978), p. 429.
3. Shoemaker, *op. cit.*, p. 646.
4. Hackler, Timothy, "That Ol' Devil Moon," *Milwaukee Journal,* March 18, 1979, Sunday magazine 48.
5. "The Earth: Size, Computation of Time, Seasons," *The World Almanac & Book of Facts 1977* (New York: Newspaper Enterprise Association, 1977), p. 763.
6. Burke, *op. cit.*, p. 429.
7. Shoemaker, *op. cit.*, p. 646a.
8. *Ibid.*, p. 646.
9. "More Moonlets," *New York Times,* May 22, 1979, C2.
10. Wilford, John Noble, "Pioneer Craft Detects 11th Moon and a 7th Ring in Orbit of Saturn," *New York Times,* September 7, 1979, A1, D16.
11. "Jupiter's World," *Science News,* 1979, *115* (10), 148.
12. Rensberger, Boyce, "Cosmic Clues on Jupiter's Moons," *The New York Times,* February 27, 1979, C2.
13. Gingerich, Owen, "Moon," *Collier's Encyclopedia,* vol. 16, rev. ed. (New York: Macmillan Educational Corp., 1978), p. 522.
14. Shoemaker, *op. cit.*, p. 646a.
15. Burke, *op. cit.*, pp. 429, 436.
16. Shoemaker, *op. cit.*, p. 646a.
17. *Ibid.*
18. Burke, *op. cit.*, p. 432.
19. Hackler, *op. cit.*, Sunday magazine 48.
20. Burke, *op. cit.*, p. 432.
21. *Ibid.*, pp. 432–433.
22. *Ibid.*, p. 432.
23. *Ibid.*
24. Urey, Harold, "Moon, Origin and History of," *Collier's Encyclopedia,* vol. 16, rev. ed. (New York: Macmillan Educational Corp., 1978), p. 528.
25. Burke, *op. cit.*, p. 432.
26. Gingerich, *op. cit.*, p. 526.

27. Shoemaker, *op. cit.*, p. 646a.
28. Urey, *op. cit.*, p. 523.

CHAPTER 11: OCEAN TIDES

1. Proudman, Joseph, and Groves, Gordon, "Tides," *Encyclopaedia Britannica,* vol. 22 (Chicago: Encyclopaedia Britannica, 1965), pp. 194–195.
2. *Ibid.*
3. *Ibid.*
4. Sarton, George, "Lunar Influences on Living Things," *Isis,* 1939, *30,* 497.
5. Reid, Robert, "Tide," *World Book,* vol. 19 (Chicago: Field Enterprises, 1977), p. 218.
6. Proudman, *op. cit.,* pp. 194–195.
7. Sarton, *op. cit.,* p. 497.
8. Proudman, *op. cit.,* pp. 194–195.
9. Sarton, *op. cit.,* p. 497.
10. *Ibid.*
11. Emery, C. Eugene, Jr., "It Must Be a Full Moon," Providence (R.I.) *Sunday Journal,* January 8, 1978, Sunday magazine 5.
12. Osborn, Roger Dean, "The Moon and the Mental Hospital: An Investigation of One Area of Folklore," *Journal of Psychiatric Nursing and Mental Health Services,* 1968, *6,* 89.
13. Reid, *op. cit.,* p. 220.
14. *Ibid.,* p. 219.
15. Emery, *op. cit.,* Sunday magazine 7.
16. Hartley, William and Ellen, "Moon Madness," *Science Digest,* September 1972, 31.
17. "Tides," *Van Nostrand's Scientific Encyclopedia,* ed. Douglas M. Considine, 5th ed. (New York: Van Nostrand Reinhold, 1976), p. 2203.
18. Proudman, *op. cit.,* p. 194.
19. Ottewell, Guy. *The 1979 Lunar Calendar,* ed. Nancy Passmore (Boston: Luna Press, 1978), p. 17.
20. "Tides," *op. cit.,* (and "Tidal Energy," *loc. cit.*), pp. 2200, 2203.
21. Proudman, *op. cit.,* p. 194.
22. Reid, *op. cit.,* p. 220.
23. "Tidal Energy," *op. cit.,* pp. 2200, 2202.
24. *Ibid.*
25. Reid, *op. cit.,* p. 220.
26. "Tidal Energy," *op. cit.,* pp. 2200, 2202.
27. Proudman, *op. cit.,* p. 200.
28. Raymond, Charles, "Bay of Fundy," *Encyclopaedia Britannica,* vol. 9 (Chicago: Encyclopaedia Britannica, 1965), p. 1011.
29. Proudman, *op. cit.,* p. 200.

30. Ketchum, Bostwick, "Bay of Fundy," *World Book*, vol. 2 (Chicago: Field Enterprises, 1977), p. 130.
31. Proudman, *op. cit.*, p. 200.
32. Raymond, *op. cit.*, p. 1011.
33. Reid, *op. cit.*, p. 218.

CHAPTER 12: ATMOSPHERIC TIDES

1. Sarton, George, "Lunar Influences on Living Things," *Isis*, 1939, *30*, 498.
2. *Ibid.*, p. 499.
3. Kiser, William; Carpenter, Thomas; and Brier, Glenn, "The Atmospheric Tides at Wake Island," *Monthly Weather Review*, 1963, *91*, 569.
4. Brier, Glenn, "Diurnal and Semidiurnal Atmospheric Tides in Relation to Precipitation Variations," *Monthly Weather Review*, 1965, *93* (2), 93.
5. *Ibid.*
6. Stolov, Harold, "Tidal Wind Fields in the Atmosphere," *Journal of Meteorology*, 1955, *12*, 117–140.
7. Kiser, *op. cit.*, pp. 566–572.
8. Brier, *op. cit.*, p. 93.
9. Proudman, Joseph, and Groves, Gordon, "Tides," *Encyclopaedia Britannica*, vol. 22 (Chicago: Encyclopaedia Britannica, 1965), p. 205.
10. Knight, Peter, "Atmosphere (Earth)," *Van Nostrand's Scientific Encyclopedia*, ed. Douglas M. Considine, 5th ed. (New York: Van Nostrand Reinhold, 1976), p. 227.
11. Reid, Robert, "Tide," *World Book*, vol. 19 (Chicago: Field Enterprises, 1977), p. 220.

CHAPTER 13: THE EIFFEL EFFECT

1. Stetson, Harlan, "Modern Evidence for Differential Movement of Certain Points on the Earth's Surface," *Science*, 1944, *100*, 114–115.
2. *Ibid.*, p. 113.
3. *Ibid.*, p. 115.
4. *Ibid.*, pp. 115–116.
5. *Ibid.*, p. 113.
6. *Ibid.*
7. Menaker, Walter, and Menaker, Abraham, "Lunar Periodicity in Human Reproduction: A Likely Unit of Biological Time," *American Journal of Obstetrics and Gynecology*, 1959, *77* (4), 911.
8. Stetson, *op. cit.*, p. 116.
9. *Ibid.*
10. Melchoir, Paul. *The Earth Tides* (Oxford: Pergamon Press, 1966), pp. 2–9.

11. *Ibid.*, pp. 2, 8.
12. *Ibid.*
13. Small, Collie, "A Full Moon Can Beam Disaster," *Boston Herald American,* December 13, 1978, 15.
14. Timmins, Clark. *Planting by the Moon* (Chicago: Aries Press, 1939), pp. 19–22.

CHAPTER 14: EARTHQUAKES

1. "Calif. Rushes Quake Area Aid," *Boston Herald,* July 22, 1952, 15, 26; "California Quake Damage High in Millions," *op. cit.*, July 23, 6; "Quake Hits Calif. City," *op. cit.*, August 23, 1, 2; "Quake Damage Seen $20-Million, State Aid Looms 'Drop in Bucket,'" *Boston Sunday Herald,* August 24, 10.
2. "11 Die in Quake in So. California Mountain Town," *Boston Traveler,* July 21, 1952, 1, 6.
3. Ravitz, Leonard J., "Electrodynamic Field Theory in Psychiatry," *Southern Medical Journal,* 1953, *46* (7), 658.
4. Endicott, William, and Hager, Philip, "Strong Earthquake Jolts San Francisco," *The Boston Globe,* August 7, 1979, 3.
5. Carlsen, William, "San Franciscans Stunned as Quake, Worst in 68 Years, Strikes the City," *New York Times,* August 7, 1979, A1, B7.
6. Stetson, Harlan, "Modern Evidence for Differential Movement of Certain Points on the Earth's Surface," *Science,* 1944, *100,* 117.
7. *Ibid.*
8. Cooke, Robert, "Quakes Linked to Moon's Pull," *Boston Globe,* April 24, 1978, p. 7.
9. "Scientists Find Link Between Quakes and 'Earth Tides,'" *Tech Talk,* April 26, 1978, 9.
10. *Ibid.*
11. Sarton, George, "Lunar Influences on Living Things," *Isis,* 1939, *30,* 499.
12. Hopson, Janet, and Rogers, Michael, "The Last Eclipse," *Science News,* 1979, *115* (9), 139.
13. Shirk, Gertrude, "Earthquake Cycles," *Cycles,* 1978, *29* (2), 47.
14. Timmins, Clark. *Planting by the Moon* (Chicago: Aries Press, 1939), p. 19.
15. *Ibid.*, p. 18.

CHAPTER 15: MOON WEATHER

1. Carter, George, "Lemuria," *Encyclopaedia Britannica,* vol. 13 (Chicago: Encyclopaedia Britannica, 1965), p. 937.

2. "Atlantis," *Encyclopaedia Britannica,* vol. 2 (Chicago: Encyclopaedia Britannica, 1965), p. 698.
3. Kelley, Douglas, "Mania and the Moon," *Psychoanalytic Review,* 1942, *29,* 423.
4. *Ibid.*
5. *Ibid.*
6. *Ibid.*
7. Timmins, Clark. *Planting by the Moon* (Chicago: Aries Press, 1939), pp. 11–12.
8. White, William, "Moon Myth in Medicine," *Psychoanalytic Review,* 1914, *1* (3), 242.
9. *Ibid.*
10. Timmins, *op. cit.,* p. 12.
11. Bradley, D.A.; Woodbury, M.A.; and Brier, G.W., "Lunar Synodical Period and Widespread Precipitation," *Science,* 1962, *137,* 748.
12. Timmins, *op. cit.,* p. 12.
13. Bradley, *op. cit.,* p. 748.
14. Smiley, Charles, "Tidal Forces and the Formation of Hurricanes," *Nature,* 1954, *173,* 397.
15. Carpenter, Thomas, *et al.,* "Observed Relationships Between Lunar Tidal Cycles and Formation of Hurricanes and Tropical Storms," *Monthly Weather Review,* 1972, *100* (6), 451–460.
16. Osborn, Roger Dean, "The Moon and the Mental Hospital: An Investigation of One Area of Folklore," *Journal of Psychiatric Nursing and Mental Health Services,* 1968, *6,* 89.
17. Carpenter, *op. cit.,* pp. 451–460.
18. *Ibid.*
19. Osborn, *op. cit.,* p. 89.
20. Bradley, *op. cit.,* p. 749.
21. *Ibid.*
22. Huff, Darrell. *Cycles in Your Life* (New York: W.W. Norton, 1964), p. 111.
23. Adderley, E.E., and Bowen, E.G., "Lunar Component in Precipitation Data," *Science,* 1962, *137,* 749–750.
24. Brier, Glenn, "Diurnal and Semidiurnal Atmospheric Tides in Relation to Precipitation Variations," *Monthly Weather Review,* 1965, *93* (2), 100.
25. *Ibid.,* p. 95.
26. *Ibid.,* p. 100.
27. Wylie, Francis, "Sharper Tide Forecasts," *New York Times,* December 29, 1978, A23.
28. *Ibid.*
29. News reports in the *Boston Globe* and *Boston Herald America* from January 23 to January 29, 1979.
30. Bird, David, "Eclipse, Winds and Rain Bring Tidal Flooding," *New York Times,* February 27, 1979, B1.

31. Dwyer, Timothy, "Sleet Was a Surprise: It's Layer-Cake Weather," *Boston Globe,* February 27, 1979, p. 21.
32. "Wild, Crazy February Bows Out Pleasantly," *Boston Herald American,* March 5, 1979, 5.
33. Wylie, *op. cit.,* p. A23.

CHAPTER 16: THE AQUATIC WORLD

1. Chamberlin, William Henry, "Fiji," *Encyclopaedia Britannica,* vol. 9 (Chicago: Encyclopaedia Britannica, 1951), pp. 231–233.
2. Burrows, William, "Periodic Spawning of 'Palolo' Worms in Pacific Waters," *Nature,* 1945, *155,* 48.
3. *Ibid.*
4. Fox, H. Munro, "Lunar Periodicity in Reproduction," *Proceedings of the Royal Society of London, Series B,* 1923, *95,* 543–544.
5. Sarton, George, "Lunar Influences on Living Things," *Isis,* 1939, *30,* 504.
6. Cloudsley-Thompson, J.L. *Rhythmic Activity in Animal Physiology and Behavior* (New York: Academic Press, 1961), p. 86.
7. *Ibid.*
8. *Ibid.*
9. Sarton, *op. cit.,* p. 503.
10. Fox, *op. cit.,* p. 524.
11. *Ibid.,* p. 525.
12. *Ibid.,* p. 523.
13. *Ibid.*
14. *Ibid.,* p. 524.
15. *Ibid.,* p. 525.
16. *Ibid.,* p. 530.
17. *Ibid.,* p. 544.
18. *Ibid.*
19. Huntsman, A.G., "*Odontosyllis* at Bermuda and Lunar Periodicity," *Journal of the Fisheries Research Board of Canada,* 1948, 7 (6), 366–367.
20. Cottrell, John, "Moon Madness: Does It Really Exist?" *Science Digest,* October 1969, 28.
21. *Ibid.*
22. Stahl, Doris Ann, "The Relevance of Hard but Unusual Data upon Commanding Officers in Their Utilization of Manpower," Thesis for M.P.A., #396, John Jay College of Criminal Justice, 1974, p. 20.
23. Huntsman, *op. cit.,* pp. 363–369.
24. *Ibid.,* pp. 366–367.
25. Sarton, *op. cit.,* p. 504.
26. Cloudsley-Thompson, *op. cit.,* p. 82.

27. Kahn, Marvin, "The Tune of a Different Tide," *Science News*, 1979, *115* (1), 3.
28. Timmins, Clark, *Planting by the Moon* (Chicago: Aries Press, 1939), p. 27.
29. Mason, James, "A Possible Lunar Periodicity in the Breeding of the Scallop, *Pecten maximus*," *Annals and Magazine of Natural History*, 1958, *1* (9), 601–602.
30. Cloudsley-Thompson, *op. cit.*, p. 88.
31. *Ibid.*, p. 89.
32. Fingerman, Milton, "Lunar Rhythmicity in Marine Organisms," *American Naturalist*, 1957, *91* (858), 170.
33. Sarton, *op. cit.*, p. 504.
34. Walker, Boyd, "A Guide to the Grunion," *California Fish and Game*, 1952, *38*, 409–420.
35. *Ibid.*, p. 417.
36. *Ibid.*, pp. 417–418.
37. Sarton, *op. cit.*, pp. 504–505.
38. Huntsman, *op. cit.*, pp. 366–367.
39. Andrews, Edson, "Moon Talk: The Cyclic Periodicity of Postoperative Hemorrhage," *Journal of the Florida Medical Association*, 1960, *46* (11), 1364.
40. Ray, Harendranath, and Chakraverty, Mukunda, "Lunar Periodicity in the Conjugation of *Conchophthirius lamellidens* Ghosh," *Nature*, 1934, *134*, 664.
41. Brown, Frank A., Jr., "Hypothesis of Environmental Timing of the Clock," *The Biological Clock: Two Views*, ed. Brown, Hastings, and Palmer (New York: Academic Press, 1970), pp. 48–50.
42. Brown, Frank A., Jr., "Persistent Activity Rhythms in the Oyster," *American Journal of Physiology*, 1954, *178*, 510–514.
43. Guyselman, J. Bruce, "Solar and Lunar Rhythms of Locomotor Activity in the Crayfish *Cambarus virilis*," *Physiological Zoology*, 1957, *30* (1), 70–87.
44. Stutz, Audrey, "Tidal and Diurnal Activity Rhythms in the Striped Shore Crab *Pachygrapsus crassipes*," *Journal of Interdisciplinary Cycle Research*, 1978, *9* (1), 41–48.
45. Sandeen, Muriel; Stephens, Grover; and Brown, Frank A., Jr., "Persistent Daily and Tidal Rhythms of Oxygen Consumption in Two Species of Marine Snails," *Physiological Zoology*, 1954, *27* (4), 350–356.
46. Brown, F.A., Jr.; Fingerman, M.; Sandeen, M.L.; and Webb, H.M., "Persistent Diurnal and Tidal Rhythms of Color Change in the Fiddler Crab, *Uca pugnax*," *Journal of Experimental Zoology*, 1953, *123*, 29–60.
47. Cloudsley-Thompson, *op. cit.*, pp. 83–84.
48. *Ibid.*, p. 84.
49. *Ibid.*, p. 85.
50. *Ibid.*, pp. 81–83.

51. Fingerman, *op. cit.*, pp. 167–178.
52. Kahn, Peter, and Pompea, Stephen, "Nautiloid Growth Rhythms and Dynamical Evolution of the Earth-Moon System," *Nature*, 1978, *275* (5681), 606.
53. *Ibid.*
54. West, Susan, "Moon History In A Seashell," *Science News*, 1978, *114* (25), 428.
55. Kahn, *op. cit.*, p. 606.
56. *Ibid.*, pp. 606–609.
57. "A Natural Clock," *New York Times*, January 9, 1979, C2.
58. Bunning, Erwin, *The Physiological Clock* (London: English Universities Press, 1973), p. 183.
59. Fox, *op. cit.*, pp. 544–546.
60. *Ibid.*, p. 544.
61. Sarton, *op. cit.*, p. 504.
62. Cloudsley-Thompson, *op. cit.*, p. 85.
63. *Ibid.*, p. 88.
64. Fingerman, *op. cit.*, p. 170.
65. Madariaga, Salvador de, "Columbus, Christopher," *Encyclopaedia Britannica*, vol. 6 (Chicago: Encyclopaedia Britannica, 1965), p. 112.
66. *Ibid.*
67. Morison, Samuel Eliot, "Columbus, Christopher," *World Book*, vol. 4 (Chicago: Field Enterprises, 1977), p. 692.
68. Beazley, Sir Charles Raymond, *et al.*, "Columbus, Christopher," *Encyclopaedia Britannica*, vol. 6 (Chicago: Encyclopaedia Britannica, 1951), p. 80.
69. Madariaga, *op. cit.*, p. 112.
70. "Columbus, Christopher," *Compton's Encyclopedia*, vol. 5 (Chicago: F.E. Compton, 1972), p. 476.
71. Beazley, *op. cit.*, p. 80.
72. *Ibid.*
73. Morison, *op. cit.*, pp. 692–693.
74. Madariaga, *op. cit.*, p. 112.
75. "Columbus, Christopher," *op. cit.*, p. 476.
76. Beazley, *op. cit.*, p. 80.
77. *Ibid.*
78. *Ibid.*
79. *Ibid.*
80. Madariaga, *op. cit.*, p. 112.
81. *Ibid.*
82. *Ibid.*
83. *Ibid.*
84. "Columbus, Christopher," *op. cit.*, p. 478.
85. *Ibid.*
86. *Ibid.*
87. Beazley, *op. cit.*, p. 80.

88. Crawshay, L.R., "Possible Bearing of a Luminous Syllid on the Question of the Landfall of Columbus," *Nature,* 1935, *136,* 559.
89. Beazley, *op. cit.,* p. 80.
90. "Columbus, Christopher," *op. cit.,* p. 478.
91. Crawshay, *op. cit.,* p. 559.
92. *Ibid.*
93. *Ibid.,* p. 560.
94. *Ibid.*

CHAPTER 17: ABOARD NOAH'S ARK

1. Cowgill, Ursula; Bishop, Alison; Andrew, R.J.; and Hutchinson, G.E., "An Apparent Lunar Periodicity in the Sexual Cycle of Certain Prosimians," *Proceedings of the National Academy of Sciences,* 1962, *48,* 239.
2. *Ibid.,* pp. 239, 241.
3. Ellis, Havelock. *Studies in the Psychology of Sex,* vol. 1 (New York: Random House, 1942), p. 92.
4. Dewan, Edmond, "On the Possibility of a Perfect Method of Birth Control by Periodic Light Stimulation," *American Journal of Obstetrics and Gynecology,* 1967, *99,* 1016.
5. Ramanthan, O., "Light and Sexual Periodicity in Indian Buffaloes," *Nature,* 1932, *130,* 169.
6. *Ibid.,* p. 170.
7. Cloudsley-Thompson, J.L., *Rhythmic Activity in Animal Physiology and Behavior* (New York: Academic Press, 1961), p. 91.
8. Palmer, John, "The Many Clocks of Man," *Cycles,* 1971, *22* (2), 40.
9. Harrison, J.L., "Moonlight and the Pregnancy of Malayan Forest Rats," *Nature,* 1952, *170,* 73–74.
10. Harrison, J.L., "Breeding Rhythms of Selangor Rodents," *Bulletin of the Raffles Museum,* 1952, *24,* 109–131.
11. *Ibid.,* p. 122.
12. Harrison, J.L., "Moonlight and the Pregnancy of Malayan Forest Rats," *op. cit.,* pp. 73–74.
13. Harrison, J.L., "The Moonlight Effect on Rat Breeding," *Bulletin of the Raffles Museum,* 1954, *25,* 166–170.
14. Cloudsley-Thompson, *op. cit.,* p. 93.
15. *Ibid.*
16. *Ibid.,* p.35.
17. *Ibid.*
18. *Ibid.,* p. 34.
19. Brown, Frank A., Jr., and Park, Young H., "Synodic Monthly Modulation of the Diurnal Rhythm of Hamsters," *Proceedings of the Society for Experimental Biology and Medicine,* 1967, *125,* 713–715.
20. Brown, Frank A., Jr., "Propensity for Lunar Periodicity in Hamsters and Its Significance for Biological Clock Theories," *Proceedings of the Society for Experimental Biology and Medicine,* 1965, *120,* 792–797.

21. Klinowska, Margaret, "Lunar Rhythms in Activity, Urinary Volume and Acidity in the Golden Hamster (*Mesocricetus auratus* Waterhouse)," *Journal of Interdisciplinary Cycle Research,* 1970, *1* (4), 317–322.
22. Klinowska, Margaret, "A Comparison of the Lunar and Solar Activity Rhythms of the Golden Hamster (*Mesocricetus auratus* Waterhouse)," *Journal of Interdisciplinary Cycle Research,* 1972, *3* (2), 145–150.
23. Brown, F.A., Jr.; Shriner, J.; and Ralph, C.L., "Solar and Lunar Rhythmicity in the Rat in 'Constant Conditions' and the Mechanism of Physiological Time Measurement," *American Journal of Physiology,* 1956, *184,* 491–496.
24. Terracini, Emma, and Brown, F.A., Jr., "Periodisms in Mouse 'Spontaneous' Activity Synchronized with Major Geophysical Cycles," *Physiological Zoology,* 1962, *35* (1), 27–37.
25. Cloudsley-Thompson, *op. cit.,* pp. 91–92.
26. Stutz, Audrey, "Synodic Monthly Rhythms in the Mongolian Gerbil *Meriones unguiculatus," Journal of Interdisciplinary Cycle Research,* 1973, *4* (3), 229–236.
27. *Ibid.,* pp. 233–234.
28. Ralph, Charles, "Persistent Rhythms of Activity and O_2-Consumption in the Earthworm," *Physiological Zoology,* 1957, *30* (1), 41–55.
29. Harker, Janet, "Diurnal Rhythms in the Animal Kingdom," *Biological Reviews,* 1958, *33,* 49.
30. Rounds, Harry, "A Lunar Rhythm in the Occurrence of Blood-Borne Factors in Cockroaches, Mice and Men," *Comparative Biochemical Physiology,* 1975, *50-C,* 193.
31. Oliven, John F., "Moonlight and Nervous Disorders," *American Journal of Psychiatry,* 1943, *99,* 580.

CHAPTER 18: DIANA'S GREEN THUMB

1. Frazier, Kendrick, "Stars, Sky and Culture," *Science News,* 1979, *116* (5), 90–93.
2. Anderson, Joan. *The '80 Lunar Calendar,* ed. Nancy Passmore (Boston: Luna Press, 1979), p. 15.
3. Hale, Jud, ed. *The Old Farmer's Almanac 1979* (Berlin, N.H.: Yankee, 1978), pp. 168–171.
4. Timmins, Clark. *Planting by the Moon* (Chicago: Aries Press, 1939), p. 49.
5. McDaniel, Walton Brooks, "The Moon, Werewolves, and Medicine," *Transactions & Studies of the College of Physicians of Philadelphia,* 1950, *18,* 114.
6. Stahl, William H., "Moon Madness," *Annals of Medical History,* 1937, *9,* 261.
7. Hale, *op. cit.,* p. 76.
8. Timmins, *op. cit.,* p. 48.

9. Anderson, *op. cit.*, p. 15.
10. Timmins, *op. cit.*, pp. 35–43.
11. Andrews, Edson, "Moon Talk: The Cyclic Periodicity of Postoperative Hemorrhage," *Journal of the Florida Medical Association*, 1960, *46* (11), 1364.
12. *Ibid.*
13. Terracini, Emma, and Brown, F.A., Jr., "Periodism in Mouse 'Spontaneous' Activity Synchronized with Major Geophysical Cycles," *Physiological Zoology*, 1962, *35* (1), 34.
14. Brown, Frank A., Jr., and Chow, Carol, "Lunar-Correlated Variations in Water Uptake by Bean Seeds," *Biological Bulletin*, 1973, *145*, 265–278.
15. *Ibid.*, p. 273.
16. Andrews, *op. cit.*, p. 1365.
17. Rhyne, W.P., "Spontaneous Hemorrhage," *Journal of the Medical Association of Georgia*, 1966, *55*, 505.
18. Dixon, Bernard, "Plant Sensations," *Omni*, December 1978, 24.
19. *Ibid.*

CHAPTER 19: REPRODUCTION

1. Ellis, Havelock. *Studies in the Psychology of Sex*, vol. 1 (New York: Random House, 1942), p. 86.
2. "The Moon and Medicine," *Clinical Excerpts*, 1940, *14* (8), 4.
3. Stahl, William H., "Moon Madness," *Annals of Medical History*, 1937, *9*, 250.
4. Timmins, Clark, *Planting by the Moon* (Chicago: Aries Press, 1939), p. 30.
5. "The Moon and Medicine," *op. cit.*, p. 5.
6. *Ibid.*
7. *Ibid.*
8. *Ibid.*
9. Kelley, Douglas, "Mania and the Moon," *Psychoanalytic Review*, 1942, *29*, 422.
10. *Ibid.*
11. "The Moon and Medicine," *op. cit.*, p. 4.
12. *Ibid.*
13. *Ibid.*
14. Kelley, *op. cit.*, p. 422.
15. Stahl, *op. cit.*, p. 250.
16. *Ibid.*
17. Oliven, John F., "Moonlight and Nervous Disorders," *American Journal of Psychiatry*, 1943, *99*, 580.
18. Stahl, *op. cit.*, p. 250.
19. Foreman, Judy, "Run for Cover, There's a Full Moon," *Boston Globe*, December 14, 1978, 33.
20. Soyka, Fred. *The Ion Effect* (New York: Bantam Books, 1978), p. 64.

21. Stahl, *op. cit.*, p. 254.
22. Palmer, John D., "The Many Clocks of Man," *Cycles*, 1971, *22* (2), 40.
23. Menaker, Walter, and Menaker, Abraham, "Lunar Periodicity in Human Reproduction: A Likely Unit of Biological Time," *American Journal of Obstetrics and Gynecology*, 1959, 77 (4), 906. (The Menakers emphasized that the human menstrual cycle is indeed the same length as the synodic month, notwithstanding the widespread, erroneous notion that the menstrual cycle is only 28 days long, a fiction which is, as John Palmer noted, perpetuated by some elementary biology textbooks.)
24. Andrews, Edson, "Moon Talk: The Cyclic Periodicity of Postoperative Hemorrhage," *Journal of the Florida Medical Association*, 1960, *46* (11), 1366.
25. Menaker, *op. cit.*, pp. 905–914. (The three-day "window period" employed here by the Menakers is used for clarity in statistical analysis. It compensates for the fact that the precise moment of the full moon may be at 11:59 P.M., for example, of any given day. Statisticians point out that any full-moon phenomena being studied would belong as much to the following calendar day as to the present one, or, if the full-moon instant were at an especially early hour, to the previous day.)
26. *Ibid.*, p. 906.
27. *Ibid.*
28. *Ibid.*
29. *Ibid.*
30. *Ibid.*, p. 908.
31. *Ibid.*
32. *Ibid.*
33. *Ibid.*, p. 310.
34. Menaker, Walter, "Lunar Periodicity with Reference to Live Births," *American Journal of Obstetrics and Gynecology*, 1967, *98* (7), 1002–1004.
35. Small, Collie, "A Full Moon Can Beam Disaster," *Boston Herald American*, December 13, 1978, 15.
36. McDonald, Robert, "Lunar and Seasonal Variations in Obstetric Factors," *Journal of Genetic Psychology*, 1966, *108*, 83.
37. *Ibid.*, p. 81.
38. Huff, Darrell. *Cycles in Your Life* (New York: W.W. Norton, 1964), p. 115.
39. *Ibid.*, pp. 115–116.
40. McDonald, *op. cit.*, pp. 81–87.
41. Schnurman, Albert, "The Effect of the Moon on Childbirth," *Virginia Medical Monthly*, 1949, *76*, 78.
42. Laycock, T., "On Lunar Influences; Being A Fourth Contribution to Proleptics," *The Lancet*, 1843, *2*, 443.
43. Foissac, P., "The Influence of the Lunar Phases on the Physical and Moral Man," *St. Louis Medical and Surgical Journal*, 1855, *13*, 503.
44. Palmer, *op. cit.*, p. 40.

45. Dietz, Jean, "Women Said More Sexual at Ovulation," *Boston Globe,* November 23, 1978, 35.
46. *Ibid.*
47. *Ibid.*
48. Kelley, *op. cit.,* p. 413.
49. Palmer, *op. cit.,* p. 41.
50. *Ibid.,* p. 40.
51. *Ibid.,* p. 41.
52. Oliven, *op. cit.,* p. 580.
53. Rounds, Harry, "A Lunar Rhythm in the Occurrence of Blood-Borne Factors in Cockroaches, Mice and Men," *Comparative Biochemical Physiology,* 1975, *50-C,* 193.
54. Malek, Jiří; Gleich, J.; and Maly, V. "Characteristics of the Daily Rhythm of Menstrustion and Labor," *Annals of the New York Academy of Sciences,* 1962, *98,* 1042–1055.
55. Oliven, *op. cit.,* p. 580.
56. Stahl, *op. cit.,* p. 251.
57. Sarton, George, "Lunar Influences on Living Things," *Isis,* 1939, *30,* 501.
58. Stahl, *op. cit.,* p. 251.
59. Ellis, *op. cit.,* p. 87.
60. *Ibid.*
61. Ward, E.H.P., The Moon and Insanity," *Medical Record,* 1919, *96,* 320.
62. *Ibid.*
63. Foissac, *op. cit.,* p. 505.
64. *Ibid.,* p. 504.
65. Menaker *et al., op. cit.,* p. 911.
66. Osley, M.; Summerville, D.; and Borst, L.B., "Natility and the Moon," *American Journal of Obstetrics and Gynecology,* 1973, *117,* 413–415.
67. Ostrander, Sheila, and Schroeder, Lynn, "Birth Control by Astrology?" *McCall's,* May 1972, 84. (The authors noted that Jonas's theory had not been tested or corroborated in the United States.)
68. *Ibid.,* p. 87.
69. *Ibid.*
70. *Ibid.*
71. *Ibid.,* pp. 87–88.
72. *Ibid.,* p. 84.

CHAPTER 20: MALE PERIODS

1. Delaney, Janet, *et al. The Curse* (New York: Mentor, 1977), p. 213.
2. Ramey, Estelle, "Men's Cycles (They Have Them Too, You Know)," *Ms.,* 1972, spring, 8, 11–14.
3. Emery, C. Eugene, Jr., "It Must Be A Full Moon," Providence (R.I.) *Sunday Journal,* January 8, 1978, Sunday magazine 5.
4. *Ibid.*

5. Ramey, *op. cit.*, p. 12.
6. *Ibid.*
7. Delaney, *op. cit.*, pp. 217–218.
8. Ellis, Havelock. *Studies in the Psychology of Sex*, vol. 1 (New York: Random House, 1942), p. 106.
9. *Ibid.*, p. 107.
10. Stahl, Doris Ann, "The Relevance of Hard but Unusual Data upon Commanding Officers in Their Utilization of Manpower," Thesis for M.P.A., #396, John Jay College of Criminal Justice, 1974, p. 23.
11. Luce, Gay G., ed. *Biological Rhythms in Psychiatry and Medicine* (Public Health Service Publication #2088; Washington, D.C.: U.S. Govt. Printing Office, 1970), p. 2.
12. Ellis, *op. cit.*, p. 107.
13. *Ibid.*
14. *Ibid.*, p. 108.
15. Luce, *op. cit.*, p. 2.
16. Stone, Michael, "Madness and the Moon Revisited," *Psychiatric Annals*, 1976, *6* (4), 47–60.
17. Ellis, *op. cit.*, p. 108.
18. *Ibid.*, p. 109.
19. *Ibid.*, p. 110.
20. *Ibid.*, p. 111.
21. *Ibid.*, p. 110.
22. *Ibid.*, pp. 118–120.
23. *Ibid.*, pp. 120–121.
24. *Ibid.*, pp. 116–117.
25. *Ibid.*, pp. 112–113.
26. Oliven, John F., "Moonlight and Nervous Disorders," *American Journal of Psychiatry*, 1943, *99*, 580.
27. Oberndorf, C.P., "Sexual Periodicity in the Male," *Medical Record*, 1913, *84*, 18–19.
28. *Ibid.*, pp. 19–20.
29. *Ibid.*, p. 19.
30. Delaney, *op. cit.*, p. 213.
31. Luce, *op. cit.*, pp. 110–111.
32. Ramey, *op. cit.*, pp. 8, 11–14.
33. *Ibid.*, p. 11.
34. Delaney, *op. cit.*, p. 214.
35. Trautman, Robert, "Women Physically Unfit for Presidency?" *Boston Globe*, August 2, 1970, 41, 42.
36. Delaney, *op. cit.*, p. 216.

CHAPTER 21: MURDER AND MAYHEM

1. Timmins, Clark. *Planting by the Moon* (Chicago: Aries Press, 1939), p. 28.

2. *Ibid.*, pp. 28–29.
3. *Ibid.*
4. Cottrell, John, "Moon Madness: Does It Really Exist?" *Science Digest*, October 1969, 26.
5. *Ibid.*
6. Lerner, Richard, "Mental Tests Ordered for Sara Moore," *Boston Herald American*, September 24, 1975, p. 25.
7. Aarons, Leroy F., "She Said She Didn't Get a Chance for Second Shot," *Boston Globe*, September 23, 1975, 1, 2.
8. Thomas, Helen, "President Escapes Assassin's Bullet," *Boston Globe*, September 23, 1975, 1, 2.
9. McDowell, Edwin, "Theories on Man's Dark Deeds Come Out by the Light of the Full Moon," *New York Times*, January 24, 1978, B1.
10. Emery, C. Eugene, Jr., "It Must Be a Full Moon," *Providence* (R.I.) *Sunday Journal*, January 8, 1978, Sunday magazine 5.
11. *Ibid.*
12. McDowell, *op. cit.*, p. B1.
13. Foreman, Judy, "Run for Cover, There's a Full Moon," *Boston Globe*, December 14, 1978, 33.
14. Katzeff, Paul, "Howl: There's a Full Moon Out Tonight," *Boston Herald American*, March 6, 1977, Sunday magazine 24.
15. Ziegler, Mel, "A Lunar Loss of Marbles," *San Francisco Chronicle*, May 2, 1977, 2.
16. Timmins, *op. cit.*, p. 28.
17. Oliven, John F., "Moonlight and Nervous Disorders," *American Journal of Psychiatry*, 1943, *99*, 581.
18. Katzeff, *op. cit.*, Sunday magazine 24.
19. Foreman, *op. cit.*, p. 33.
20. Small, Collie, "A Full Moon Can Beam Disaster," *Boston Herald American*, December 13, 1978, 15.
21. *Ibid.*, p. 17.
22. *Ibid.*, p. 15.
23. *Ibid.*
24. Seigel, Max H., "Berkowitz Is Judged Competent; A Murder Trial Is Set for May 8," *New York Times*, April 25, 1978, pp. 1, 24.
25. Kelley, Douglas, "Mania and the Moon," *Psychoanalytic Review*, 1942, *29*, 408.
26. "Mrs. Snyder and Gray Electrocuted Less Than 10 Months from Arrest," *Boston Herald*, January 13, 1928, 16.
27. "Art Editor Is Slain, Wife Bound, Gagged; Girl 9, Spreads Alarm," *Boston Herald*, March 20, 1927, 8.
28. "Snyder's Wife Admits Helping Kill Husband," *Boston Herald*, March 22, 1927, 1.
29. "Mrs. Snyder and Gray. . . ." *op. cit.*, p. 16.
30. Lieber, Arnold, and Sherin, Carolyn, "Homicides and the Lunar Cycle: Toward a Theory of Lunar Influence on Human Emotional Disturbance," *American Journal of Psychiatry*, 1972, *129*, (1), 69–74.

31. *Ibid.*, p. 72.
32. Brown, Frank A., Jr., and Park, Y.H., "Synodic Monthly Modulation of the Diurnal Rhythm of Hamsters," *Proceedings of the Society for Experimental Biology and Medicine,* 1967, *125,* 712–715.
33. Lieber, Arnold, "Lunar Effect on Homicides: A Confirmation," *International Journal of Chronobiology,* 1973, *1,* (4), 338–339.
34. *Ibid.*
35. *Ibid.*, p. 339.
36. Lieber and Sherin, *op. cit.*, p. 73.
37. Hartley, William and Ellen, "Moon Madness," *Science Digest,* September 1972, 29–30.
38. Stahl, Doris Ann, "The Revelance of Hard but Unusual Data upon Commanding Officers in Their Utilization of Manpower," Thesis for M.P.A., #396, John Jay College of Criminal Justice, 1974, p. i.
39. *Ibid.*, pp. 54–59.
40. *Ibid.*, p. 57.
41. *Ibid.*, p. 53.
42. *Ibid.*, p. 41.
43. *Ibid.*
44. Tasso, Jodi, and Miller, Elizabeth, "The Effects of the Full Moon on Human Behavior," *Journal of Psychology,* 1976, *93,* 81.
45. *Ibid.*, p. 83.
46. Huff, Darrell. *Cycles in Your Life* (New York: W.W. Norton, 1964), pp. 112–113.
47. Monahan, D. Leo, "Keeping Winning in Mind," *Boston Herald American,* February 4, 1979 C7.
48. Polnaszek, Frank, interview with author, March 22, 1979.
49. Abel, Allen, "Statistics Prove Hockey Is Lunacy," *Toronto Globe and Mail,* November 14, 1977, page unknown.
50. Hine, Tom, "Goal-starved Whalers Beaten 4–1," *Hartford Courant,* February 5, 1979, 29, 30.
51. Monahan, D. Leo, "Referee's Whistle Frustrates Bruins," *Boston Herald American,* final edition, February 5, 1977, 13.
52. Fitzgerald, Tom, "Flames Decision Bruins, 6–3; Call the Fights A Draw," *Boston Globe,* February 5, 1977, 17.
53. Monahan, D. Leo, "Bruins Incensed Over Plett's 'Foul,'" *Boston Herald American,* first edition, February 5, 1977, 13.
54. *Ibid.*
55. Monahan, "Referee's Whistle. . ." *op. cit.*, p. 13.
56. Fitzgerald, *op. cit.*, p. 17.
57. Abel, *op. cit.*, page unknown.
58. *Ibid.*
59. *Ibid.*

CHAPTER 22: MADNESS

1. Stone, Michael, "Madness and the Moon Revisited," *Psychiatric Annals,* 1976, *6* (4), 55.
2. *Ibid.*
3. *Ibid.*
4. Rounds, Harry, "A Lunar Rhythm in the Occurrence of Blood-Borne Factors in Cockroaches, Mice and Men," *Comparative Biochemical Physiology,* 1975, *50-C,* 193.
5. Foreman, Judy, "Run for Cover, There's a Full Moon," *Boston Globe,* December 14, 1978, 33.
6. *Ibid.*
7. *Ibid.*
8. *Ibid.*
9. Stair, Thomas, "Lunar Cycles and Emergency-Room Visits," *New England Journal of Medicine,* 1978, *298* (23), 1318–1319.
10. Beaumier, Mrs. Dorothy, letter to author, March 7, 1977.
11. Foreman, *op. cit.,* p. 33.
12. Kelley, Douglas, "Mania and the Moon," *Psychoanalytic Review,* 1942, *29,* 416.
13. White, William, "Moon Myth in Medicine," *Psychoanalytic Review,* 1914, *1* (3), 243.
14. Andrews, Edson, "Moon Talk: The Cyclic Periodicity of Postoperative Hemorrhage," *Journal of the Florida Medical Association,* 1960, *46* (11), 1365.
15. Osborn, Roger Dean, "The Moon and the Mental Hospital: An Investigation of One Area of Folklore," *Journal of Psychiatric Nursing and Mental Health Services,* 1968, *6,* 88–93.
16. *Ibid.,* p. 91.
17. *Ibid.*
18. *Ibid.,* pp. 90–91.
19. *Ibid.,* p. 92.
20. *Ibid.,* p. 93.

21. In the chapter, "Reproduction," we saw that births and ovulation occur more often at the full moon than at any other time of the lunar month; menstruation is usually around the new moon. This is especially interesting in light of the Osborn study here, describing a peak in female psychiatric admissions during the last lunar quarter, which precedes the new moon. It is that time preceding menstruation, presumably at the new moon, which Gay Luce, editor of *Biological Rhythms in Psychiatry and Medicine,* described as the period of "premenstrual tension" when an "estimated 60 percent of all women suffer some palpable change" like "mild irritation, depression, headache, decline in attention or vision. . . . Some become jittery, others weep, suffer insomnia, vertigo, or even nymphomania.

"The roster of premenstrual complaints includes respiratory ailments, the activation of such chronic illnesses as arthritis or ulcers, along with gastrointestinal complaints, altered appetite, and notable changes in blood-sugar levels."

22. Blackman, Sheldon, and Catalina, Don, "The Moon and the Emergency Room," *Perceptual and Motor Skills,* 1973, *37,* 625.
23. *Ibid.*
24. Pokorny, Alex, "Moon Phases and Mental Hospital Admissions," *Journal of Psychiatric Nursing and Mental Health Services,* 1968, *6,* 326.
25. *Ibid.*
26. *Ibid.*, p. 327.
27. Ravitz, Leonard J., "Electrodynamic Field Theory in Psychiatry," *Southern Medical Journal,* 1953, *46* (7), 658.
28. Ravitz, Leonard J., "Comparative Clinical and Electrocyclic Observations on Twin Brothers Concordant as to Schizophrenia," *Journal of Nervous and Mental Disease,* 1955, *121,* 85.
29. Geller, Sheldon, and Shannon, Herbert, "The Moon, Weather and Mental Hospital Contacts: Confirmation and Explanation of the Transylvania Effect," *Journal of Psychiatric Nursing and Mental Health Services,* 1976, *14,* 16.
30. *Ibid.,* p. 13.
31. *Ibid.,* p. 16.
32. Weiskott, Gerald, and Tipton, George, "Moon Phases and State Hospital Admissions," *Psychological Reports,* 1975, *37,* 486.
33. Laycock, T., "On Lunar Influences; Being A Fourth Contribution to Proleptics," *The Lancet,* 1843, *2,* 442.
34. Stahl, Doris Ann, "The Revelance of Hard but Unusual Data upon Commanding Officers in Their Utilization of Manpower," Thesis for M.P.A., #396, John Jay College of Criminal Justice, 1974, p. 3.
35. Fitzpatrick, JoAnn, "Getting Even," *Boston Herald American,* February 18, 1979, Sunday magazine 21.
36. Cottrell, John, "Moon Madness: Does It Really Exist?" *Science Digest,* October 1969, 26.
37. Ziegler, Mel, "A Lunar Loss of Marbles," *San Francisco Chronicle,* May 2, 1977, 2.
38. *Ibid.*
39. *Ibid.*
40. Foreman, *op. cit.,* p. 33.
41. C., Sylvia, interview with author, November 24, 1978.
42. McDowell, Edwin, "Theories on Man's Dark Deeds Come Out by the Light of the Full Moon," *New York Times,* January 24, 1978, B1.
43. Ziegler, *op. cit.,* p. 2.
44. Emery, C. Eugene, Jr., "It Must Be A Full Moon," Providence (R.I.) *Sunday Journal,* January 8, 1978, Sunday magazine 7.
45. Sarton, George, "Lunar Influences on Living Things," *Isis,* 1939, *30,* 495.
46. *Ibid.*

47. *Ibid.*
48. Ravitz, Leonard J., "Electrocyclic Phenomena and Emotional States," *Journal of Clinical and Experimental Psychopathology,* 1952, *13* (2), 94.

CHAPTER 23: SUICIDE

1. Small, Collie, "A Full Moon Can Beam Disaster," *Boston Herald American,* December 13, 1978, 15.
2. Ziegler, Mel, "A Lunar Loss of Marbles," *San Francisco Chronicle,* May 2, 1977, 2.
3. Lester, David; Brockopp, Gene; and Priebe, Kitty, "Association Between a Full Moon and Completed Suicide," *Psychological Reports,* 1969, *25,* 598.
4. Jones, Paul, and Jones, Susan, "Lunar Association with Suicide," *Suicide and Life-Threatening Behavior,* 1977, 7 (1), 36.
5. *Ibid.,* p. 37.
6. *Ibid.,* pp. 34–36.
7. De Voge, Susan, and Mikawa, James, "Moon Phases and Crisis Calls: A Spurious Relationship," *Psychological Reports,* 1977, *40,* 389.
8. *Ibid.*
9. Taylor, L.J., and Diespecker, D.D., "Moon Phases and Suicide Attempts in Australia," *Psychological Reports,* 1972, *31,* 112.
10. Ossenkopp, K.P., and Ossenkopp, Margitta, "Self-Inflicted Injuries and the Lunar Cycle: A Preliminary Report," *Journal of Interdisciplinary Cycle Research,* 1973, *4* (4), 339, 342.
11. *Ibid.*
12. *Ibid.,* p. 343.
13. *Ibid.,* p. 339.
14. *Ibid.,* pp. 339–340.
15. Pokorny, Alex, "Moon Phases, Suicide, and Homicide," *American Journal of Psychiatry,* 1964, *121,* 66.
16. Foissac, P., "The Influence of the Lunar Phases on the Physical and Moral Man," *St. Louis Medical and Surgical Journal,* 1855, *13,* 513.

CHAPTER 24: BIOLOGICAL RHYTHMS

1. Luce, Gay G., ed. *Biological Rhythms in Psychiatry and Medicine* (Public Health Service Publication #2088; Washington, D.C.: U.S. Govt. Printing Office, 1970), p. 8.
2. *Ibid.*
3. Brown, Frank A., Jr., "Hypothesis of Environmental Timing of the Clock," *The Biological Clock: Two Views,* ed. Brown, Hastings, and Palmer (New York: Academic Press, 1970), p. 3.

4. Miles, L.E.M.; Raynal, D.M.; and Wilson, M.A., "Blind Man Living in Normal Society Has Circadian Rhythms of 24.9 Hours," *Science,* 1977, *198,* 421–423.
5. *Ibid.,* p. 423.
6. *Ibid.,* p. 422.
7. *Ibid.*
8. *Ibid.,* p. 423.
9. *Ibid.*
10. Aschoff, Jurgen, "Human Circadian Rhythms in Activity, Body Temperature and Other Functions," *Life Sciences and Space Research,* vol. 5, A.H. Brown and F.G. Favorite, eds. (Amsterdam: North-Holland Publishing Co., 1967), p. 165.
11. *Ibid.,* pp. 165–166.
12. *Ibid.,* pp. 166–168.
13. Stahl, Doris Ann, "The Relevance of Hard but Unusual Data upon Commanding Officers in Their Utilization of Manpower," Thesis for M.P.A., #396, John Jay College of Criminal Justice, 1974, pp. 27–28.
14. Luce, *op. cit.,* p. 2.
15. Sarton, George, "Lunar Influences on Living Things," *Isis,* 1939, *30,* 506–507.
16. *Ibid.,* p. 506.
17. Laycock, T., "Lunar Influence; Being A Fourth Contribution to Proleptics," *The Lancet,* 1843, *2,* 441.
18. *Ibid.,* pp. 440–441.
19. Foissac, P., "The Influence of the Lunar Phases on the Physical and Moral Man," *St. Louis Medical and Surgical Journal,* 1855, *13,* 510.
20. *Ibid.*
21. Laycock, *op. cit.,* pp. 440–441.
22. *Ibid.*
23. Foissac, *op. cit.,* p. 510.
24. *Ibid.,* p. 503.
25. Laycock, *op. cit.,* pp. 440–441.
26. Foissac, *op. cit.,* p. 503.
27. Timmins, Clark. *Planting by the Moon* (Chicago: Aries Press, 1939), p. 30.
28. Stone, Michael, "Madness and the Moon Revisited," *Psychiatric Annals,* 1976, *6* (4), 47.
29. Oliven, John F., "Moonlight and Nervous Disorders," *American Journal of Psychiatry,* 1943, *99,* 581.
30. Laycock, *op. cit.,* p. 442.
31. Andrews, Edson, "Moon Talk: The Cyclic Periodicity of Postoperative Hemorrhage," *Journal of the Florida Medical Association,* 1960, *46* (11), 1365.
32. Stahl, *op. cit.,* p. 23.
33. Laycock, *op. cit.,* p. 441.

34. Kelley, Douglas, "Mania and the Moon," *Psychoanalytic Review,* 1942, *29,* 411.
35. Katzeff, Paul, "Howl: There's a Full Moon Out Tonight," *Boston Herald American,* March 6, 1977, Sunday magazine 26. Also, additional notes taken during interview with author.
36. Rosenstock, Harvey, and Vincent, Kenneth, "A Case of Lycanthropy," *American Journal of Psychiatry,* 1977, *134* (10), 1148.
37. Oliven, *op. cit.*, p. 583.
38. Laycock, *op. cit.*, p. 441.
39. Andrews, *op. cit.*, p. 1365.
40. Oliven, *op. cit.*, p. 583.
41. Timmins, *op. cit.*, p. 27.
42. *Ibid.*
43. Sadger, J., *Sleep Walking and Moon Walking* (Nervous and Mental Disease Monograph Series No. 31; Washington, D.C.: Nervous and Mental Disease Publishing Co., 1920), pp. 27–30.
44. *Ibid.*, p. 30.
45. *Ibid.*, p. 31.
46. *Ibid.*
47. *Ibid.*, p. 30.
48. *Ibid.*, p. 2.
49. *Ibid.*
50. *Ibid.*, p. 5.
51. *Ibid.*, p. 3.
52. *Ibid.*, p. 17.
53. *Ibid.*, p. 12.
54. *Ibid.*, pp. 13–14.
55. *Ibid.*, p. 16.
56. *Ibid.*, p. 22.
57. *Ibid.*
58. Huff, Darrell. *Cycles in Your Life* (New York: W.W. Norton, 1964), p. 116.
59. Laycock, *op. cit.*, p. 442.
60. Kelley, *op. cit.*, pp. 415–416.
61. Laycock, *op. cit.*, p. 442.
62. *Ibid.*, p. 443.
63. *Ibid.*, p. 441.
64. Foissac, *op. cit.*, p. 510.
65. Gauquelin, Michel, "Genetic Sensitivity to External Factors During the Daily Cycle of the Deliveries," *Journal of Interdisciplinary Cycle Research,* 1971, *2* (2), 227.
66. Gauquelin, Michel. *Les Hommes et les Astres* (Paris: Denoel, 1960), p. 200.
67. Gauquelin, "Genetic. . . ," *op. cit.*, p. 230.
68. *Ibid.*, pp. 231–232.
69. Laycock, *op. cit.*, p. 442.

CHAPTER 25: BLEEDING

1. Rhyne, W.P., "Spontaneous Hemorrhage," *Journal of the Medical Association of Georgia,* 1966, *55,* 505.
2. Andrews, Edson, "Moon Talk: The Cyclic Periodicity of Postoperative Hemorrhage," *Journal of the Florida Medical Association,* 1960, *46* (11), 1366.
3. *Ibid.,* p. 1363.
4. *Ibid.*
5. *Ibid.*
6. Hackler, Timothy, "That Ol' Devil Moon," *Milwaukee Journal,* March 18, 1979, Sunday magazine 52.
7. Rhyne, *op. cit.,* p. 506.
8. Foissac, P., "The Influence of the Lunar Phases on the Physical and Moral Man," *St. Louis Medical and Surgical Journal,* 1855, *13,* 509.
9. Laycock, T., "Lunar Influence; Being A Fourth Contribution to Proleptics," *The Lancet,* 1843, *2,* 443.
10. Foissac, *op. cit.,* p. 509.
11. White, William, "Moon Myth in Medicine," *Psychoanalytic Review,* 1914, *1* (3), 249.
12. Laycock, *op. cit.,* p. 439.
13. Andrews, *op. cit.,* pp. 1365–1366.
14. *Ibid.*
15. Rounds, Harry, "A Lunar Rhythm in the Occurrence of Blood-Borne Factors in Cockroaches, Mice and Men," *Comparative Biochemistry and Physiology,* 1975, *50-C,* 194.
16. *Ibid.,* p. 195.
17. *Ibid.*

CHAPTER 26: MOONLIGHT

1. Foissac, P., "The Influence of the Lunar Phases on the Physical and Moral Man," *St. Louis Medical and Surgical Journal,* 1855, *13,* 505.
2. Fox, H. Munro, "Lunar Periodicity in Reproduction," *Proceedings of the Royal Society of London, Series B,* 1923, *95,* 545.
3. Kelley, Douglas, "Mania and the Moon," *Psychoanalytic Review,* 1942, *29,* 415.
4. Dewan, Edmond, "On the Possibility of a Perfect Method of Birth Control by Periodic Light Stimulation," *American Journal of Obstetrics and Gynecology,* 1967, *99,* 1016–1019.
5. Luce, Gay G. *Biological Rhythms in Psychiatry and Medicine* (Public Health Service Publication #2088; Washington, D.C.: U.S. Govt. Printing Office, 1970), pp. 130–131.
6. Stahl, Doris Ann, "The Relevance of Hard but Unusual Data upon Commanding Officers in Their Utilization of Manpower," Thesis for

M.P.A., #396, John Jay College of Criminal Justice, 1974, p. 21.
7. Dewan, *op. cit.*, p. 1017.
8. Luce, *op. cit.*, p. 131.
9. *Ibid.*
10. Rush, Anne Kent. *Moon, Moon* (Berkeley, Calif.: Moon Books, 1976), p. 300.
11. Passmore, Nancy. *The 1977 Lunar Calendar* (Boston: Luna Press, 1976), p. 13.
12. *Ibid.*
13. *Ibid.*
14. Rush, *op. cit.*, p. 300.
15. Luce, *op. cit.*, p. 128.
16. Cowgill, Ursula, *et al.*, "An Apparent Lunar Periodicity in the Sexual Cycle of Certain Prosimians," *Proceedings of the National Academy of Sciences,* 1962, *48,* 241.
17. Stahl, *op. cit.*, p. 21.
18. Luce, *op. cit.*, p. 131.
19. Fox, *op. cit.*, p. 543.
20. Cloudsley-Thompson, J.L. *Rhythmic Activity in Animal Physiology and Behavior* (New York: Academic Press, 1961), pp. 91–92.
21. *Ibid.*, p. 93.
22. *Ibid.*, p. 91.
23. Bunning, Erwin. *The Physiological Clock* (London: English Universities Press, 1973), p. 183.
24. *Ibid.*
25. Fox, *op. cit.*, pp. 545–546.
26. Semmens, Elizabeth, "Effect of Moonlight on the Germination of Seeds," *Nature,* 1923, *111,* 49–50.
27. Gates, Frank, "Influence of Moonlight on Movements of Leguminous Leaflets," *Ecology,* 1923, *4,* 37–39.
28. Cowgill, *op. cit.*, p. 241.
29. Klinowska, Margaret, "A Comparison of the Lunar and Solar Activity Rhythms of the Golden Hamster (*Mesocricetus auratus* Waterhouse), *Journal of Interdisciplinary Cycle Research,* 1972, *3* (2), 145–150.
30. Clark, L.B., "Factors in the Lunar Cycle Which May Control Reproduction in the Atlantic Palolo," *Biological Bulletin,* 1941, *81,* 278.
31. *Ibid.*
32. Rensberger, Boyce, "16 Hours of Light Each Day Raises Cows' Milk Flow," *New York Times,* June 15, 1978, 23.
33. *Ibid.*
34. *Ibid.*
35. Luce, *op. cit.*, p. 123.
36. *Ibid.*, pp. 123, 129.
37. *Ibid.*, p. 130.
38. *Ibid.*

39. *Ibid.*
40. *Ibid.*
41. Kaiser, I.H., and Halberg, Franz, "Circadian Periodic Aspects of Birth," *Annals of the New York Academy of Sciences,* 1962, *98,* 1056–1067.
42. Luce, *op. cit.*, p. 130.
43. Charles, Enid, "The Hour of Birth," *British Journal of Preventive and Social Medicine,* 1953, *7,* 43–59.
44. Simpson, A.S., "Are More Babies Born At Night?" *British Medical Journal,* 1952, *2,* 831.
45. Shettles, Landrum, "Hourly Variation In Onset of Labor And Rupture of Membranes," *American Journal of Obstetrics and Gynecology,* 1960, *79,* 177–179.
46. Luce, *op. cit.*, p. 123.
47. *Ibid.*, p. 129.
48. *Ibid.*, p. 124.
49. *Ibid.*
50. *Ibid.*, p. 128.
51. Degucki, Takeo, "Circadian Rhythm of Serotonin N-acetyltransferase Activity in Organ Culture of Chicken Pineal Gland," *Science,* 1979, *203,* 1245–1247.
52. Luce, *op. cit.*, p. 128.
53. Schmeck, Harold, "Manic-Depressive Cycle Tied to 'Clock' Defect," *New York Times,* December 5, 1978, C1.
54. Semmens, *op. cit.*, p. 49.
55. *Ibid.*
56. Webster, Bayard, "Polarized Light Leads the Dance of the Bees," *New York Times,* November 13, 1979, C1, C3.
57. Stahl, William H., "Moon Madness," *Annals of Medical History,* 1937, *9,* 258.
58. Spalding, J.F., *et al.*, "Influence of the Visible Color Spectrum on Activity in Mice," *Laboratory Animal Care,* 1969, *19* (1), 50–54.
59. Ott, John Nash, "Some Responses of Plants and Animals to Variations in Wavelengths of Light Energy," *Annals of the New York Academy of Sciences,* 1964, *117,* 625–626.
60. *Ibid.*, p. 632.
61. *Ibid.*, pp. 632–633.
62. *Ibid.*, p. 632.
63. McDaniel, Walton Brooks, "The Moon, Werewolves, and Medicine," *Transactions & Studies of the College of Physicians of Philadelphia,* 1950, *18,* 122.
64. *Ibid.*
65. King, Howard, "Medicine and the Moon: Beliefs of Other Days," *Medical Record,* 1917, *92,* 1031.

CHAPTER 27: BIOLOGICAL TIDES

1. Katzeff, Paul, "Howl: There's a Full Moon Out Tonight," *Boston Herald American,* March 6, 1977, Sunday magazine 25.
2. Menaker, Walter, and Menaker, Abraham, "Lunar Periodicity in Human Reproduction: A Likely Unit of Biological Time," *American Journal of Obstetrics and Gynecology,* 1959, *77* (4), 911.
3. Foreman, Judy, "Run for Cover, There's A Full Moon," *Boston Globe,* December 14, 1978, 33.
4. Jones, Paul, and Jones, Susan, "Lunar Association with Suicide," *Suicide and Life-Threatening Behavior,* 1977, *7* (1), 31–32.
5. *Ibid.,* p. 32.
6. Kerry, Raphael, and Owen, Goronwy, "Lithium Carbonate as a Mood and Total Body Water Stabilizer," *Archives of General Psychiatry,* 1970, *22,* 301–303.
7. Stone, Michael, "Madness and the Moon Revisited," *Psychiatric Annals,* 1976, *6* (4), 59–60.
8. *Ibid.*

CHAPTER 28: "P.I." IN THE SKY

1. Rossiter, Al, Jr., "How Animals Sense Coming Earthquakes Is Traced," *Boston Herald American,* December 27, 1978, 10.
2. Carlsen, William, "San Franciscans Stunned as Quake, Worst in 68 Years, Strikes the City," *New York Times,* August 7, 1979, A1, B7.
3. Endicott, William, and Hager, Philip, "Strong Earthquake Jolts San Francisco," *Boston Globe,* August 7, 1979, 3.
4. Rossiter, *op. cit.,* p. 10.
5. Soyka, Fred. *The Ion Effect* (New York: Bantam Books, 1978), p. 22.
6. Luce, Gay G. *Biological Rhythms in Psychiatry and Medicine* (Public Health Service Publication #2088; Washington, D.C.: U.S. Govt. Printing Office, 1970), p. 13.
7. Soyka, *op. cit.,* p. 22.
8. Ravitz, Leonard J., "Electrocyclic Phenomena and Emotional States," *Journal of Clinical and Experimental Psychopathology,* 1952, *13* (2), 94–95.
9. Holzer, Robert, "Electricity, Atmospheric," *Encyclopaedia Britannica,* vol. 8 (Chicago: Encyclopaedia Britannica, 1965), p. 184.
10. Biggs, E.K., "Lunar and Planetary Influences on Geomagnetic Disturbances," *Journal of Geophysical Research,* 1963, *68* (13), 4104.
11. Soyka, *op. cit.,* p. 19.
12. *Ibid.,* pp. 21–23.
13. *Ibid.,* p. 20.
14. *Ibid.,* p. 26.
15. *Ibid.,* pp. 21–23.

16. Rossiter, *op. cit.*, p. 10.
17. Soyka, *op. cit.*, pp. 23–25.
18. *Ibid.*, p. 20.
19. *Ibid.*, pp. 20–21.
20. Cottrell, John, "Moon Madness: Does It Really Exist?" *Science Digest*, October 1969, 29.
21. Soyka, *op. cit.*, pp. 23–25.
22. *Ibid.*, pp. 20, 25.
23. "Biological Effects of Ions (Again)," *Science News*, 1978, *114* (15), 247.
24. Soyka, *op. cit.*, pp. 127–128.
25. *Ibid.*
26. *Ibid.*, p. 53.
27. *Ibid.*, p. 55.
28. *Ibid.*, pp. 32–39, 56.
29. *Ibid.*, p. 23.
30. Hackler, Timothy, "That Ol' Devil Moon," *Milwaukee Journal*, March 18, 1979, Sunday magazine 50, 52.
31. Carlson, Peter, "Does Weather Reign Over Our Lives?" *Boston Herald American*, February 28, 1979, 11.
32. Hackler, *op. cit.*, Sunday magazine 50, 52.
33. Soyka, *op. cit.*, p. 23.
34. *Ibid.*, pp. 35–36.
35. *Ibid.*, pp. 49–50.
36. *Ibid.*, pp. 124–125.

CHAPTER 29: WEATHER EFFECTS

1. Geller, Sheldon, and Shannon, Herbert, "The Moon, Weather and Mental Hospital Contacts: Confirmation and Explanation of the Transylvania Effect," *Journal of Psychiatric Nursing and Mental Health Services*, 1976, *14*, 13–17.
2. *Ibid.*, pp. 13–14.
3. Jones, Paul, and Jones, Susan, "Lunar Association with Suicide," *Suicide and Life-Threatening Behavior*, 1977, *7* (1), 32.
4. Carlson, Peter, "Does Weather Reign Over Our Lives?" *Boston Herald American*, February 28, 1979, 11.
5. Bokonjic, R., and Zec, N., "Strokes and the Weather: A Quantitative Statistical Study," *Journal of Neurological Sciences*, 1968, *6*, 483–491.
6. *Ibid.*, p. 483.
7. "Study Finds Weather Plays Role in Mental Health," *New York Times*, May 10, 1974, 18.
8. Bouma, Janneke, and Tromp, S.W., "Daily, Monthly and Yearly Fluctuations in Total Number of Suicides and Suicide Attempts in the Western Part of The Netherlands," *Journal of Interdisciplinary Cycle Research*, 1972, *3* (3–4), 269.

9. Bokonjic, *op. cit.*, pp. 483–491.
10. Geller, *op. cit.*, pp. 13–14.
11. *Ibid.*
12. Jones, *op. cit.*, p. 32.
13. Andrews, Edson, "Moon Talk: The Cyclic Periodicity of Postoperative Hemorrhage," *Journal of the Florida Medical Association,* 1960, *46* (11), 1364.
14. "Study Finds Weather Plays Role in Mental Health," *op. cit.*, p. 18.
15. Thomson, Daniel, "The Ebb and Flow of Infection," *Journal of the American Medical Association,* 1976, *235,* 269–272.
16. Carlson, *op. cit.*, pp. 11, 14.
17. "Brain," *Van Nostrand's Scientific Encyclopedia,* 5th ed. (New York: Van Nostrand Reinhold, 1976), p. 351.
18. Petersen, William, "Psychotic and Somatic Interrelations," *Journal of the American Medical Association,* 1940, *115* (19), 1587.
19. *Ibid.*, p. 1588.
20. Carlson, *op. cit.*, p. 11.
21. *Ibid.*

CHAPTER 30: MAGNETISM AND ELECTRICITY

1. "Space Travel," *Compton's Encyclopedia,* vol. 19 (Chicago: E.F. Compton, 1972), p. 341c.
2. Shoemaker, Eugene, "Moon," *World Book,* vol. 13 (Chicago: Field Enterprises, 1977), p. 650.
3. MacLeod, Mathew, "Lucian," *Encyclopaedia Britannica,* vol. 14 (Chicago: Encyclopaedia Britannica, 1965), p. 394.
4. "Space Travel," *op. cit.*, p. 341c.
5. Harley, Timothy. *Moon Lore* (Rutland, Vt.: Charles E. Tuttle, 1970), p. 47.
6. Bowen, E.G., "A Lunar Effect on the Incoming Meteor Rate," *Journal of Geophysical Research,* 1963, *68* (5), 1401–1403.
7. Bigg, E.K., "A Lunar Influence on Ice Nucleus Concentrations," *Nature,* 1963, *197* (4863), 172–173.
8. Adderley, E.E., "The Influence of the Moon on Atmospheric Ozone," *Journal of Geophysical Research,* 1963, *68,* (5), 1405–1408.
9. Bigg, E.K., "The Influence of the Moon on Geomagnetic Disturbances," *Journal of Geophysical Research,* 1963, *68* (5), 1409–1413.
10. Bigg, E.K., "Lunar and Planetary Influences on Geomagnetic Disturbances," *Journal of Geophysical Research,* 1963, *68* (13), 4099–4104.
11. Bell, B., and Defouw, R.J., "Concerning a Lunar Modulation of Geomagnetic Activity," *Journal of Geophysical Research,* 1964, *69* (15), 3169–3174.
12. Stolov, Harold, and Cameron, A.G.W., "Variations of Geomagnetic Activity with Lunar Phase," *Journal of Geophysical Research,* 1964, *69* (23), 4975–4982.

13. Dodson, Helen, and Hedeman, Ruth, "An Unexpected Effect in Solar Cosmic Ray Data Related to 29.5 Days," *Journal of Geophysical Research,* 1964, *69* (19), 3965–3971.
14. Stolov, *op. cit.,* p. 4975.
15. Chapman, Sydney, and Bartels, Julius, *Geomagnetism,* vols. 1 & 2 (Oxford: Oxford University Press, 1940), pp. 159, 244–271.
16. Timmins, Clark. *Planting by the Moon* (Chicago: Aries Press, 1939), p. 17.
17. Sarton, George, "Lunar Influences on Living Things," *Isis,* 1939, *30,* 502.
18. Ravitz, Leonard J., "Electrodynamic Field Theory in Psychiatry," *Southern Medical Journal,* 1953, *46* (7), 658.
19. Ravitz, Leonard J., "Electrocyclic Phenomena and Emotional States," *Journal of Clinical and Experimental Psychopathology,* 1952, *13* (2), 94–95.
20. Brown, Frank A., Jr. "Hypothesis of Environmental Timing of the Clock," *The Biological Clock: Two Views,* Brown, Hastings, and Palmer, eds. (New York: Academic Press, 1970), pp. 48–56.
21. Brown, Frank A., Jr., "Biological Clocks: Endogenous Cycles Synchronized by Subtle Geophysical Rhythms," *BioSystems,* 1976, *8,* 67–81.
22. Fisher, Allen, "Mysteries of Bird Migration," *National Geographic,* 1979, *156* (2), 185–186.
23. Walcott, Charles, and Green, Robert, "Orientation of Homing Pigeons Altered by a Change in the Direction of an Applied Magnetic Field," *Science,* 1974, *184,* 180–182.
24. Fisher, *op. cit.,* p. 186.
25. Begley, Sharon, and Carey, John, "The Migration Enigma," *Newsweek,* October 15, 1979, 111–113.
26. Webster, Bayard, "Pigeons' Instincts Tied to Moon," *New York Times,* December 26, 1978, C3.
27. Fisher, *op. cit.,* p. 186.
28. Walcott, *op. cit.,* pp. 180–182.
29. Fisher, *op. cit.,* p. 186.
30. Palmer, John D., "Organismic Spatial Orientation in Very Weak Magnetic Fields," *Nature,* 1963, *198,* 1061–1062.
31. *Ibid.,* p. 1062.
32. Brown, "Hypothesis. . . ," *op. cit.,* pp. 45–47.
33. Persinger, Michael, "Prenatal Exposure to an ELF Rotating Magnetic Field, Ambulatory Behavior, and Lunar Distance at Birth: A Correlation," *Psychological Reports,* 1971, *28,* 435–438.
34. Brown, Frank A., Jr., and Scow, Kate, "Magnetic Induction of a Circadian Cycle in Hamsters," *Journal of Interdisciplinary Cycle Research,* 1978, *9* (2), 137–145.
35. Barnothy, Jeno, "Growth-rate of Mice in Static Magnetic Fields," *Nature,* 1963, *200,* 86–87.
36. Audus, L.J., "Magnetotropism: A New Plant-Growth Response," *Nature,* 1960, *185,* 132–134.

37. "Blame Moon in Triangle?" Miami *Herald,* December 5, 1976, page unknown.
38. Walcott, Charles; Gould, James; and Kirschvink, J.L., "Pigeons Have Magnets," *Science,* 1979, *205,* 1027–1029.
39. Gould, James; Kirschvink, J.L.; and Deffeyes, K.S., "Bees Have Magnetic Remanence," *Science,* 1978, *201,* 1026–1028.
40. Frankel, Richard; Blakemore, Richard; and Wolfe, Ralph, "Magnetite in Freshwater Magnetotactic Bacteria," *Science,* 1979, *203,* 1355–1356.
41. "Magnetite Is Found in Bacteria," *Tech Talk,* April 18, 1979, 1, 3.
42. "Lodestone Compass Inside Bacteria," *Science News,* 1979, *115* (17), 278.
43. "Magnetite Is Found in Bacteria," *op. cit.,* p. 1.
44. *Ibid.,* p. 3.
45. Begley, *op. cit.,* p. 115.
46. Gould, *op. cit.,* p. 1027.
47. Walcott, "Pigeons. . . ," *op. cit.,* p. 1028.
48. Gould, *op. cit.,* p. 1026.
49. Rose, Kenneth Jon, "Magnetic Sense of Sharks," *Omni,* October 1978, 49.
50. Tromp, Solco, "Research Project on Terrestrial Biological, Medical and Biochemical Phenomena, Caused or Triggerred by Possible Extra-Terrestrial Physical Force," *Cycles,* 1970, *21* (2), 26.
51. Brown, "Biological Clocks: Endogenous. . . ," *op. cit.,* p. 74.
52. Rose, *op. cit.,* p. 49.
53. Brown, "Biological Clocks: Endogenous. . . ," *op. cit.,* p. 74.
54. Rose, *op. cit.,* p. 49.
55. *Ibid.*
56. Gould, *op. cit.,* p. 1026.
57. The electromagnetic spectrum includes everything from the lowest frequency radio waves through infrared radiation, visible light, ultraviolet radiation, and x-rays to gamma rays, which have high frequencies. Each of those forms of electromagnetic radiation is made of the same thing: atomic particles with both a magnetic and electric charge. What distinguishes one from another is wavelength, or the number of "vibrations" in a given distance. Gamma rays, for example, vibrate fastest, which means they have the highest "frequency" and the shortest "wavelength" (that is, they squeeze more vibrations—or waves—into a given distance traveled). Radio waves have the lowest frequency.
58. Gold, Michael, "The Radiation Syndrome," *Science 80,* 1979, *1* (1), 78–84.
59. Brown, F.A., Jr.; Park, Y.H.; and Zeno, J., "Diurnal Variation in Organismic Response to Very Weak Gamma Radiation," *Nature,* 1966, *211* (5051), 830–833.
60. Brown, F.A., and Chow, Carol S., "Interorganismic and Environmental Influences Through Extremely Weak Electromagnetic Fields," *Biological Bulletin,* 1973, *144* (3), 437–461.

61. Mulder, J.B., "Animal Behavior and Electromagnetic Energy Waves," *Laboratory Animal Science,* 1971, *21* (3), 389–390.
62. *Ibid.,* p. 390.
63. Malek, Jiří; Gleich, J.; and Maly, V., "Characteristics of the Daily Rhythm of Menstruation and Labor," *Annals of the New York Academy of Sciences,* 1962, *98,* 1042.
64. Malin, S.R.C., and Srivastava, B.J., "Correlation between Heart Attacks and Magnetic Activity," *Nature,* 1979, *277* (5698), 646–648.
65. "Heart Attacks Tied to Magnetic Change," *New York Times,* April 24, 1979, C5.
66. Luce, Gay G. *Biological Rhythms in Psychiatry and Medicine* (Public Health Service Publication #2088; Washington, D.C.: U.S. Govt. Printing Office, 1970), p. 14.
67. Friedman, Howard; Becker, Robert; and Bachman, Charles, "Geomagnetic Parameters and Psychiatric Hospital Admissions," *Nature,* 1963, *200,* 626–628.
68. *Ibid.,* p. 626.
69. Friedman, Howard; Becker, Robert; and Bachman, Charles, "Psychiatric Ward Behavior and Geophysical Parameters," *Nature,* 1965, *205,* 1050–1052.
70. Friedman, Howard; Becker, Robert; and Bachman, Charles, "Effect of Magnetic Fields on Reaction Time Performance," *Nature,* 1967, *213,* 949–950.
71. Hackler, Timothy, "That Ol' Devil Moon," *Milwaukee Journal,* March 18, 1979, Sunday magazine 50.
72. Stahl, Doris Ann, "The Relevance of Hard but Unusual Data upon Commanding Officers in Their Utilization of Manpower," Thesis for M.P.A., #396, John Jay College of Criminal Justice, 1974, p. 28.
73. Luce, *op. cit.,* pp. 13–14.
74. Ossenkopp, K.P., and Ossenkopp, Margitta, "Self-Inflicted Injuries and the Lunar Cycle: A Preliminary Report," *Journal of Interdisciplinary Cycle Research,* 1973, *4* (4), 343.
75. *Ibid.,* pp. 343–344.
76. Jasper, Herbert, "Nervous System," *World Book,* vol. 14 (Chicago: Field Enterprises, 1977), p. 126.
77. Ravitz, "Electrocyclic. . .," *op. cit.,* pp. 69–70.
78. Seely, Samuel, "Electric Field," *World Book,* vol. 6 (Chicago: Field Enterprises, 1977), p. 123.
79. Burr, H.S., and Northrup, F.S.C., "Evidence for the Existence of an Electro-Dynamic Field in Living Organisms," *Proceedings of the National Academy of Sciences,* 1939, *25,* 284–288.
80. Ravitz, "Electrocyclic. . .," *op. cit.,* pp. 69–70, 96.
81. Burr, *op. cit.,* p. 287.
82. *Ibid.*
83. Becker, Robert, "Electromagnetic Forces and Life Processes," *Technology Review,* 1972, *75* (2), 32–38.

84. Burr, H.S., "Moon-Madness," *Yale Journal of Biology and Medicine,* 1943, *16,* 249–256.
85. Ravitz, "Electrocyclic. . .," *op. cit.,* p. 98.
86. *Ibid.,* p. 74.
87. *Ibid.*
88. *Ibid.,* p. 97.
89. Ravitz, "Electrodynamic. . .," *op. cit.,* p. 651.
90. Ravitz, Leonard J., "Comparative Clinical and Electrocyclic Observations on Twin Brothers Concordant as to Schizophrenia," *Journal of Nervous and Mental Disease,* 1955, *121,* 72–87.
91. Jannino, Edmund, "Jack the Ripper, 1962 Version," *International Meeting in Forensic Immunology, Medicine, Pathology and Toxicology, 3rd,* London, 1963, Discussion papers, 94–96.
92. *Ibid.,* p. 94.

Bibliography

Aarons, Leroy F., "She Said She Didn't Get a Chance for Second Shot," *Boston Globe,* September 23, 1975, 1.

Abel, Allen, "Statistics Prove Hockey Is Lunacy," *Toronto Globe and Mail,* November 14, 1977, page unknown.

Abrahamsen, David, "Unmasking 'Son of Sam's' Demons," *New York Times,* July 1, 1979, Sunday magazine 20–22.

Adderley, E.E., "The Influence of the Moon on Atmospheric Ozone," *Journal of Geophysical Research,* 1963, *68* (5), 1405–1408.

Adderley, E.E., and Bowen, E.G., "Lunar Component in Precipitation Data," *Science,* 1962, *137,* 749–750.

"A Natural Clock," *New York Times,* January 9, 1979, C2.

Andrews, Edson J., "Moon Talk: The Cyclic Periodicity of Postoperative Hemorrhage," *Journal of the Florida Medical Association,* 1960, *46* (11), 1362–1366.

"Art Editor Is Slain, Wife Bound, Gagged; Girl 9, Spreads Alarm," *Boston Herald,* March 20, 1927, 1, 8.

Aschoff, Jurgen, "Human Circadian Rhythms in Activity, Body Temperature and Other Functions," *Life Sciences and Space Research,* vol. 5, A.H. Brown and F.G. Favorite, eds. (Amsterdam: North-Holland Publishing, 1967), pp. 159–173.

"Atlantis," *Encyclopaedia Britannica,* vol. 2 (Chicago: Encyclopaedia Britannica, 1965), pp. 698–699.

"Attorneys Ask Change of Venue Due to Prejudice," *Boston Herald,* March 26, 1927, 2.

Audus, L.J., "Magnetotropism: A New Plant-Growth Response," *Nature,* 1960, *185,* 132–134.

Balmforth, Ed E., "Teng's New Year Plan," *New York Times,* January 17, 1979, A 22.

Baring-Gould, Sabine. *The Book of Were-Wolves: Being an Account of a Terrible Superstition* (New York: Causeway Books, 1973).

Barnard, Allen. *The Harlot Killer* (New York: Dodd, Mead, 1953).

Barnothy, Jeno M., "Growth-rate of Mice in Static Magnetic Fields," *Nature,* 1963, *200,* 86–87.

Bauer, S.F., and Hornick, E.J., "Lunar Effects on Mental Illness," *American Journal of Psychiatry,* 1968, *125,* 696–697.

Baxavanis, John J., and Petropulos, John A., "Greece," *World Book,* vol. 8 (Chicago: Field Enterprises, 1977), pp. 350–357.

Beaumier, Dorothy, letter to author, March 7, 1977.

Beazley, Sir Charles Raymond, *et al.,* "Columbus, Christopher," *Encyclopaedia Britannica,* vol. 6 (Chicago: Encyclopaedia Britannica, 1951), pp. 78–83.

Becker, Robert O., "Electromagnetic Forces and Life Processes," *Technology Review,* 1972, *75* (2), 32–38.

Begley, Sharon, and Carey, John, "The Migration Enigma," *Newsweek,* October 5, 1979, 111–116.

Bell, B., and DeFouw, R.J., "Concerning a Lunar Modulation of Geomagnetic Activity," *Journal of Geophysical Research,* 1964, *69* (15), 3169–3174.

Bigg, E.K., "A Lunar Influence on Ice Nucleus Concentrations," *Nature,* 1963, *197* (4863), 172–173.

———, "Lunar and Planetary Influences on Geomagnetic Disturbances," *Journal of Geophysical Research,* 1963, *68* (13), 4099–4104.

———, "Lunar Influences on the Frequency of Magnetic Storms," *Journal of Geophysical Research,* 1964, 69 (23), 4971–4974.

———, "The Influence of the Moon on Geomagnetic Disturbances," *Journal of Geophysical Research,* 1963, *68* (5), 1409–1413.

"Biological Effects of Ions (Again)," *Science News,* 1978, *114* (15), 247.

Bird, David, "Eclipse, Winds and Rain Bring Tidal Flooding," *New York Times,* February 27, 1979, B1.

Blackman, Sheldon, and Catalina, Don, "The Moon and the Emergency Room," *Perceptual and Motor Skills,* 1973, *37,* 624–626.

"Blame Moon in Triangle?" Miami *Herald,* December 5, 1976, page unknown.

Bokonjic, R., and Zec, N., "Strokes and the Weather: A Quantitative Statistical Study," *Journal of the Neurological Sciences,* 1968, *6,* 483–491.

Bos, G.J., "Possible Relationship between Sun Spot Cycles and Fluctuations in Frequency of Mongolism," *Journal of Interdisciplinary Cycle Research,* 1972, *3* (3–4), 267–268.

Bouma, Janneke J., and Tromp, S.W., "Daily, Monthly and Yearly Fluctuations in Total Number of Suicides and Suicide Attempts in the Western Part of The Netherlands," *Journal of Interdisciplinary Cycle Research,* 1972, *3* (3–4), 269–270.

Bowen, E.G., "A Lunar Effect on the Incoming Meteor Rate," *Journal of Geophysical Research,* 1963, *68* (5), 1401–1403.

Bradley, Donald A., and Woodbury, Max A., "Lunar Synodical Period and Widespread Precipitation," *Science,* 1962, *137,* 748–749.

"Brain," *Van Nostrand's Scientific Encyclopedia,* 5th ed. (New York: Van Nostrand Reinhold, 1976), pp. 350–357.

Brier, Glenn W., "Diurnal and Semidiurnal Atmospheric Tides in Relation to Precipitation Variations," *Monthly Weather Review,* 1965, *93* (2), 93–100.

Brown, Frank A., Jr., "Biological Clocks," *Oceanology International,* July-August 1967, reprint.

———, "Biological Clocks: Endogenous Cycles Synchronized by Subtle Geophysical Rhythms," *BioSystems,* 1976, *8,* 67–81.

———, letter to author, November 25, 1979.

———, "Persistent Activity Rhythms in the Oyster," *American Journal of Physiology,* 1954, *178,* 510–514.

———, "Propensity for Lunar Periodicity in Hamsters and Its Significance for Biological Clock Theories," *Proceedings of the Society for Experimental Biology and Medicine,* 1965, *120,* 792–797.

———, "The 'Clocks' Timing Biological Rhythms," *American Scientist,* 1972, *60* (6), 756–766.

Brown, F.A., Jr., and Chow, Carol S., "Interorganismic and Environmental Influences Through Extremely Weak Electromagnetic Fields," *Biological Bulletin,* 1973, *144* (3), 437–461.

———, "Lunar-Correlated Variations in Water Uptake by Bean Seeds," *Biological Bulletin,* 1973, *145,* 265–278.

Brown, F.A., Jr.; Fingerman, M.; Sandeen, M.L.; and Webb, H.M., "Persistent Diurnal and Tidal Rhythms of Color Change in the Fiddler Crab, *Uca Pugnax,*" *Journal of Experimental Zoology,* 1953, *123,* 29–60.

Brown, F.A., Jr.; Hastings, J. Woodland; and Palmer, John D. *The Biological Clock: Two Views* (New York: Academic Press, 1970).

Brown, F.A., Jr., and Park, Young H., "A Persistent Monthly Variation in Responses of Planarians to Light, and Its Annual Modulation," *International Journal of Chronobiology,* 1975, *3,* 57–62.

———, "Synodic Monthly Modulation of the Diurnal Rhythm of Hamsters," *Proceedings of the Society for Experimental Biology and Medicine,* 1967, *125,* 712–715.

Brown, F.A., Jr.; Park, Y.H.; and Zeno, Joseph R., "Diurnal Variation in Organismic Response to Very Weak Gamma Radiation," *Nature,* 1966, *211* (5051), 830–833.

Brown, F.A., Jr., and Scow, Kate M., "Magnetic Induction of a Circadian Cycle in Hamsters," *Journal of Interdisciplinary Cycle Research,* 1978, *9* (2), 137–145.

Brown, F.A., Jr.; Shriner, J.; and Ralph, C.L., "Solar and Lunar Rhythmicity in the Rat in 'Constant Conditions' and the Mechanism of Physiological Time Measurement," *American Journal of Physiology,* 1956, *184,* 491–496.

Brown, F.A., Jr.; Webb, H.M.; and Bennett, Miriam F., "Proof for an Endogenous Component in Persistent Solar and Lunar Rhythmicity in Organisms," *Proceedings of the National Academy of Sciences,* 1955, *41,* 93–100.

Browne, Malcolm W., "Doomsday Debate: How Near Is the End?" *New*

York Times, November 11, 1978, C1.
———, "Total Eclipse of the Sun Races Across West," *New York Times,* February 27, 1979, A1.
Bunning, Erwin. *The Physiological Clock,* rev. 3rd ed. (London: English Universities Press, 1973).
Burke, James D., "Moon," *Encyclopedia Americana,* vol. 19, int'l rev. ed. (Danbury, Conn.: Americana Corp., 1978), pp. 429–437.
Burr, H.S., "Moon-Madness," *Yale Journal of Biology and Medicine,* 1943, *16,* 249–256.
Burr, H.S., and Northrup, F.S.C., "Evidence for the Existence of an Electro-Dynamic Field in Living Organisms," *Proceedings of the National Academy of Sciences,* 1939, *25,* 284–288.
Burrows, William, "Periodic Spawning of 'Palolo' Worms in Pacific Waters," *Nature,* 1945, *155,* 47–48.
C., Sylvia, interview with author, November 24, 1978.
"Calendar," *Encyclopaedia Britannica,* vol. 4 (Chicago: Encyclopaedia Britannica, 1965), pp. 611–628.
"The Calendar," *Information Please Almanac 1979* (New York: Viking Press, 1978), pp. 422–424.
"California Quake Damage High In Millions," *Boston Herald,* July 23, 1952, 6.
"California Rushes Quake Area Aid," *Boston Herald,* July 22, 1952, 15, 26.
Carlsen, William R., "San Franciscans Stunned as Quake, Worst in 68 Years, Strikes the City," *New York Times,* August 7, 1979, A1, B7.
Carlson, Peter, "Does Weather Reign Over Our Lives?" *Boston Herald American,* February 28, 1979, 11.
Carpenter, Thomas H.; Holle, Ronald L.; and Fernandez-Partagas, Jose J., "Observed Relationships Between Lunar Tidal Cycles and Formation of Hurricanes and Tropical Storms," *Monthly Weather Review,* 1972, *100* (6), 451–460.
Carter, George Francis, "Lemuria," *Encyclopaedia Britannica,* vol. 13 (Chicago: Encyclopaedia Britannica, 1965), p. 937.
Chamberlin, William Henry, "Fiji," *Encyclopaedia Britannica,* vol. 9 (Chicago: Encyclopaedia Britannica, 1951), pp. 231–233.
Chapman, L.J., "A Search for Lunacy," *Journal of Nervous and Mental Disease,* 1961, *132,* 171–174.
Chapman, Sydney, and Bartels, Julius, *Geomagnetism,* vols. 1, 2 (Oxford: Oxford University Press, 1940), pp. 159, 244–271, 690–800.
Charles, Enid, "The Hour of Birth," *British Journal of Preventive and Social Medicine,* 1953, 7, 43–59.
Chartrand, Mark R., III, "A Bit of Lunacy," *Omni,* July 1979, 18, 131.
———, "Happy New Year," *Omni,* January, 1979, 20, 22.
Charriere, Henri. *Papillon* (New York: Pocket Books, 1971).
Chibnall, Mary, letter to author, October 9, 1978.
Clark, L.B., "Factors in the Lunar Cycle Which May Control Reproduction in the Atlantic Palolo," *Biological Bulletin,* 1941, *81,* 278.

Cloudsley-Thompson, J.L. *Rhythmic Activity in Animal Physiology and Behavior* (New York: Academic Press, 1961).

"Columbus, Christopher," *Compton's Encyclopedia,* vol. 5 (Chicago: F.E. Compton, 1972), pp. 474–479.

"Coming Up: Lots of Snow But Milder," *Boston Herald American,* October 30, 1978, 1, 7.

Cooke, Robert, "Oceans May Help Forecast Weather," *Boston Globe,* October 30, 1978, 14.

———, "Quakes Linked to Moon's Pull," *Boston Globe,* April 24, 1978, 7.

———, "Scientists Keep Weather Eye on Sun," *Boston Evening Globe,* October 11, 1978, 76.

Copper, Basil. *The Werewolf in Legend, Fact & Art* (New York: St. Martin's Press, 1977).

Cottrell, John, "Moon Madness: Does It Really Exist?" *Science Digest,* October 1969, 24–29.

Cowgill, Ursula M.; Bishop, Alison; Andrew, R.J.; and Hutchinson, G.E., "An Apparent Lunar Periodicity in the Sexual Cycle of Certain Prosimians," *Proceedings of the National Academy of Sciences,* 1962, *48,* 239–241.

Crawshay, L.R., "Possible Bearing of a Luminous Syllid on the Question of the Landfall of Columbus," *Nature,* 1935, *136,* 559–560.

"The Crime of Epilepsy," *Science News,* 1978, *114* (7), 101.

Davidson, T.W., and Martyn, D.F., "A Supposed Dependence of Geomagnetic Storminess on Lunar Phase," *Journal of Geophysical Research,* 1964, *69* (19), 3973–3979.

———, "A Supposed Dependence of Meteor Rates on Lunar Phase," *Journal of Geophysical Research,* 1964, *69* (19), 3981–3987.

Delaney, Janice; Lupton, Mary Jane; and Toth, Emily. *The Curse* (New York: Mentor, 1977), chapters 26 & 27.

Delury, George E., ed. *The World Almanac & Book of Facts 1977* (New York: Newspaper Enterprise Association, 1976).

De Voge, Susan D., and Mikawa, James K., "Moon Phases and Crisis Calls: A Spurious Relationship," *Psychological Reports,* 1977, *40,* 387–390.

Dewan, Edmond M., "On the Possibility of a Perfect Method of Birth Control by Periodic Light Stimulation," *American Journal of Obstetrics and Gynecology,* 1967, *99,* 1016–1019.

Dietz, Jean, "Women Said More Sexual at Ovulation," *Boston Globe,* November 23, 1978, 35.

Dixon, Bernard, "Plant Sensations," *Omni,* December 1978, 24.

Dobyns, Zipporah, rev. of *Cosmic Influences on Human Behavior* by Michel Gauquelin, *Psychology Today,* 1974, *8* (4), 16 & 131.

Dodson, Helen W., and Hedeman, E. Ruth, "An Unexpected Effect in Solar Cosmic Ray Data Related to 29.5 Days," *Journal of Geophysical Research,* 1964, *69* (19), 3965–3971.

Dwyer, Timothy, "Sleet Was a Surprise: It's Layer-Cake Weather," *Boston Globe,* February 27, 1979, 21.

Eisler, Robert. *Man Into Wolf: An Anthropological Interpretation of Sadism, Masochism, and Lycanthropy* (New York: Greenwood Press, 1969).

"Electricity & Weather," *Omni,* October 1978, 48.

"11 Die in Quake In So. California Mountain Town," *Boston Traveler,* July 21, 1952, 1, 6.

Ellis, Havelock. *Studies in the Psychology of Sex,* vol. 1 (New York: Random House, 1942).

Ellison, Samuel P., Jr., "Earth," *World Book,* vol. 6 (Chicago: Field Enterprises, 1977), pp. 10–16g.

Emery, C. Eugene, Jr., "It Must Be A Full Moon," Providence (R.I.) *Sunday Journal,* January 8, 1978, Sunday magazine 4–9.

Endicott, William, and Hager, Philip, "Strong Earthquake Jolts San Francisco," *Boston Globe,* August 7, 1979, 3.

Fingerman, Milton, "Lunar Rhythmicity in Marine Organisms," *American Naturalist,* 1957, *91* (858), 167–178.

Fisher, Allan C., "Mysteries of Bird Migration," *National Geographic,* 1979, *156* (2), 154–193.

Fitzgerald, Tom, "Flames Decision Bruins, 6–3; Call the Fights A Draw," *Boston Globe,* February 5, 1977, 17.

Fitzpatrick, JoAnn, "Getting Even," *Boston Herald American,* February 18, 1979, Sunday magazine 20–22.

Fodor, Nandor, "Lycanthropy as a Psychic Mechanism," *Journal of American Folklore,* 1945, *58* (227), 310–316.

Foissac, P., "The Influence of the Lunar Phases on the Physical and Moral Man," *St. Louis Medical and Surgical Journal,* 1855, *13,* 502–517.

Foreman, Judy, "Run for Cover; There's a Full Moon," *Boston Globe,* December 14, 1978, 33.

Fox, H. Munro, "Lunar Periodicity in Reproduction," *Nature,* 1932, *130,* 23.

———, "Lunar Periodicity in Reproduction," *Proceedings of the Royal Society of London, Series B,* 1923, *95,* 523–550.

Fox, Selena, and Alan, Jim, interview with author, August 2, 1979.

Frankel, Richard B., interview with author, November 8, 1979.

Frankel, Richard B.; Blakemore, Richard P.; and Wolfe, Ralph S., "Magnetite in Freshwater Magnetotactic Bacteria," *Science,* 1979, *203,* 1355–1356.

Frazer, James George. *The Golden Bough,* 3rd ed. (New York: Macmillan, 1935).

Frazier, Kendrick, "Stars, Sky and Culture," *Science News,* 1979, *116* (5), 90–93.

Friedman, Howard, and Becker, Robert O., "Psychiatric Ward Behavior and Geophysical Parameters," *Nature,* 1965, *205,* 1050–1052.

Friedman, Howard; Becker, Robert O.; and Bachman, Charles H., "Effect of Magnetic Fields on Reaction Time Performance," *Nature,* 1967, *213,* 949–950.

———, "Geomagnetic Parameters and Psychiatric Hospital Admissions," *Nature,* 1963, *200,* 626–628.

Frye, Richard Nelson, "Darius," *World Book,* vol. 5 (Chicago: Field Enterprises, 1977), p. 30.

———, "Marathon," *World Book,* vol. 13 (Chicago: Field Enterprises, 1977), p. 150.

"Full Moon Means Trouble," *Winnipeg Free Press,* October 12, 1977, page unknown.

Gates, Frank C., "Influence of Moonlight on Movements of Leguminous Leaflets," *Ecology,* 1923, *4,* 37–39.

Gauquelin, Michel, "Genetic Sensitivity to External Factors During the Daily Cycle of the Deliveries," *Journal of Interdisciplinary Cycle Research,* 1971, *2* (2), 227–232.

———. *Les Hommes et les Astres* (Paris: Denoel, 1960), p. 200.

Geller, Sheldon H., and Shannon, Herbert W., "The Moon, Weather and Mental Hospital Contacts: Confirmation and Explanation of the Transylvania Effect," *Journal of Psychiatric Nursing and Mental Health Services,* 1976, *14,* 13–17.

Gill, David; Eddington, Arthur S.; and Jones, Harold S., "Telescope," *Encyclopaedia Britannica,* vol. 21 (Chicago: Encyclopaedia Britannica, 1951), 908–912.

Gingerich, Owen, "Moon," *Collier's Encyclopedia,* vol. 16, rev. ed. (New York: Macmillan Educational Corp., 1978), pp. 522–527.

Giuliani, Judith, "Full Moon Awareness," *Boston Herald American,* December 23, 1978, 6.

Goddard, John, "Dionne Quints—45 Years Later," *Boston Herald American,* May 28, 1979, 10.

Gold, Michael, "The Radiation Syndrome," *Science 80,* 1979, *1* (1), 78–84.

Gordon, Donald A., "Sensitivity of the Homing Pigeon to the Magnetic Field of the Earth," *Science,* 1948, *108,* 710–711.

Gould, James L.; Kirschvink, J.L.; and Deffreyes, K.S., "Bees Have Magnetic Remanence," *Science,* 1978, *201,* 1026 1028

"Gray As 'Mental Slave' of Woman," *Boston Herald,* March 28, 1927, 2.

Gunn, D.L., and Jenkins, P.M., "Lunar Periodicity in Homo Sapiens," *Nature,* 1937, *39,* 841.

Guyselman, J. Bruce, "Solar and Lunar Rhythms of Locomotor Activity in the Crayfish *Cambarus virilis,*" *Physiological Zoology,* 1957, *30* (1), 70–87.

Hackler, Timothy, "That Ol' Devil Moon," *Milwaukee Journal,* March 18, 1979, Sunday magazine 46–52.

Hale, Jud, ed. *The Old Farmer's Almanac 1979* (Dublin, N.H.: Yankee, 1978).

Hammond, Nicholas Geoffrey L., "Marathon, Battle of," *Encyclopaedia Britannica,* vol. 14 (Chicago: Encyclopaedia Britannica, 1965), pp. 845–846.

Harker, Janet E., "Diurnal Rhythms in the Animal Kingdom," *Biological*

Reviews, 1958, *33,* 1–52.

Harley, Timothy, *Moon Lore* (Rutland, Vt.: Charles E. Tuttle, 1970).

Harrison, J.L., "Breeding Rhythms of Selangor Rodents," *Bulletin of the Raffles Museum,* 1952, *24,* 109–131.

———, "Moonlight and the Pregnancy of Malayan Forest Rats," *Nature,* 1952, *170,* 73–74.

———, "The Moonlight Effect on Rat Breeding," *Bulletin of the Raffles Museum,* 1954, *25,* 166–170.

Hartley, William, and Hartley, Ellen, "Moon Madness," *Science Digest,* September 1972, 28–33.

Hawkins, Gerald S., "Stonehenge: A Neolithic Computer," *Nature,* 1964, *202* (4939), 1258–1261.

———, "Stonehenge Decoded," *Nature,* 1963, *200* (4904), 306–308.

Hine, Tom, "Goal-Starved Whalers Beaten, 4–1," *Hartford Courant,* February 5, 1977, 29, 30.

Holzer, Robert E., "Electricity, Atmospheric," *Encyclopaedia Britannica,* vol. 8 (Chicago: Encyclopaedia Britannica, 1965), pp. 184–192.

Hopson, Janet, and Rogers, Michael, "The Last Eclipse," *Science News,* March 3, 1979, *115* (9), 137–139.

Huff, Darrell. *Cycles in Your Life* (New York: W.W. Norton, 1964).

Huntsman, A.G., "*Odontosyllis* at Bermuda and Lunar Periodicity," *Journal of the Fisheries Research Board of Canada,* 1948, *7* (6), 363–369.

Inman, W.S., "The Moon, the Seasons, and Man," *British Journal of Medical Psychology,* 1951, *24,* 267–276.

Jannino, Edmund A., "Jack the Ripper, 1962 Version," *International Meeting in Forensic Immunology, Medicine, Pathology and Toxicology, 3rd,* London, 1963, Discussion papers, 94–96.

———, letter to author, April 14, 1978.

Jasper, Herbert H., "Nervous System," *World Book,* vol. 14 (Chicago: Field Enterprises, 1977), 124–126.

Johnson, L.G., "Diurnal Patterns of Metabolic Variations in Chick Embryos," *Biological Bulletin,* 1966, *131* (2), 308–318.

Jones, Paul K., and Jones, Susan L., "Lunar Association with Suicide," *Suicide and Life-Threatening Behavior,* 1977, *7* (1), 31–39.

Jordan, Charles L., "Tidal Forces and the Formation of Hurricanes," *Nature,* 1955, *175,* 38–39.

"Jupiter's World," *Science News,* 1979, *115* (10), 147–149.

Kagan, Donald, "Greece, Ancient," *World Book,* vol. 8 (Chicago: Field Enterprises, 1977), pp. 358–369.

Kahn, Marvin E., "The Tune of a Different Tide," *Science News,* 1979, *115* (1), 3.

Kahn, Peter G.K., and Pompea, Stephen M., "Nautiloid Growth Rhythms and Dynamical Evolution of the Earth-Moon System," *Nature,* 1978, *275* (5681), 606.

Kaiser, I.H., and Halberg, Franz, "Circadian Periodic Aspects of Birth,"

Annals of the New York Academy of Sciences, 1962, *98,* 1056–1067.

Katzeff, Paul, "Howl: There's A Full Moon Out Tonight," *Boston Herald American,* March 6, 1977, Sunday magazine 24–26.

Kelley, Douglas, "Mania and the Moon," *Psychoanalytic Review,* 1942, *29,* 406–426.

Kerry, Raphael J., and Owen, Goronwy, "Lithium Carbonate As a Mood and Total Body Water Stabilizer," *Archives of General Psychiatry,* 1970, *22,* 301–303.

Ketchum, Bostwick H., "Bay of Fundy," *World Book,* vol. 2 (Chicago: Field Enterprises, 1977), p. 130.

King, Howard D., "Medicine and the Moon: Beliefs of Other Days," *Medical Record,* 1917, *92,* 1030–1032.

King, J.W., "Weather and the Earth's Magnetic Field," *Nature,* 1974, *247,* 131–134.

Kiser, William L.; Carpenter, Thomas H.; and Brier, Glenn W., "The Atmospheric Tides at Wake Island," *Monthly Weather Review,* 1963, *91,* 566–572.

Klinowska, Margaret, "A Comparison of the Lunar and Solar Activity Rhythms of the Golden Hamster (*Mesocriceius auratus* Waterhouse)," *Journal of Interdisciplinary Cycle Research,* 1972, *3* (2), 145–150.

Knight, Peter S., "Atmosphere (Earth)," *Van Nostrand's Scientific Encyclopedia,* 5th ed. (New York: Van Nostrand Reinhold, 1976), pp. 215, 227.

Langdon, Stephen H.; Muller, W. Max; and Scott, James G., eds. *The Mythology of All Races* (New York: Cooper Square Publishers, 1964).

Laycock, T., "Lunar Influence; Being a Fourth Contribution to Proleptics," *The Lancet,* 1843, *2,* 438–444.

Lerner, Richard, "Mental Tests Ordered for Sara Moore," *Boston Herald American,* September 24, 1975, 25.

Lester, David; Brockopp, Gene W.; and Priebe, Kitty, "Association Between A Full Moon and Completed Suicide," *Psychological Reports,* 1969, *25,* 598.

Lieber, Arnold L., "Lunar Effect on Homicides: A Confirmation," *International Journal of Chronobiology,* 1973, *1* (4), 338–339.

———, "On the Moon Again," *American Journal of Psychiatry,* 1975, *132* (6), 669–670.

Lieber, Arnold L., and Sherin, Carolyn R., "Homicides and the Lunar Cycle: Toward a Theory of Lunar Influence on Human Emotional Disturbances," *American Journal of Psychiatry,* 1972, *129* (1), 69–74.

Lilienfeld, D.M., "Lunar Effect on Mental Illness," *American Journal of Psychiatry,* 1969, *125,* 1454.

Lockard, Robert B., "Experimental Inhibition of Activity of Kangaroo Rats in the Natural Habitat by an Artificial Moon," *Journal of Comparative and Physiological Psychology,* 1975, *89* (3), 263–266.

"Lodestone Compass Inside Bacteria," *Science News,* 1979, *115* (17), 278.

Luce, Gay G., ed. *Biological Rhythms in Psychiatry and Medicine* (Public Health Service Publication #2088; Washington, D.C.: U.S. Govt. Printing Office, 1970).

MacLeod, Mathew D., "Lucian," *Encyclopaedia Britannica,* vol. 14 (Chicago: Encyclopaedia Britannica, 1965), pp. 394–395.

Madariaga, Salvador de, "Columbus, Christopher," *Encyclopaedia Britannica,* vol. 6 (Chicago: Encyclopaedia Britannica, 1965), pp. 111–115.

"Magnetite Is Found in Bacteria," *Tech Talk,* April 18, 1979, 1, 3.

Malek, Jiří; Gleich, J.; and Maly, V., "Characteristics of the Daily Rhythm of Menstruation and Labor," *Annals of the New York Academy of Sciences,* 1962, *98,* 1042–1055.

Malin, S.R.C., and Srivastava, B.J., "Correlation between Heart Attacks and Magnetic Activity," *Nature,* 1979, *277* (5698), 646–648.

"Marathon," *Encyclopaedia Britannica,* vol. 14 (Chicago: Encyclopaedia Britannica, 1951), pp. 857–858.

Marshak, Alexander, "Lunar Notation on Upper Paleolithic Remains," *Science,* 1964, *146,* 743–745.

Mason, James, "A Possible Lunar Periodicity in the Breeding of the Scallop, *Pecten maximus* (L.)," *Annals and Magazine of Natural History,* 1958, *1* (9), 601–602.

Mather, K., and Newell, J., "Seed Germination and the Moon," *Journal of the Royal Horticultural Society,* 1941, *66,* 358–366.

Mather, M., "The Effect of Temperature and the Moon on Seedling Growth," *Journal of the Royal Horticultural Society,* 1942, *67,* 264–270.

McDaniel, Walton Brooks, "The Moon, Werewolves, and Medicine," *Transactions & Studies of the College of Physicians of Philadelphia,* 1950, *18,* 113–122.

McDowell, Edwin, "Theories on Man's Dark Deeds Come Out by the Light of the Full Moon," *New York Times,* January 24, 1978, B1.

McDonald, Robert L., "Lunar and Seasonal Variations in Obstetric Factors," *Journal of Genetic Psychology,* 1966, *108,* 81–87.

Melchoir, Paul. *The Earth Tides* (Oxford: Pergamon Press, 1966).

Menaker, Walter, "Lunar Periodicity with Reference to Live Births," *American Journal of Obstetrics and Gynecology,* 1967, *98* (7), 1002–1004.

Menaker, Walter, and Menaker, Abraham, "Lunar Periodicity in Human Reproduction: A Likely Unit of Biological Time," *American Journal of Obstetrics and Gynecology,* 1959, *77* (4), 905–914.

Michel, F.C.; Dessler, A.J.; and Walter, G.K., "A Search for Correlation between *K*p and the Lunar Phase," *Journal of Geophysical Research,* 1964, *68* (19), 4177–4181.

Miles, L.E.M.; Raynal, D.M.; and Wilson, M.A., "Blind Man Living in Normal Society Has Circadian Rhythms of 24.9 Hours," *Science,* 1977, *198,* 421–423.

"Mistletoe Kiss of Death for Some Trees," *Boston Evening Globe,* December 11, 1978, 5.

Monahan, D. Leo, "Bruins Incensed Over Plett's 'Foul,'" *Boston Herald American,* first edition, February 5, 1977, 13.

———, "Keeping Winning in Mind," *Boston Herald American,* February 4, 1979 C7.

———, "Referee's Whistle Frustrates Bruins," *Boston Herald American,* final edition, February 5, 1977, 13.

"The Moon and Medicine," *Clinical Excerpts,* 1940, *14* (8), 3–11.

Moore, Patrick, *Suns, Myths and Men,* rev. ed. (New York: W.W. Norton, 1968).

"More Moonlets," *New York Times,* May 22, 1979, C2.

"More on Sun-Weather Correlations," *Science News,* 1978, *114* (16), 264.

Morison, Samuel Eliot, "Columbus, Christopher," *World Book,* vol. 4 (Chicago: Field Enterprises, 1977), pp. 690–697.

Morris, William and Mary. *Morris Dictionary of Word and Phrase Origins* (New York: Harper & Row, 1977).

"Mrs. Snyder and Gray Electrocuted Less Than 10 Months from Arrest," *Boston Herald,* January 13, 1928, 16.

"Mrs. Snyder and Gray Face Indictments for First Degree Murder," *Boston Herald,* March 23, 1927, 1, 9.

Mulder, J.B., "Animal Behavior and Electromagnetic Energy Waves," *Laboratory Animal Science,* 1971, *21* (3), 389–393.

Oberndorf, C.P., "Sexual Periodicity in the Male," *Medical Record,* 1913, *84,* 18–20.

Oliven, John F., "Moonlight and Nervous Disorders," *American Journal of Psychiatry,* 1943, *99,* 579–584.

"On Baffin Island, Universal Sounds of Joy and Wonder," *New York Times,* February 27, 1979, C4.

Osborn, Roger Dean, "The Moon and the Mental Hospital: An Investigation of One Area of Folklore," *Journal of Psychiatric Nursing and Mental Health Services,* 1968, *6,* 88–93.

Osley, M.; Summerville, D.; and Borst, L.B., "Natility and the Moon," *American Journal of Obstetrics and Gynecology,* 1973, *117,* 413–415.

Ossenkopp, K.P., and Ossenkopp, Margitta D., "Self-Inflicted Injuries and the Lunar Cycle: A Preliminary Report," *Journal of Interdisciplinary Cycle Research,* 1973, *4* (4), 337–348.

Ostrander, Sheila, and Schroeder, Lynn, "Birth Control by Astrology?" *McCall's,* May 1972, 84–88.

Ott, John Nash, "Some Responses of Plants and Animals to Variations in Wavelengths of Light Energy," *Annals of the New York Academy of Sciences,* 1964, *117,* 624–635.

Palmer, C.E., "The Impulsive Generation of Certain Changes in the Tropospheric Circulation," *Journal of Meteorology,* 1953, *10* (1), 1–9.

Palmer, J.D., "Organismic Spatial Orientation in Very Weak Magnetic Fields," *Nature,* 1963, *198* (4885), 1061–1062.

———, "The Many Clocks of Man," *Cycles,* 1971, *22* (2), 36–41.

Passmore, Nancy, interview with author, September 1, 1979.

———, editor, *The 1977 Lunar Calendar* (Boston: Luna Press, 1976).

———, editor and publisher, *The 1978 Lunar Calendar* (Boston: Luna Press, 1977).

———, *The 1979 Lunar Calendar* (Boston: Luna Press, 1978).

———, *The '80 Lunar Calendar* (Boston: Luna Press, 1979).

"Patricia Hearst Tells of Her Kidnapping in Affidavit," *Boston Herald American,* September 24, 1975, 2.

"Patty Kidnapers Seen at Large," *Boston Herald American,* October 17, 1975, 2.

Persinger, Michael A., "Prenatal Exposure to an ELF Rotating Magnetic Field, Ambulatory Behavior, and Lunar Distance at Birth: A Correlation," *Psychological Reports,* 1971, *28,* 435–438.

Petersen, William F., and Reese, Hans H., "Psychotic and Somatic Interrelations," *Journal of the American Medical Association,* 1940, *115* (9), 1587–1591.

Pochobradsky, J., "Independence of Human Menstruation on Lunar Phases and Days of the Week," *American Journal of Obstetrics and Gynecology,* 1974, *118,* 1136–1138.

Pokorny, Alex D., "Moon Phases and Mental Hospital Admissions," *Journal of Psychiatric Nursing and Mental Health Services,* 1968, *6,* 325–327.

———, "Moon Phases, Suicide, and Homicide," *American Journal of Psychiatry,* 1964, *121,* 66–67.

Pokorny, Alex D., and Jachimczyk, Joseph, "The Questionable Relationship Between Homicides and the Lunar Cycle," *American Journal of Psychiatry,* 1974, *131* (7), 827–829.

Pokorny, Alex D., and Mefferd, R.B., "Geomagnetic Fluctuation and Disturbed Behavior," *Journal of Nervous and Mental Disease,* 1966, *143,* 140–151.

"Preaching Pan, Isis and 'Om,'" *Time,* August 6, 1979, 84.

Proudman, Joseph, and Groves, Gordon W., "Tides," *Encyclopaedia Britannica,* vol. 22 (Chicago: Encyclopaedia Britannica, 1965), pp. 193–205.

"Quake Damage Seen $20-Million, State Aid Looms 'Drop in Bucket,'" *Boston Sunday Herald,* August 24, 1952, 10.

"Quake Hits California City," *Boston Herald,* August 23, 1952, 1, 2.

"Quakes Strike California; Los Angeles Hit," *Boston Traveler,* August 23, 1952, 1, 3.

Ralph, Charles L., "Persistent Rhythms of Activity and O_2-Consumption in the Earthworm," *Physiological Zoology,* 1957, *30* (1), 41–55.

Ramanathan, O., "Light and Sexual Periodicity in Indian Buffaloes," *Nature,* 1932, *130,* 169–170.

Ramey, Estelle, "Men's Cycles (They Have Them Too, You Know)," *Ms.,* 1972, Spring, *8,* 11–14.

Ravitz, Leonard J., "Electrocyclic Phenomena and Emotional States," *Journal of Clinical and Experimental Psychopathology,* 1952, *13* (2), 69–106.

———, "Comparative Clinical and Electrocyclic Observations on Twin Brothers Concordant as to Schizophrenia," *Journal of Nervous and Mental Disease,* 1955, *121,* 72–87.

———, "Electrodynamic Field Theory in Psychiatry," *Southern Medical Journal,* 1953, *46* (7), 650–660.

Ray, Harendranath, and Chakraverty, Mukunda, "Lunar Periodicity in the Conjugation of *Conchophthririus lamellidens* Ghosh," *Nature,* 1934, *134,* 664–665.

Raymond, Charles W., "Bay of Fundy," *Encyclopaedia Britannica,* vol. 9 (Chicago: Encyclopaedia Britannica, 1965), p. 1011.

Reid, Robert O., "Tide," *World Book,* vol. 19 (Chicago: Field Enterprises, 1977), pp. 218–220.

Rensberger, Boyce, "Cosmic Clues on Jupiter's Moons," *New York Times,* February 27, 1979, C2.

———, "16 Hours of Light Each Day Raises Cows' Milk Flow," *New York Times,* June 15, 1978, 23.

Rhyne, W.P., "Spontaneous Hemorrhage," *Journal of the Medical Association of Georgia,* 1966, *55,* 505–506.

Rimland, B., "Epilepsy and Crime: Biological?" *Science News,* 1978, *114* (16), 259.

Rippmann, E.T., "The Moon and the Birth Rate," *American Journal of Obstetrics and Gynecology,* 1957, *74,* 148–150.

Rose, Jon Kenneth, "Magnetic Sense of Sharks," *Omni,* October 1978, 49.

Rosenstock, Harvey A., and Vincent, Kenneth R., "A Case of Lycanthropy," *American Journal of Psychiatry,* 1977, *134* (10), 1147–1149.

Rossiter, Al, Jr., "How Animals Sense Coming Earthquakes Is Traced," *Boston Herald American,* December 27, 1978, 10.

Rosten, Leo. *The Joys of Yiddish* (New York: Pocket Books, 1970).

Rounds, Harry D., "A Lunar Rhythm in the Occurrence of Bloodborne Factors in Cockroaches, Mice and Men," *Comparative Biochemistry and Physiology,* 1975, *50 C,* 193–197.

Rush, Anne Kent. *Moon, Moon* (Berkeley, Calif.: Moon Books, 1976).

"Ruth and Judd Facing Another Sanity Inquiry," New York *Daily News,* October 28, 1927, 42.

"Ruth and Judd Worried Over Children's Fourth," New York *Daily News,* July 4, 1927, 7.

Sadger, J., *Sleep Walking and Moon Walking,* trans. Louise Brink (Nervous and Mental Disease Monograph Series No. 31; Washington, D.C.: Nervous and Mental Disease Publishing Co., 1920).

Sandeen, Muriel L.; Stephens, Grover C.; and Brown, Frank A., Jr., "Persistent Daily and Tidal Rhythms of Oxygen Consumption in Two Species of Marine Snails," *Physiological Zoology,* 1954, *27* (4), 350–356.

Sarton, George, "Lunar Influences on Living Things," *Isis,* 1939, *30,* 495–507.

Schmeck, Harold M., Jr., "Manic-Depressive Cycle Tied to 'Clock' Defect," *New York Times,* December 5, 1978, C1.

Schnurman, Albert G., "The Effect of the Moon on Childbirth," *Virginia*

Medical Monthly, 1949, *76,* 78.

"Scientists Find Link Between Quakes and 'Earth Tides,'" *Tech Talk,* April 26, 1978, 9.

Seeley, Samuel, "Electric Field," *World Book,* vol. 6 (Chicago: Field Enterprises, 1977), p. 123.

Selzer, M., and Payne, C., "Automobile Accidents, Suicides and Unconscious Motivation," *American Journal of Psychiatry,* 1962, *119,* 237–240.

Semmens, Elizabeth Sidney, "Effect of Moonlight on the Germination of Seeds," *Nature,* 1923, *111,* 49–50.

Shapiro, J.L.; Streiner, D.L.; and Gray, A.L., "The Moon and Mental Illness," *Perceptual Motor Skills,* 1970, *30,* 827–830.

Sheppard, Lancelot Capel, "Devil," *Encyclopaedia Britannica,* vol. 7 (Chicago: Encyclopaedia Britannica, 1965), pp. 327–329.

Shettles, Landrum B., "Hourly Variation in Onset of Labor and Rupture of Membranes," *American Journal of Obstetrics and Gynecology,* 1960, *79,* 177–179.

Shirk, Gertrude, "Earthquake Cycles," *Cycles,* 1978, *29* (2), 47.

———, "Moon People," *Cycles,* 1978, *29* (3), 71.

Shoemaker, Eugene M., "Moon," *World Book,* vol. 13 (Chicago: Field Enterprises, 1977), pp. 646–651.

Shurley, Jay T.; Pierce, Chester M.; Natani, Kirmach; and Brooks, Robert E., "Sleep and Activity Patterns at South Pole Station: A Preliminary Report," *Archives of General Psychiatry,* 1970, *22,* 385–389.

Simpson, A.S., "Are More Babies Born At Night?" *British Medical Journal,* 1952, *2,* 831.

Skilling, William, and Richardson, Robert S. *Astronomy* (New York: Henry Holt, 1954).

———, *Sun, Moon and Stars,* 2nd ed. rev. (New York: McGraw-Hill, 1964).

"SLA Diary Details Patty's Role," *Boston Herald American,* October 18, 1975, 1.

Slaughter, J.W., "The Moon In Childhood and Folklore," *American Journal of Psychology,* 1902, *13* (2), 294–318.

Small, Collie, "A Full Moon Can Beam Disaster," *Boston Herald American,* December 13, 1978, 15.

Smiley, Charles H., "Tidal Forces and the Formation of Hurricanes," *Nature,* 1954, *173,* 397.

Smith, Peter J., "Magnetics, Climate and Eccentricity," *Nature,* 1979, *277,* 354.

"Snyder's Wife Admits Helping Kill Husband," *Boston Herald,* March 22, 1927, 1, 9.

Sofaer, Anna; Zinser, Volker; and Sinclair, Rolf M., "A Unique Solar Marking Construct," *Science,* 1979, *206* (4416), 283–291.

"Solar Activity May Alter Atmospheric Electricity," *Tech Talk,* September 27, 1978, 12.

"Solar Eclipse—'Awesome,'" *Boston Herald American,* February 27, 1979, 29.

Solomon, Dr. Neil, "Magnet Helps Broken Bone," *Boston Globe,* September 20, 1979, 42.

Soyka, Fred, with Edmonds, Alan. *The Ion Effect* (New York: Bantam Books, 1977).

"Space Travel," *Compton's Encyclopedia,* vol. 19 (Chicago: E.F. Compton, 1972), pp. 341–348d.

Spalding, J.F.; Archuleta, R.F.; and Holland, L.M., "Influence of the Visible Color Spectrum on Activity in Mice," *Laboratory Animal Care,* 1969, *19* (1), 50–54.

Stahl, Doris Ann, "The Relevance of Hard but Unusual Data upon Commanding Officers in Their Utilization of Manpower," Thesis for M.P.A., #396, John Jay College of Criminal Justice, 1974.

Stahl, William Harris, "Moon Madness," *Annals of Medical History,* 1937, *9,* 248–263.

Stair, Thomas, "Lunar Cycles and Emergency-Room Visits," *New England Journal of Medicine,* 1978, *298* (23), 1318–1319.

"State Lunacy Board to Re-Examine Ruth," New York *Daily News,* July 1, 1927, 12.

Stetson, Harlan T., "Modern Evidence for Differential Movement of Certain Points on the Earth's Surface," *Science,* 1944, *100,* 113–117.

Stevens, Susan S., "Beware of the Full Moon in February," United Press International wire service transmission #482, "A" wire, June 21, 1978.

Stevens, William K., "Lunar Research Thrives in Wake of Apollo," *New York Times,* July 17, 1979, C1, C3.

Stolov, Harold L., "Tidal Wind Fields in the Atmosphere," *Journal of Meteorology,* 1955, *12,* 117–140.

Stolov, Harold L., and Cameron, A.G.W., "Variations of Geomagnetic Activity with Lunar Phase," *Journal of Geophysical Research,* 1964, *69* (23), 4975–4982.

Stone, Michael H., "Madness and the Moon Revisited," *Psychiatric Annals,* 1976, *6* (4), 47–60.

"Study Finds Weather Plays Role In Mental Health," *New York Times,* May 10, 1974, 18.

Stutz, Audrey M., "Synodic Monthly Rhythms in the Mongolian Gerbil *Meriones unguiculatus,*" *Journal of Interdisciplinary Cycle Research,* 1973, *4* (3), 229–236.

———, "Tidal and Diurnal Activity Rhythms in the Striped Shore Crab *Pachygrapsus crassipes,*" *Journal of Interdisciplinary Cycle Research,* 1978, *9* (1), 41–48.

Summers, Montague. *The Werewolf* (New Hyde Park: University Books, 1966).

"Sun and Weather: An Electric Link," *Science News,* 1978, *113* (21), 340.

"The Sun and Weather: 'Things Are Popping,'" *Science News,* 1978, *112* (26 & 27), 423.

Surawicz, Frida G., and Banta, Richard, "Lycanthropy Revisited," *Canadian Psychiatric Association Journal,* 1975, *20* (7), 537–542.

Tasso, Jodi, and Miller, Elizabeth, "The Effects of the Full Moon on Human Behavior," *Journal of Psychology,* 1976, *93,* 81–83.

Taylor, L.J., and Diespecker, D.D., "Moon Phases and Suicide Attempts in Australia," *Psychological Reports,* 1972, *31,* 112.

Tchijevsky, A.L., "Physical Factors of the Historical Process," *Cycles,* 1971, *22* (1), 11–27.

Terracini, Emma D., and Brown, Frank A., Jr., "Periodism in Mouse 'Spontaneous' Activity Synchronized with Major Geophysical Cycles," *Physiological Zoology,* 1962, *35* (1), 27–37.

Thomas, Helen, "President Escapes Assasin's Bullet," *Boston Globe,* September 23, 1975, 1.

Thomson, Daniel, "The Ebb and Flow of Infection," *Journal of the American Medical Association,* 1976, *235,* 269–272.

"Tidal Energy," *Van Nostrand's Scientific Encyclopedia,* 5th ed. (New York: Van Nostrand Reinhold, 1976), pp. 2199–2202.

"Tides," *Van Nostrand's Scientific Encyclopedia,* 5th ed. (New York: Van Nostrand Reinhold, 1976), pp. 2202–2203.

Timmins, Clark. *Planting by the Moon* (Chicago: Aries Press, 1939).

Trapp, Carl E., "Lunacy and the Moon," *American Journal of Psychiatry,* 1937, *94,* 339–343.

Trautman, Robert, "Women Physically Unfit for Presidency?" *Boston Globe,* August 2, 1970, 41, 42.

Tromp, Solco W., "Research Project on Terrestrial Biological, Medical and Biochemical Phenomena, Caused or Triggered by Possible Extra-Terrestrial Physical Forces," *Cycles,* 1970, *21* (2), 26–28.

"Two Faces of Mistletoe," *Boston Globe,* December 12, 1978, page unknown.

Urey, Harold C., "Moon, Origin and History of," *Collier's Encyclopedia,* vol. 16, rev. ed. (New York: Macmillan Educational Corp., 1978), pp. 527–530.

Walcott, Charles, and Green, Robert P., "Orientation of Homing Pigeons Altered by a Change in the Direction of an Applied Magnetic Field," *Science,* 1974, *184,* 180–182.

Walcott, Charles; Gould, James L.; and Kirschvink, J.L., "Pigeons Have Magnets," *Science,* 1979, *205,* 1027–1029.

Walker, Boyd D., "A Guide to the Grunion," *California Fish and Game,"* 1952, *38,* 409–420.

Ward, E.H.P., "The Moon and Insanity," *Medical Record,* 1919, *96,* 318–320.

Webster, Bayard, "History and Longevity's Secret Hunted in Clamshells," *The New York Times,* November 21, 1978, C2.

———, "Physicist Challenges Theory on Sunspots," *New York Times,* July 17, 1979, C3.

———, "Pigeons' Instincts Tied to Moon," *New York Times,* December 26, 1978, C3.

———, "Polarized Light Leads The Dance of the Bees," *New York Times,* November 13, 1979, C1, C3.

Weiskott, G.N., "Moon Phases and Telephone Counselling Calls," *Psychological Reports,* 1974, *35,* 752–754.

Weiskott, Gerald N., and Tipton, George B., "Moon Phases and State Hospital Admissions," *Psychological Reports,* 1975, *37,* 486.

West, Susan, "Intruding Stratosphere," *Science News,* 1978, *114* (7), 105.

———, "Moon History In A Seashell," *Science News,* 1978, *114* (25), 426–428.

Wheeler, Raymond Holder, "The Effect of Climate on Human Behavior in History," *Cycles,* 1978, *29* (1), 7–17.

White, William A., "Moon Myth in Medicine," *Psychoanalytic Review,* 1914, *1* (3), 241–256.

"Wild, Crazy February Bows Out Pleasantly," *Boston Herald American,* March 5, 1979, 5.

Wilford, John Noble, "Cloud of Charged Particles Discovered Around Jupiter," *New York Times,* March 1, 1979, B20.

Wolfe, Tom, "Columbus and the Moon," *New York Times,* July 20, 1979, A25.

Wylie, Francis, "Sharper Tide Forecasts," *New York Times,* December 29, 1978, A23.

Xanthakis, John, "Possible Sun-Weather Correlation," *Nature,* 1978, *275* (5682), 775.

Ziegler, Mel, "A Lunar Loss of Marbles," *San Francisco Chronicle,* May 2, 1977, 2.